# The Bible Speaks Today

*Series editors:* Alec Motyer (OT)
John Stott (NT)
Derek Tidball (Bible Themes)

# The Message of Creation

# The Bible Speaks Today Series

**Creation**
David Wilkinson

**The Cross**
Derek Tidball

**The Living God**
Peter Lewis

**The Resurrection**
Paul Beasley-Murray

**Salvation**
Philip Graham Ryken

**Genesis 1—11**
David Atkinson

**Genesis 12—50**
Joyce G. Baldwin

**Numbers**
Raymond Brown

**Deuteronomy**
Raymond Brown

**Judges**
Michael Wilcock

**Ruth**
David Atkinson

**Chronicles**
Michael Wilcock

**Nehemiah**
Raymond Brown

**Job**
David Atkinson

**Psalms 1—72**
Michael Wilcock

**Psalms 73—150**
Michael Wilcock

**Proverbs**
David Atkinson

**Ecclesiastes**
Derek Kidner

**Song of Songs**
Tom Gledhill

**Isaiah**
Barry Webb

**Jeremiah**
Derek Kidner

**Ezekiel**
Christopher J. H. Wright

**Daniel**
Ronald S. Wallace

**Hosea**
Derek Kidner

**Amos**
J. A. Motyer

**Joel, Micah &**
**Habakkuk**
David Prior

**Matthew**
Michael Green

**Sermon on the Mount**
**(Matthew 5—7)**
John R. W. Stott

**Mark**
Donald English

**Luke**
Michael Wilcock

**John**
Bruce Milne

**Acts**
John R. W. Stott

**Romans**
John R. W. Stott

**1 Corinthians**
David Prior

**2 Corinthians**
Paul Barnett

**Galatians**
John R. W. Stott

**Ephesians**
John R. W. Stott

**Philippians**
J. A. Motyer

**Colossians & Philemon**
R. C. Lucas

**1 & 2 Thessalonians**
John R. W. Stott

**1 Timothy & Titus**
John R. W. Stott

**2 Timothy**
John R. W. Stott

**Hebrews**
Raymond Brown

**James**
J. A. Motyer

**1 Peter**
Edmund P. Clowney

**2 Peter & Jude**
Dick Lucas &
Christopher Green

**John's Letters**
David Jackman

**Revelation**
Michael Wilcock

# The Message of Creation

*Encountering the Lord of the Universe*

David Wilkinson

InterVarsity Press

*InterVarsity Press*
*P.O. Box 1400, Downers Grove, IL 60515-1426*
*World Wide Web: www.ivpress.com*
*E-mail: mail@ivpress.com*

*Inter-Varsity Press*
*38 De Montfort Street, Leicester LE1 7GP, England*
*World Wide Web: www.ivpbooks.com*
*E-mail: ivp@uccf.org.uk*

*InterVarsity Press® is the book-publishing division of InterVarsity Christian Fellowship/USA®, a
student movement active on campus at hundreds of universities, colleges and schools of nursing in
the United States of America, and a member movement of the International Fellowship of
Evangelical Students. For information about local and regional activities, write Public Relations
Dept., InterVarsity Christian Fellowship/USA, 6400 Schroeder Rd., P.O. Box 7895, Madison, WI
53707-7895.*

*Inter-Varsity Press is the book-publishing division of the Universities and Colleges Christian
Fellowship (formerly the Inter-Varsity Fellowship), a student movement linking Christian Unions
in universities and colleges throughout the United Kingdom and the Republic of Ireland, and a
member movement of the International Fellowship of Evangelical Students. For information about
local and national activities write to UCCF, 38 De Montfort Street, Leicester LE1 7GP, England.*

*USA ISBN 0-8308-2405-7*
*UK ISBN 0-85111-269-2*

*Printed in the United States of America* ∞

British Library Cataloguing in Publication Data
*A catalogue record for this book is available from the British Library.*

Library of Congress Cataloging-in-Publication Data has been requested.

| P | 19 | 18 | 17 | 16 | 15 | 14 | 13 | 12 | 11 | 10 | 9 | 8 | 7 | 6 | 5 | 4 | 3 | 2 | 1 |
|---|----|----|----|----|----|----|----|----|----|----|----|----|----|----|----|----|----|----|----|
| Y | 18 | 17 | 16 | 15 | 14 | 13 | 12 | 11 | 10 | 09 | 08 | 07 | 06 | 05 | 04 | 03 | 02 | | |

*In memory of Bertha and Donald English,*
*mentors and friends who lived their love of God's Word.*

# Contents

General preface                                                         9
Preface                                                                11

## The beginning of creation                                           15

1. Genesis 1:1–25      The Creator of heaven and earth                 17
2. Genesis 1:26 – 2:3  The Creator of human beings                     31
3. Genesis 2:4–25      The Creator provides                            46
4. Genesis 3:1–24      The Creator rejected                            62

## The songs of creation                                               79

5. Proverbs 8:22–36    The wisdom of God                               81
6. Psalm 8             The majesty of God                              88
7. Psalm 19            The glory of God                                96
8. Psalm 148           The universal praise of God                   105

## The Lord of creation                                               113

9. Luke 8:22–25        The wind and waves obey him                    115
10. John 1:1–18        The Word became flesh                          125
11. Colossians 1:15–20 Supreme in all things                          140
12. Hebrews 1:1–14     Heir of all things                             157

## The lessons of creation                                            167

13. Genesis 9:1–17     A new trust                                    169
14. Job 38:1 – 42:17   A new understanding                            181
15. Isaiah 40:9–31     A new strength                                 194
16. Acts 17:16–34      A new life                                     205

## The fulfilment of creation 217

17. Isaiah 65:17–25  The Creator of a new heaven and earth 219
18. Romans 8:18–30  The Creator liberates 229
19. 2 Peter 3:3–16  The Creator transforms 244
20. Revelation 21:1–8  The Creator accepted 257

Appendix 271
Study guide 280

# General preface

THE BIBLE SPEAKS TODAY describes three series of expositions, based on the books of the Old and New Testaments, and on Bible themes that run through the whole of Scripture. Each series is characterized by a threefold ideal:

- to expound the biblical text with accuracy
- to relate it to contemporary life, and
- to be readable.

These books are, therefore, not 'commentaries', for the commentary seeks rather to elucidate the text than to apply it, and tends to be a work rather of reference than of literature. Nor, on the other hand, do they contain the kind of 'sermons' which attempt to be contemporary and readable without taking Scripture seriously enough.

The contributors to The Bible Speaks Today series are all united in their convictions that God still speaks through what he has spoken, and that nothing is more necessary for the life, health and growth of Christians than that they should hear what the Spirit is saying to them through his ancient – yet ever modern – Word.

ALEC MOTYER
JOHN STOTT
DEREK TIDBALL
*Series Editors*

# Preface

One of the highlights of my childhood was our annual holiday at Scarborough. It was not a long journey from the north-east of England to this seaside town and I looked forward to it eagerly. Scarborough was a place of beaches, funfairs and mini-golf and I wanted to get there as quickly as possible. However, my grandparents who came with us saw things differently. They viewed the car journey to Scarborough as a treat in itself. They loved to stop at places along the way, whether it be villages, monuments or toilets! My parents therefore found themselves in something of a quandary, caught between my needs to get there as quickly as possible and their parents wanting to stop on the way.

I feel something of that quandary in the writing of this book. The doctrine of creation is before us and there is a systematic theologian who wants to use the Bible to get there as soon as possible. Yet to do that is to miss a great deal along the way. Then there is the biblical scholar and preacher who wants to spend time with the Bible passages themselves and see them as of interest in their own right. Not only do I feel under pressure from different readers of this book; I also feel the tension myself. I love systematic theology and try to teach a little of it. Part of me wants to engage with the doctrine of creation and set it out logically in headings, subheadings and sub-subheadings! Yet part of me wants to let the Bible speak for itself with a richness that always defies neat subheadings.

So this book is a kind of journey. Some will want to get to the destination quickly, but that is not what we shall do. We have twenty 'villages' to visit on the way in pursuing the doctrine of creation and opening up its biblical themes. The large number of passages and their diversity is testimony to how important this doctrine is within the biblical literature. These villages will be different sizes with a variety of things within them. That means some of the chapters will be short, while some of them will be long. Sometimes we shall need time with various guidebooks in order to understand better what is going on; at other times it will be fairly obvious. My concern is to let the passages speak for themselves rather than manipulate them in order to give convenient systematic development. That may mean that the same doctrinal ground is repeated, but it will be interesting to see how the same ground is covered in different biblical forms.

I have tried to put the villages in some sort of overall direction, but if you are expecting a motorway journey with convenient service stations I am afraid that you will be disappointed. We shall need to cross backward and forward a number of times in the course of the journey. To help us I have arranged the passages in five groups with a short introduction at the transition between sections.

Most biblical commentaries do have a more direct journey, for they follow the linear form of a book or letter. The value of a commentary on a particular book is the ability to develop gradually the biblical writer's context and approach. All of the preparation time in terms of author, background, context and form can be done in one block at the start and then referred back to and developed at appropriate points. In this book, which looks at twenty passages taken from thirteen different books of the Bible, the preparation time is severely limited. I have given short pictures of the issues involved and then suggested further reading for those who want to engage with the books at greater depth.

As with any villages there are a number of ways in and a number of ways out. I have therefore chosen one way in and another way out of each Bible passage. This of course is not to say that in order to preach the passage you have to take this particular route. Yet my hope is that it will encourage readers to see different routes and to devise their own. In addition, the character of the village often determines how you explore it. I have therefore attempted to use a variety of structures in the exposition that best communicate the text.

The invitation to contribute to this new series filled me with both excitement and apprehension. The excitement was in part due to the privilege of joining a series that had had a profound effect on my own Christian journey. The Bible Speaks Today series had introduced me to a way of approaching Scripture that became foundational for my own Christian discipleship and ministry. Commentaries by John Stott, Dick Lucas and Donald English had impressed me with their holding together of faithfulness to the biblical text and application to the questions of today. The opportunity to join my teachers was exciting, especially in a subject that I care so deeply about.

I initially approached the biblical doctrine of creation not as a theologian. As a research astrophysicist the passages on creation within the Bible were of utmost importance in attempting to live with integrity as a scientist and follower of Jesus. My research sometimes posed difficult questions for those passages, yet at the same time those passages encouraged my work as a scientist. As I read the Word of God in my Bible study, so I saw his works in my science. As I switched my area of research, the significance of those passages for the theologian also excited me. They provided the context for the great drama of a God who came into the world and died for me. They continue to open my eyes to the greatness of God 'who made the stars also'.

Finally, these passages have always excited me as a pastor and a preacher. The passages dealing with creation, as we shall see, are not there simply for intellectual speculation. Embedded in the whole story of God's gracious actions in the world, they reassure, challenge, humble, give hope and supremely call for worship.

Yet alongside the excitement, I write this with a great deal of apprehension. I am nowhere near the standard of my teachers and am first and foremost a preacher rather than a professional biblical scholar. I pray that I can show the same faithfulness to the biblical text and relate it to contemporary questions that so impressed me as a student.

However, a further cause of apprehension is in the task of choosing a selection of biblical texts in order to expound a particular theme. I am conscious that various passages traditionally used to speak about creation may not have creation as their primary focus, and indeed contain a great deal more than just the doctrine of the creation. I recall a number of occasions of being asked to speak on a subject and being given the biblical passage that the church thought went best with the subject. The only trouble was that as I got into the text it was clear that the subject did not quite fit and I was left with trying to fit the subject together with the text in a somewhat artificial way. I have tried to avoid such a trap in this work. I have tried to let the passages speak, sometimes about creation and sometimes about other themes and issues.

Yet I believe in the aim of this series, for it demonstrates the unity in the diversity of the Bible. This unity exists in the way that particular passages build upon other passages. The Bible is self-referencing in that sense, and we shall see that very clearly even with the diversity of time and place in which the passages were written. The unity is also there in the fundamental conviction that behind the diversity there is one inspiration who speaks his Word to us in a variety of human authors in different forms of literature, contexts and time periods. The passages dealing with the doctrine of creation are really about the one Creator who reveals himself as the one and only God in the person of Jesus Christ and the work of the Holy Spirit. Thus the attempt to explore the biblical themes of creation that run throughout the Scriptures is both possible and necessary.

My hope and prayer is that you will be excited by the journey. Many of us have reduced the themes of creation in our mind to God starting the Universe off. The biblical picture of creation is far richer than that, seeing Father, Son and Spirit in the beginning, the sustaining and another beginning. Creation is meant not to be an end in itself but a way of orientating ourselves to the Creator who gives us life and love.

This book has been preached and lectured before it was written. My thanks go to students at Cranmer Hall and the Wesley Study Centre in St Johns College, Durham, and students at Asbury Theological Seminary in Kentucky who have helped me sharpen the focus and kept pushing me back to the text. Churches and student groups have kindly invited to me to preach these texts, and I am grateful for that opportunity. It will be apparent to the reader that I hold the conviction that only as the Bible is used in mission and ministry does it become the full instrument of God's work through the Holy Spirit.

I am thankful for the creative and supportive environment at the Centre for Christian Communication in St Johns College, which has enabled me to do this work. Its Director, Geoffrey Stevenson, Rev. Dr Steve Croft, the Warden of Cranmer Hall, and Bishop Stephen Sykes, the Principal of St Johns, have been constant in their support and encouragement. The previous Principal, Rev. David Day, and the Methodist Church created the Fellowship I am privileged to hold, which gives the space for writing and preaching. Alison Wilkinson, Karen George, Blair Carlson and Tony Watkins kindly read the manuscript and suggested changes, but all mistakes remain my responsibility. Derek Tidball and Colin Duriez acted as wise and gracious editors.

None of this would be possible without the love and understanding of my wife, Alison, and my children, Adam and Hannah. They are a constant source of joy, wisdom and noise. Without them this book would have been finished in half the time but it would not have been so much fun!

David Wilkinson
St John's College
Durham, 2002

# The beginning of creation

We begin by exploring the first three chapters of Genesis, looking at the beginning of God's creation.

These passages are rich in theology and worship. We also find in the passages some questions that have divided Christians, and questions that require us to understand the nature of the biblical literature. We shall therefore have to look at the disagreements between Christians and also issues of how we interpret God's Word.

However, more importantly we shall see an overwhelming sense of the need to respond to our Creator God. These chapters breathe the astonishing nature of this God, the ugliness of our rejection of him and the invitation to worship him. They speak into many contemporary questions of modern science, human nature and what is wrong with the world.

They are the Bible's introduction to the Lord of creation.

# 1. Genesis 1:1–25
# The Creator of heaven and earth

## 'Let's start at the very beginning'

Julie Andrews in *The Sound of Music* enthused that the very beginning was a very good place to start. It would seem an obvious thing to say about exploring the biblical doctrine of creation, as well as the basics of music for a family of Austrian children dressed in old curtains!

Yet Genesis 1 has become a minefield for evangelical Christians in recent years. Controversy over the dating of the Universe has caused at worst Christians questioning each other's faith and at the very least a hesitancy amongst preachers to preach on the chapter. For some, a particular interpretation of the chapter has become a test of biblical orthodoxy. If you do not take a particular understanding of Genesis 1 then some will say you give up on the authority of the Bible itself.

In this there are three important dangers. The first is that it does not recognize that Christians equally committed to the authority of the Bible have followed a number of different interpretations as to the dating of the Universe and Genesis 1. The Appendix lists at least five, some of which have a long history and all of which have been advocated by leading evangelical Christians. The fact that there exist different interpretations should caution us against believing that our interpretation is the only one possible. There needs to be humility that allows us to talk to one another while respecting one another's integrity.

Second, there is a danger of confusing a commitment to biblical authority with a commitment to a particular interpretation of a Bible passage. As we shall see throughout this book, each passage has to be understood in its own context and style of literature. A commitment to biblical authority encourages us to work harder at a more faithful interpretation of the biblical text, which does justice to its original setting while allowing it to speak into our own setting.

The third danger is much more subtle yet even more important. The controversy over the dating question often obscures for us the main points of Genesis 1. In the disagreement over the details we lose the very things that the writer inspired by the Holy Spirit wants to communicate.

Not so far from where I write this chapter is the magnificent Durham Cathedral. I still marvel at its simple beauty and the faith of those who built it. I remember the first time I visited it. There was so much to see on the walls that I spent most of my time reading the inscriptions and looking at the paintings. But then my friend said, 'Look up.' There above us was the most breathtaking roof, with those incredible stone arches. I had been spending my time on important details, but was missing the great sight.

Whether the Universe was made in seven days a few thousand years ago, or whether it was created over billions of years, is an important question. Yet it is not central to the message of Genesis 1. Here we have the overture to the Bible. The scene is being set by introducing some of the fundamental themes that will feature in more detail later in the book. And this is an overture about the central character. It is about the character who is introduced in the first verse, and who is central to the close of this overture (Gen. 2:1–3). This is not a passage about the 'how' of creation, nor even primarily about the 'why' of creation. Rather, it is a passage about the 'who' of creation, and is an overture that introduces us to the Creator God:

> [1]*In the beginning God created the heavens and the earth.* [2]*Now the earth was formless and empty, darkness was over the surface of the deep, and the Spirit of God was hovering over the waters.*
> [3]*And God said, 'Let there be light,' and there was light.* [4]*God saw that the light was good, and he separated the light from the darkness.* [5]*God called the light 'day,' and the darkness he called 'night.' And there was evening, and there was morning – the first day.*
> [6]*And God said, 'Let there be an expanse between the waters to separate water from water.'* [7]*So God made the expanse and separated the water under the expanse from the water above it. And it was so.* [8]*God called the expanse 'sky.' And there was evening, and there was morning – the second day.*

*⁹And God said, 'Let the water under the sky be gathered to one place, and let dry ground appear.' And it was so. ¹⁰God called the dry ground 'land,' and the gathered waters he called 'seas.' And God saw that it was good.*

*¹¹Then God said, 'Let the land produce vegetation: seed-bearing plants and trees on the land that bear fruit with seed in it, according to their various kinds.' And it was so. ¹²The land produced vegetation: plants bearing seed according to their kinds and trees bearing fruit with seed in it according to their kinds. And God saw that it was good. ¹³And there was evening, and there was morning – the third day.*

*¹⁴And God said, 'Let there be lights in the expanse of the sky to separate the day from the night, and let them serve as signs to mark seasons and days and years, ¹⁵and let them be lights in the expanse of the sky to give light on the earth.' And it was so. ¹⁶God made two great lights – the greater light to govern the day and the lesser light to govern the night. He also made the stars. ¹⁷God set them in the expanse of the sky to give light on the earth, ¹⁸to govern the day and the night, and to separate light from darkness. And God saw that it was good. ¹⁹And there was evening, and there was morning – the fourth day.*

*²⁰And God said, 'Let the water teem with living creatures, and let birds fly above the earth across the expanse of the sky.' ²¹So God created the great creatures of the sea and every living and moving thing with which the water teems, according to their kinds, and every winged bird according to its kind. And God saw that it was good. ²²God blessed them and said, 'Be fruitful and increase in number and fill the water in the seas, and let the birds increase on the earth.' ²³And there was evening, and there was morning – the fifth day.*

*²⁴And God said, 'Let the land produce living creatures according to their kinds: livestock, creatures that move along the ground, and wild animals, each according to its kind.' And it was so. ²⁵God made the wild animals according to their kinds, the livestock according to their kinds, and all the creatures that move along the ground according to their kinds. And God saw that it was good.*

(Gen. 1:1–25)

This may be an artificial way to divide up the first chapter but many preachers and commentators move too quickly to verses 26–31 and look at the the Creator God in relation to human beings. Yet here in verses 1–25 are the majestic sights of the fundamental assertions in the Bible concerning the Creator God in relation to the Universe.

19

They are themes that run throughout the Bible, but are highlighted in Genesis 1.[1]

Genesis 1:1 – 2:3 is framed by two sections that remind us what this is all about. Verses 1–3 of chapter 2 echo the opening verse. This is about the heavens and the earth and the God who created them. What then do we learn about this God?

## 1. No other creator!

*In the beginning God created the heavens and the earth* (1:1). The first thing we need to know is that God is the sole creator of the Universe. Everything in heaven and earth owes its existence to the sovereign will of God.

Now you may say that's not too exciting! It's a fairly obvious point and we need not have gone to all the trouble of reading a commentary to find out something that is so obvious that most readers assume it. However, before we move on too quickly it is worth seeing that the writer, no doubt facing similar assumptions, thinks that the point is so important that it needs to be developed and indeed reinforced very strongly indeed.

This happens a number of times in the text, in ways that can often be overlooked by the modern reader. The points are interwoven into the cultural setting of the writer. Look for example at the first part of verse 16: *God made two great lights – the greater light to govern the day and the lesser light to govern the night.* What is the writer referring to? It is fairly clear that the reference is to the Sun and the Moon. Indeed, the Good News Bible unfortunately here changes the words in the translation to 'Sun' and 'Moon'. However, in Hebrew, it is the greater and lesser lights. Why are the Sun and the Moon not called by their respective names? The most probable answer is that in many neighbouring cultures they were the names of gods. Genesis 1 seems to be attacking this false theological idea, by saying that they are not gods but simply lights created by the one true God. This is reinforced by the way the Sun and Moon are given the role of simply giving light

---

[1] For a fuller discussion of questions of authorship, origin and context of these chapters see H. Blocher, *In the Beginning* (IVP, 1984); E. Lucas, *Can we Believe in Genesis Today?* (IVP, 2001); D. Atkinson, *The Message of Genesis 1–11*, The Bible Speaks Today (IVP, 1990); J. E. Hartley, *Genesis*, New International Biblical Commentary on the Old Testament (Paternoster, 2000); W. Brueggemann, *Genesis*, Interpretation (John Knox, 1982); D. Kidner, *Genesis*, Tyndale Old Testament Commentaries (IVP, 1967); G. von Rad, *Genesis: A Commentary*, tr. J. Marks (Westminster, 1972); G. J. Wenham, *Genesis 1–15*, Word Biblical Commentary (Word, 1987); C. Westermann, *Genesis 1–11*, tr. J. J. Scullion (SPCK, 1984); U. Cassuto, *A Commentary on the Book of Genesis*, 2 vols. (Magnes, 1961, 1964).

to the earth, and ruling the day and the night under God. There is no suggestion that they have a life of their own or are divine in any way. They are not worthy of worship but are simply creations of God.

A similar point is made in the second half of verse 16 in the brief understatement *He also made the stars*. For some the stars would be gods, controlling human destiny, but here God is so great he simply made the stars also. They are so unimportant compared to God that they almost do not merit a mention.

This is a theological attack or a polemic. It is taking well-known concepts in popular culture and religion in the ancient Near East and arguing that they are misguided. The polemic continues in the use of the verb 'create' in verse 21: *God created the great sea monsters* (RSV). The verb is used only in relation to three acts in Genesis 1. First it is used in the creation of the heavens and the earth (1:1) and in the creation of humanity (1:21). Why should such a special verb be used of great sea monsters? Again the answer is in the background of the ancient Near East and the need to assert that there is no other creator. In other creation stories, the creator has first to subdue sea monsters. Genesis 1 is criticizing this false theological view and asserting that God created everything.

Other examples run through the chapter.[2] In some creation stories the gods struggle to separate the upper waters from lower waters. In verses 6–10 God does it simply and easily. In the Egyptian stories of creation God has to create through magical utterance. Here he simply speaks and it is done. In addition, God names the various things he creates such as the heavens, the earth, the sea, as well as day and night (vv. 5, 8, 10). This is significant against the Old Testament background that to name something is to assert sovereignty over it (e.g. 2 Kgs. 23:34; 24:17).

The message conveyed by this text is that God is without peer or competitor: he has no rivals in creation. His word is supreme; that is, he speaks and it is done.

This polemic nature of Genesis 1 is important to bear in mind within the scholarly debate as to the relationship of the Genesis text to other ancient creation stories. Gunkel in 1895 raised the question of whether Genesis 1 is dependent on other creation stories. Since then many theories have been suggested regarding the relationship of the Genesis account to stories in the ancient Near East such as the Babylonian creation stories *Enuma Elish* or the Epic of Atrahasis, or Egyptian ideas of creation in such works as The Teaching of King Merikare. Some have reduced the Genesis account to a much later

---

[2] G. Hasel, 'The Polemic Nature of the Genesis Cosmology', *Evangelical Quarterly* 46 (1974), pp. 81–102.

work that has simply copied more ancient stories, while others wanting to defend the purity of Genesis as revelation direct from God have emphasized the differences.

The truth is probably more complex.[3] There are broad parallels between Genesis and the Babylonian stories such as the separation of heaven and earth, and the schema of creation followed by divine displeasure followed by flood. However, the evidence for direct dependence is weak in all these cases. For example the often quoted parallel that the Babylonian Genesis is written on seven tablets, which parallels the seven days of creation of the Hebrew account, is simply coincidence. The division of the Babylonian story bears no resemblance to its content, nor indeed to the stages of the story.

However, as Wenham has argued, the writers of Genesis probably knew the Babylonian stories.[4] Hebrew patriarchs had links with Mesopotamia, and there was a widespread distribution of cuneiform texts. While not deriving their theology from the Babylonian stories, God has set the revelation of the truth about himself into the thought forms and culture of the ancient Near East. Far from corrupting its purity, this gives the revelation even more power. God's revelation of himself is never in the abstract; it is in the reality of human history.

How do we translate to the world of today this truth that there is no other Creator? One of the most important applications is in how we view science. Cosmology has allowed us to trace the history of the Universe further back in time. Indeed, some scientists such as Stephen Hawking claim that a combination of quantum theory and general relativity will describe the initial conditions of the Universe.[5]

Yet what does this mean? Is quantum theory the creator of the Universe? Genesis 1 says a very clear 'no'! Science is extremely successful, but that success is based on the fact that it limits its area of questions. If my wife kisses me, then as a good scientist I can say that what caused that was 'neck-muscle movements reducing the distance between two pairs of lips, a reciprocal transmission of carbon dioxide and microbes, and a contraction of orbicular muscles'. I would be entirely correct in the scientific description of the reason for the kiss. But I would also be a very sad human being! There are

---

[3] See e.g. W. G. Lambert, 'A New Look at the Babylonian Background of Genesis', *Journal of Theological Studies* 16 (1965), p. 294; D. T. Tsumura, *The Earth and the Waters in Genesis 1 and 2: A Linguistic Investigation* (Sheffield Academic Press, 1989), pp. 156–157.

[4] Wenham, *Genesis 1–15*, p. xlviii.

[5] S. W. Hawking, *A Brief History of Time* (Bantam, 1988); *The Universe in a Nutshell* (Bantam, 2001); See also D. Wilkinson, *God, Time and Stephen Hawking* (Monarch, 2001).

other issues of meaning and purpose that are to do with the motives for my wife's actions; that is, she is demonstrating her love.

Genesis 1 is reminding us that in terms of questions of meaning and purpose, God is the only answer. Science may describe God's activity in creation and is to be valued for that. However, we must guard against language that suggests that science is the creator. Richard Dawkins, the Oxford Professor of the Public Understanding of Science, often presents science as the creator of life, the Universe and everything.[6]

Against such a view, a theological polemic is needed again in a society that puts its faith totally in science.

## 2. The order of faithfulness

The second major theme of Genesis 1 is given not just by the content but also the style. If God gives revelation of his nature in the reality of history, he also does it within various literary styles within the Bible. Here the style reflects a very important truth.

What is striking about the account in the first chapter of Genesis is the pattern and order to God's creation. Verses 3 to 5 show seven standard formulae that with variation comprise the descriptions of each stage of creation:

1. God said
2. God's command
3. Fulfilment of God's command
4. Description of what God created
5. God's approval
6. God named
7. Day number

On each subsequent day there may be variation in the sequence and components but this basic shape is followed. God creates with pattern and order.

Indeed, the whole chapter reflects this. Much debate between Christians has centred on the seven days, and whether they mean literally seven periods of 24 hours (see references in the Appendix). However, the structure of the seven days reflects a logical rather than

---

[6] R. Dawkins, *The Blind Watchmaker* (Penguin, 1988). See also C. Sagan, *Cosmos* (Abacus, 1983); P. Atkins, *Creation Revisited* (Freeman, 1992); D. Dennett, *Darwin's Dangerous Idea: Evolution and the Meanings of Life* (Simon & Schuster, 1995; E. O. Wilson, *Sociobiology: The New Synthesis* (Harvard University Press, 1975).

chronological order. Lucas divides up the seven-day structure as follows:

|  | The earth was |  |
|---|---|---|
| shapeless | and | empty |

| Day 1 | Day 4 |
|---|---|
| The separation of light and darkness | The creation of the lights to rule the day and the night |

| Day 2 | Day 5 |
|---|---|
| The separation of the waters to form the sky and the sea | The creation of the birds and fish to fill the sky and the sea |

| Day 3 | Day 6 |
|---|---|
| The separation of the sea from the dry land and creation of plants | The creation of the animals and humans to fill the land and eat the plants |

Day 7
The heavens and the earth were finished and God rested.[7]

That is, the first three days deal with shape and the second three with filling up that shape. The structure speaks of the order, harmony and beauty of God's creation. This logical structure does seem to indicate that the aim of the chapter is not meant to be a strict scientific record.

Furthermore, the number seven is not just present in the days. For example, the number of Hebrew words in verse 1 is seven. Verse 2 has fourteen. Verses 1 to 3 of chapter 2 have thirty-five. The word 'God' occurs thirty-five times in the chapter, the word 'Earth' twenty-one times, and the phrase 'God saw that it was good' seven times. Now one does not need to be a great mathematician to see something very subtle going on. The number seven throughout the Bible is associated with completion, fulfilment and perfection. It speaks of order and goodness.

The style reflects the content, reinforcing the message that the Universe is ordered and good because of God. The faithfulness of God is the source of the order in creation.

This too has a very important application to science. Science pro-

---

[7] Lucas, *Can we Believe?* p. 96.

ceeds on the basis of order in the Universe and our ability to discern it. So Christianity, far from being attacked by or attacking science, fundamentally affirms it. To use another image of the passage, God is the divine lawgiver appointing the stars, Sun and Moon. God gives life and fruitfulness to creation, in a way that reflects its dependence rather than independence. All things are ultimately dependent on God's faithful upholding of the Universe moment by moment, for without the Creator they would not exist.

That faithfulness expressing itself in the order of the scientific laws means that science is possible. Indeed, a number of historians of science have pointed out the importance of the Christian worldview to the growth of what we now know as science.[8] Alongside the many other influences, this worldview was because people believed that God had created the Universe as a free act, and that it was important to look at the Universe to see what it was like. The nature of the Universe could not be worked out from mere logic, as God was not subject to our understandings of what is logical. We had to examine what he had done and so came an emphasis on the value of observation. At the same time, because this God was a faithful God, the Universe should exhibit a divine order, which would be described by scientific laws. Observing the Universe would therefore lead to an understanding of those laws. Finally, because there was no other creator and God was the creator of all things, different parts of the Universe were not under different control. The science of a stone falling to the ground, was the same science of a planet orbiting the Sun. The laws of science should be consistent in different times and places, which is one of the fundamental assumptions of modern science. Therefore observation and the hope for consistent laws was encouraged by the understanding of God the Creator from Scripture.

Christians have often celebrated such faithfulness in the natural world. The long tradition of church harvest festivals give thanks to God for the faithfulness of the seasons. Indeed the well-known hymn celebrates:

> Summer and winter, and springtime and harvest,
> Sun, moon and stars in their courses above,
> Join with all nature in manifold witness,
> To Thy great faithfulness, mercy and love.[9]

[8] This is argued in various ways in R. Hooykaas, *Religion and the Rise of Modern Science* (Scottish Academic Press, 1972); S. L. Jaki, *Cosmos and Creator* (Scottish Academic Press, 1980); C. A. Russell, *Cross Currents* (Christian Impact, 1997); J. H. Brooke, *Science and Religion: Some Historical Perspectives* (CUP, 1991).

[9] William Runyon and Thomas Chisholm © 1951 Hope Publishing Co., CopyCare <www.copycare.com>. Used by permission.

It is a truth to celebrate not only in the farming community, but also in the scientific community. The courses of the Sun, Moon and stars are the result of gravity and on a greater scale general relativity. These owe their origin to God. As Kepler said, 'Science is thinking God's thoughts after him.' Those such as scientists who explore the order of the Universe, or those such as engineers who exploit its order do so because of God, whether they recognize it or not, in that science, engineering and technology are Christian ministries.

We often unconsciously form a hierarchy of Christian ministries and vocations. The top job in terms of perceived spirituality is the missionary followed by the evangelist. Then the church leader whether a pastor, preacher or prophet. Then the caring professions, such as doctors or nurses, which have long been recognized as Christian vocations. Then perhaps teachers. However, right at the bottom are usually the scientists and accountants!

The point may be overstated, but I wonder if the above hierarchy is often represented in the way that Christians pray. A friend at the forefront of genetic research who acts as salt and light in that diffi-cult arena, once said to me, 'I wish my church would occasionally pray for me in the same way that we pray for our overseas mission-aries.' How can we support those in our congregations who are involved in exploring or using the faithfulness of God in creation? I wonder too if our perspective is reflected in the way that we encour-age people to respond to the call of God in their lives. Can we encourage young people and students to study science and delight in thinking God's thoughts after him?

It is also worth noticing what this might have to say in terms of pointers to God. The order in the Universe represented by the laws of physics and their very particular arrangement has been striking to many scientists.[10] Whereas this does not lead to a proof of God, it may join with other pointers towards him. Those in the so-called intelligent-design movement use the order of the Universe to point to the existence of a Creator. As we shall see later in this book there are dangers if this is pushed too far, but it does have value.[11]

## 3. Extravagant diversity

If this talk of order and science gives the idea that God is a boring egghead who can be blamed for numerous students having to learn

---

[10] E.g. M. Rees, *Just Six Numbers: The Deep Forces That Shape the Universe* (Weidenfeld & Nicolson, 2000).
[11] W. A. Dembski, *Intelligent Design* (IVP, 1999); N. Broom, *How Blind Is the Watchmaker?* (IVP, 2001).

calculus, we need to notice another overriding theme in Genesis 1. Alongside the image of lawgiver, king and logician, the Genesis account gives us the picture of God as the great artist.

Here is creativity and diversity in abundance. Some forms of torture put prisoners in cells with no windows, blank walls and constant light, maintaining a monotony of environment. How different from the creativity of God!

*The earth was formless and empty* (v. 2), a phrase that could be translated as 'total chaos' or 'waste and void'. This formless earth could signify either nothingness or disorder. The word is often used in describing the experience of being lost in a desert without tracks or distinguishing features as a guide (Job 6:18).

It is into this monotony, disorder and darkness that God brings differentiation, contrast, structure and order. The acts of separation (vv. 3, 6, 7, 14, 18) as well as giving a sense of structure show God as giving diversity to the created order. We may at times not notice these differences, but contrasts add to our sense of beauty of the world. The contrasts of heat and cold, oceans and dry land, the brightness of a summer day and the star field of a clear night, affect all of our senses and add to our experience of the world as an awe-inspiring place.

Then into this structure comes light and life. Once again, here is diversity and creativity. When vegetation is brought forth it is of various kinds with the ability to reproduce (v. 11). As one child once said to me, 'Wouldn't it have been awful if the only vegetable God created was cabbage!'

Even in the small phrase *He also made the stars* (v. 16), is an awe-inspiring statement of the creativity of God. To a person of the ancient world, the night sky unpolluted by the street lights of the modern world was a myriad of constellations and movement. Today we are able to see even more than the ancients could. The Hubble Space Telescope and a new generation of ground-based and satellite telescopes have opened up an almost unbelievable vista of diversity.

Our Sun is a star, a million times larger than the Earth. Yet it is only one star in 100 billion stars that make up the Milky Way Galaxy. Each star is different in terms of size, lifetime, colour and temperature. In addition to the stars, vast clouds of molecular hydrogen and dust give birth to new stars and then are lit up in spectacular nebulae by their young stars. At the end of their lives the stars turn into exotic objects such as cold and dense white dwarfs, violent supernovae explosions, spinning neutron stars or colossal black holes. And the Milky Way Galaxy is only one galaxy in the 100 billion galaxies in the Universe. Once again these galaxies are in a variety of sizes and shapes, from the small Magellanic clouds visible in the southern hemisphere to vast elliptical galaxies such as M81, twenty times the size of our own Milky Way. And that's not to mention the different forms of matter and radiation that make up the Universe, some of which we have yet to discover.

Why such a Universe? People often ask why God has created a Universe with more stars than the grains of sand on the beaches of the world. After all, human life could have arisen with a special creation of one star and one planet. My answer could be that the night sky would have been very boring and very few people could ever have done research in theoretical astrophysics! More seriously, we now know that such a Universe is important in sustaining human life. However, we are still left with the question of why this kind of Universe?

The answer is surely in the extravagant diversity of God. As we shall see in a later chapter, the heavens declare the glory of God (Ps. 19:1). God is an artist who creates on a vast canvas with huge brush strokes. He celebrates diversity, making a Universe that communicates his greatness, joy and generosity. Such a God is shown throughout the Bible. In the New Testament, when Jesus turns the water into wine at the wedding in Cana, John records significantly that Jesus provided between 120 to 180 gallons of wine at a party where most of the guests were probably already well filled (John 2:6)! Why? Part of the reason is surely that God is extravagant in generosity.

Such extravagance is also seen within the animal world. In the creation of birds and fishes (vv. 20–23), once again different kinds are emphasized. The phrase in verse 20 *teem with living creatures* as a command to the water is an evocative image. As well as signifying movement it suggests the sense of abundant fertility (e.g. Exod. 1:7). The BBC television series *The Blue Planet* shows the extraordinary diversity in the oceans of the world, which parallels the diversity of space. Until now we've only touched the surface. In God's blessing is the command and opportunity for fruitfulness and increase (v. 22). This is a world where diversity increases.

Even in the animals based on the land the writer is eager to emphasize the different kinds as part of God's creation (vv. 24–25). Within that it is interesting to note that a process is involved. *Let the land produce living creatures* says God (v. 24). God builds into the natural world the process of his creativity. Thus the natural world provides an intricate tapestry bearing witness to the creativity of God.

Perhaps the image of a tapestry is too static, however. At a worship event we as a congregation were surrounded by a number of video screens each giving different pictures of the beauty of creation, the suffering of the cross, the words of Jesus, and the words of songs with which we were invited to join in. It was a dynamic experience of the greatness of God and the diversity of his creation. Creation itself is that dynamic experience of the glory of God.

In all of this, as God gives structure to the heavens and earth and fills up the emptiness with diversity, the repeated refrain is that God saw it was good. As Wenham comments here, 'God the great artist is pictured admiring his handiwork'.[12] God delights in the diversity of his creativity.

In contrast, our delight in greed destroys diversity. It is estimated that there are several million species of living things on the Earth, of which possibly fewer than 10% have been identified. Yet the American scientist Edward Wilson estimates that we as human beings currently wipe out three species every hour. This is due in large part to deforestation, which proceeds at such a rate that an area of forest equivalent to that of the British Isles is lost every year. In addition, we pollute the land and the sea with persistent pesticides, acid rain, and 2 million tonnes of rubbish daily. Greenhouse gases are raising the temperature of the Earth and the destruction of the ozone layer increases ultraviolet radiation and affects weather patterns.

All because we do not respect the world as God's creation. 'The earth is the LORD's, and everything in it' (Ps. 24:1). There is no other creator. He is the one who gives us the gift of science and technology, but then wants us to use it in a way that celebrates diversity and generosity.

It is blasphemous to destroy the diversity of the world. The extravagance and diversity of the creation reflects the glory of God. In fact, far from being a dry scientific or even theological text, this first chapter of Genesis breathes worship. Indeed, there are indications that it reflects a liturgical form; that is, it was used in worship. It is neither simple prose nor simple Hebrew poetry, but is skilfully arranged, a form recognized in the way that the NIV text is set out. It is liturgy or a meditation on the work of creation so that we can understand that the creation is related to God.

Its central concern is not to explain the how of creation, but to catch the reader up with the wonder of creation. This is not to exalt the creation itself, but is an invitation to worship the Creator. Throughout this book we shall see time after time that the Bible never speaks of the doctrine of creation purely out of intellectual curiosity. Creation is used to encourage worship, to increase faith,

[12] Wenham, *Genesis 1–15*, p. 38.

and to change perspective on our life in the light of the nature of God.

For Christians to abuse creation or even to spend too much time debating its age, misses the point. We need to ask the question 'Is the worship of the God of heaven and earth central to our own lives and to our local church?'

# 2. Genesis 1:26 – 2:3
# The Creator of human beings

## O, to be human

Steven Spielberg knows what sells. *Jaws*, *Indiana Jones*, and *ET* were box-office blockbusters, and so it was not surprising to see him producing a movie in 2001 on one of the biggest issues that will face human beings in the future. In the movie *AI: Artificial Intelligence* Spielberg uses the earlier story of Brian Aldiss to explore what it means to be human. A young boy robot gains the capacity to love, and to be loved. Does this make him human? It is a fascinating and disturbing movie. We are left with the question of whether it is the reality of love or even the reality of death that defines humanity.

It is a theme that has been explored before. Mr Data in *Star Trek: The Next Generation* struggles with the same question alongside *The Terminator* and Kubrick's own supercomputer Hal in *2001: A Space Odyssey*. This rich vein of interest in Hollywood reflects questions that are part of our society. The growth of the power of computers has been rapid. Are we reaching the stage of having to ask our computer whether we can turn it off? This is not just fear of whether artificial intelligence will take over the world, but a genuine question that if computers begin to show intelligence or even self-consciousness, then what does that mean for human beings?

The development of modern medicine also raises the question of what it means to be human.[13] The ease of abortion and genetic engineering on human embryos creates controversy over when life begins. The pressure by some for legal euthanasia locates the

---

[13] M. Jeeves, *Human Nature at the Millennium* (IVP, 1997); J. Wyatt, *Matters of Life and Death* (IVP, 1999); P. Moore, *Babel's Shadow: Genetic Technologies in a Fracturing Society* (Lion, 2000).

question in the midst of suffering, disability and death. Even popular discussion of the possibilities of human cloning often concentrates on whether the same person would result.

Against this background many people are ready to give an answer to what it means to be human. There are those who stress the physical. Richard Dawkins for example speaks of humans as simply gene-survival machines.[14] Such a reductionist view of human life has (unjustly) enrolled the findings of the Human Genome Project to say that we are simply our genes.

Others go in the opposite direction and stress the spiritual. On this view it is some eternal soul that makes us human. The mass suicide of thirty-nine members of the Heaven's Gate cult, in a mansion in San Diego in 1997, was based on the belief that a spaceship was hiding behind Comet Hale-Bopp, waiting for their eternal souls to take them to heaven.

Others have tried to specify the nature of self-consciousness as the key to being human. Daniel Dennett believes that as we understand the neuroscience of the brain more, so we shall understand consciousness.[15] However, other philosophers, such as David Chalmers, disagree, believing that there is 'an extra, irreducible ingredient' to self-consciousness.[16] The difficulty of any consensus in the area is summed up by Stuart Sutherland, who comments on self-consciousness, 'It is impossible to specify what it is, what it does, or how it evolved. Nothing worth reading has been written about it'.[17]

To all of these views the Genesis account says that the point is being missed. The physical, the spiritual and self-consciousness are all important to being human. However, the Bible defines human beings not in terms of a particular part of our bodies or minds. Instead, human beings are defined in terms of relationship, and in particular their relationship to God.

Let us return to the last part of the first chapter:

*26Then God said, 'Let us make human beings in our image, in our likeness, and let them rule over the fish of the sea and the birds of the air, over the livestock, over all the earth, and over all the creatures that move along the ground.'*

---

[14] R. Dawkins, *Unweaving the Rainbow* (Penguin, 1998), p. 285.

[15] D. C. Dennett, *Consciousness Explained* (Penguin, 1993); D. C. Dennett, *Kinds of Mind: Towards an Understanding of Consciousness* (Weidenfeld & Nicolson, 1996).

[16] D. Chalmers, *The Conscious Mind* (OUP, 1996), p. xiv.

[17] S. Sutherland, 'Consciousness', in *Macmillan Dictionary of Psychology* (Macmillan, 1995), p. 95.

*27So God created human beings in his own image,*
*in the image of God he created them;*
*male and female he created them.*

*28God blessed them and said to them, 'Be fruitful and increase*
*in number; fill the earth and subdue it. Rule over the fish of the sea*
*and the birds of the air and over every living creature that moves*
*on the ground.' 29Then God said, 'I give you every seed-bearing*
*plant on the face of the whole earth and every tree that has fruit*
*with seed in it. They will be yours for food. 30And to all the beasts*
*of the earth and all the birds of the air and all the creatures that*
*move on the ground – everything that has the breath of life in it –*
*I give every green plant for food.' And it was so.*
*31God saw all that he had made, and it was very good. And there*
*was evening, and there was morning – the sixth day.*

*2:1Thus the heavens and the earth were completed in all their vast*
*array.*

*2By the seventh day God had finished the work he had been doing;*
*so on the seventh day he rested from all his work. 3And God*
*blessed the seventh day and made it holy, because on it he rested*
*from all the work of creating that he had done.*
(Gen. 1:26 – 2:3)

As I commented, this is a somewhat artificial division of the chapter
for the purposes of this book. It must be remembered that this
section is part of the sixth day, linking in part the creation of human
beings with the creation of land animals. We also need to note that
there is a division of style in the text itself between verses 3 and 4 of
chapter 2, and indeed, in the view of many scholars, these different
sections represent two different sources of material combined by the
writer of the Genesis text. However, as the commentator Gerhard
von Rad pointed out some years ago, although they may be different, there are a number of important links between the two.[18] We
shall explore some of those links in the next chapter.

What then do we learn about human beings? In the diversity and
extravagance of God's creative activity there is something special.
The high point of the creation narrative is the creation of human
beings, for they alone are made in his image and given dominion over
the natural world.

The *Let us* of verse 26 has sometimes been used in Christian tradition to argue that the trinitarian understanding of God was there

[18] G. von Rad, *Genesis: A Commentary*, tr. J. Marks (Westminster, 1972), pp. 23–42.

from the beginning of the Old Testament. We need to be careful of such an argument. The trinitarian understanding of God as Father, Son and Holy Spirit is true but is not the primary image behind this phrase. Others have argued that the *Let us* shows the use of an earlier account that believed in a multitude of gods rather than one God. However, as we have seen in the previous chapter this does not fit with the theological polemic throughout the Genesis text.

The *Let us* introduction to the creation of human beings more likely refers to the royal 'we' or the plural of self-encouragement. Jewish commentators have seen it as an image of God addressing the heavenly court. In that it shows the importance of the creation of human beings. It is, as Wenham comments, 'a divine announcement to the heavenly court, drawing the angelic host's attention to the master stroke of creation, man'.[19]

If this is recognized as the primary use of the image, then it is not invalid for Christians looking back from the revelation of the Old and New Testaments to be reminded that the work of creation involves all three persons of the Trinity.

## Understanding the image of God

The creation of human beings is said by God to be *in our image, in our likeness* (v. 26). We need to ask first whether there is any difference between image and likeness. This is an important question because some of the early Christian commentators made a distinction.

Irenaeus (c. 180) viewed the reference to image as representing 'natural qualities' such as reason and personality, while likeness represented 'supernatural graces' such as ethical, moral and spiritual qualities. Tertullian (c. 160–225) suggested that the image of God was retained after sinning, while the lost likeness was restored through the renewing activity of the Spirit after conversion. Origen (c. 185–254) argued that the image of God referred to humanity after the fall, while likeness referred to human nature after its perfection at final consummation. Such distinctions were based in part on the need to understand the fact that human beings are both created good and are fallen, in need of redemption. By distinguishing human nature into image and likeness, then, this 'duality' of human beings could be explained.

However, the text gives little support for such a distinction. In Genesis 5:3 likeness and image are reversed compared to Genesis 1:26, showing that the terms are used interchangeably. Likeness is used here simply as a qualification of image to stress that humans are not identical to God while being a reflection of God himself.

[19] G. J. Wenham, *Genesis 1–15*, Word Biblical Commentary (Word, 1987), p. 28.

The precise meaning of 'image' is difficult because of its rarity in the Bible and uncertainty about its etymology. This is then overlaid by two thousand years of the attempt of Christian systematic theology to give a precise definition. Even a cursory glance at the history of the various interpretations of 'image' may warn us as to the dangers of too simplistic an interpretation.[20]

First, the image was seen as a physical embodiment of God. The Anthropomorphites and Audiani in the fourth century argued that God is physically embodied and human beings are physically the image of God. This must be rejected, as the Old Testament stresses the invisibility of God (e.g. Deut. 4:15–16). However, there is a sense in which the creation gives 'visibility' to the invisible God. For example Paul in Romans 1:20 states, 'For since the creation of the world God's invisible qualities – his eternal power and divine nature – have been clearly seen, being understood from what has been made, so that they are without excuse.' In the created nature of human beings, therefore, in Calvin's words, 'some sparks' of God's image glow.

Second, image has been suggested to refer to human reason, which mirrors the wisdom of God. Augustine (354–430) spoke of the 'footsteps of the Trinity' comprising intelligence, memory and will in human beings. Aquinas (1225–74) also saw the image of God in this way. While our God-given capacity of rational thought is dependent on a rational and faithful Creator, the danger of such an understanding of image leads to the 'intellectualization' of human beings. If the essence of being human is primarily intellectual thought, then the emotional and physical aspects are often neglected. It may be a good definition of what is most important to academic theologians, but disenfranchises many human beings, from those who learn about the world in non-academic ways to those who are mentally disabled.

Third, image has been linked to freedom. Being made in the image of God means that human beings are free, self-determining and self-transcending. Our free will and creative activities are a reflection of the nature of God. Once again we can acknowledge the insight of this, without allowing it to be the core definition of image of God. We are created with free will, although the nature of our freedom is very limited compared to that of God. We cannot freely create the Universe; indeed, we are constrained in our choices by the nature of the created Universe. Even in moral choices, leaving aside the question of sin, we are limited by our limited knowledge. Free will is one of the results of being created in the image of God, but it is not the only thing.

[20] See D. J. A. Clines, 'Humanity as the Image of God', in idem, *On the Way to the Postmodern: Old Testament Essays, 1967–1998*, vol. 2, *Journal for the Study of the Old Testament*, Supplement Series 293 (Sheffield Academic Press, 1998), pp. 447–498.

Fourth, our moral sense has been suggested to be what it means to be created in the image of God. God is holy and righteous and human beings reflect this moral sense. Calvin characterized image as being 'in the light of the mind, in the uprightness of the heart and in the soundness of all its parts'.[21] He interpreted two verses in the New Testament on the principle that what was restored by grace was what was marred in the fall. So Colossians 3:10, 'put on the new self, which is being renewed in knowledge in the image of its Creator', put alongside Ephesians 4:24, 'put on the new self, created to be like God in true righteousness and holiness', means that the image is true righteousness and holiness. Yet again, there is an important insight here, but perhaps it does not sum up all what it means to be made in the image of God.

The weakness of the above attempted definitions is that they actually pay little attention to the Genesis text itself. They have come from systematic considerations.

Fortunately, in recent years, studies in the language and context of the ancient Near East have helped us to a deeper understanding of image. The first thing to say is that image needs to be understood against a background of being a representative. Egyptian and Assyrian texts sometimes describe the king as the image of God, meaning God's representative on earth. Such concepts seem to be in the Genesis text. Certainly there is a close connection in the text between made in the image of God and God's command to exercise dominion over the natural world (Gen. 1:26–28). To rule (v. 26) and subdue (v. 28) are royal tasks. Furthermore, physical images of gods and kings in terms of statues erected in cities or conquered nations were viewed as representatives of the deity or king, even to the extent of a god being thought of as indwelling an idol by his spirit. The image represented the one imaged, and the presence of an absent lord.

Further, the image of God is not part of the human constitution so much as it is a description of the process of creation that makes human beings different. The image should not be imagined to be a 'part' of us, whether our body, our reason or our moral sense. It is not about something we have or something we do; it is about relationship. The Old Testament scholar Claus Westermann writes, 'human beings are created in such a way that their very existence is intended to be their relationship to God'.[22] The 'image of God' means that we are sufficiently like God that we can have an intimate relationship with him. This is often emphasized later in the Genesis account. God walks in the garden with Adam and Eve, and he speaks

---

[21] J. Calvin, *Institutes of the Christian Religion*, tr. F. L. Battles, ed. J. T. McNeill (SCM, 1961), 1.15.4.
[22] C. Westermann, *Genesis 1–11*, tr. J. J. Scullion (SPCK, 1984), p. 158.

in a different way to them than to the rest of creation. He speaks personally, while they understand and respond.

This is how the Bible understands the special nature of human beings. Not primarily that we are physically different from the rest of creation, though in many ways we are, but in the fact that he has given us an intimate relationship with himself.

This is a point that has been explored by many early and contemporary theologians. Athanasius (c. 296–373) spoke of the image of God as the capacity to relate to and partake in the life of God, while the twentieth-century theologian Emil Brunner spoke of it as 'existence for love'.[23]

It is worth at this point reflecting on the importance of taking the Bible as a whole. If some systematic theologians have perhaps neglected the Genesis text, we need to be careful of building doctrine on only one text. A study of the background of the ancient Near East and the meaning of image does not give us a full understanding of being made in the image of God.

Karl Barth was one of many theologians who pointed out the importance of seeing the image of God from the perspective of Jesus Christ. He suggested that the image of God was reflected in man-and-woman created as the sign of hope of the coming Son of Man who is himself the image of God. Christ is the image of God (Col. 1:15), through his work on the cross enabling us to 'put on the new self, which is being renewed in knowledge in the image of its Creator' (Col. 3:10). Thus when Paul describes Jesus as the image of the invisible God, he is saying that Jesus is the decisive norm for both divinity and humanity.

Therefore, as David Atkinson points out, a Christian understanding of what it means to be human begins with Jesus Christ.[24] He is the one in whom God's purposes for humanity are summed up. His life demonstrates among many things that to be human is to

- be in intimate relationship with God
- be embodied
- experience emotion
- exercise moral choice
- relate in love to other humans
- demonstrate compassion

Humanity is so fully shown in Jesus that he is the only true human being. The rest of us, marred by our rebellion against God, yet

---

[23] E. Brunner, *The Christian Doctrine of Creation and Redemption: Dogmatics*, vol. 2 (Lutterworth, 1952), p. 57.

[24] D. Atkinson, *Pastoral Ethics* (Lynx, 1994), p. 168.

created in his image and offered salvation by him, are 'Human Becomings', on the way to full humanity.

Thus image is about both creation and redemption. Our capacity for relationship with God means that we reflect something of God in our human bodies, and to some extent we reflect his reason, the capacity for free action and moral sensitivity. Yet we need to see these things from the perspective of Jesus Christ.

Some will say that this has been a long section of doctrine and definitions. Yet it is important to guard against those who would simplify the image of God too much. However, the danger is that we concentrate on human beings at the expense of God. We need to remember that the Genesis text wants us to know more about the Creator reflected in creation.

## Looking at the image of God

If Genesis 1:26–28 suggests that the image of God in human beings is about relationship and responsibility, then what does that tell us of God? What do we see reflected in the image of the creation of human beings?

### 1. A God who gives relationship

What is the high point of God's creation as recorded in Genesis? Despite the protest of some astrophysicists, it is not a black hole! The high point is humanity. God creates in his image beings who have the gift of relationship with him.

This is in stark contrast to the Babylonian creation story *Enuma Elish*. There human beings are created simply as slaves to the gods, an afterthought to relieve the gods of work and to provide them with food. In the biblical account there is no such afterthought and no slavery. Indeed, God provides food for human beings (v. 29), a theme that will be developed in the next chapter.

As we have seen, some scholars have suggested that the Genesis account reflects the metaphor of creation as the royal act of a great King. God's creative words are presented in the form and function of royal decrees. The giving of names (e.g. Gen. 1:10) is a royal expression of lordship. Yet here the King creates in his own image. This is a very personal model of creation. The Enlightenment model of the West sees the Universe as a machine with human beings able to do whatever they wish with the impersonal world. The Eastern model of the Universe as an organism sees human beings as simply part of the world. Here the biblical metaphor for the created realm is kingdom. Not in terms of a geographical place, but where the rule of the King is experienced, and human beings have a key part in this.

Christianity therefore maintains that the real meaning of the Universe is not to be found in an impersonal cosmic force, nor in a mathematical theory of everything, but in a personal God who wants to be in relationship with human beings. To be human is to be made for relationship, to love and to be loved by the God who created us.

This means that relationship is at the heart of the Universe. This is important, especially in a materialistic and consumer-dominated society. If we want to find purpose in life, we find it not in possessions nor in wealth, but in relationship with this God. In business, profit should not be everything. While important to generate wealth, we need to remember that relationship is fundamental to the Universe. This means that justice and respect to employees, suppliers and customers is as important. Christians have an important role as salt and light within the power structures of our society in witnessing to the importance of relationship.

Human life is a gift from God. I sometimes speak at churches about creation and I visited one church where, before I spoke, the leader read a poem by way of introduction. The poem started with 'God was sitting in heaven feeling very lonely and so he decided to create the Universe . . .' The poem continued, but I was stuck on the first line! It may have been a nice poem but it was not a Christian understanding of creation.

God was not lonely in heaven! God in Trinity was experiencing love within the three persons. God did not have to make the Universe in order to feel loved, as if he needed human beings. He created human beings in his image because he wanted to. A friend of mine once asked me why God created the Universe. He and his wife had just had their first child, so I turned the question back to him: 'Why have you had a baby?' The answer was not because they needed the child to provide for them in old age. They had created a baby out of their love for each other and the delight of bringing a new human life into the world. God freely creates human beings in his image, because he delights in relationship with them.

As we explore the complex ethical questions involved in the issues of life and death we must remember that human life is a gift from God, who gives the capacity of relationship whatever our age, physical abilities or mental state.

## 2. A God who gives community

Individualism is a dominant philosophy in Western culture. The 'there is no such thing as community' of the 1980s has helped to give birth to a perception that it is the individual and his or her freedom that is the important thing. In contrast, in giving an account of human beings, the Bible stresses the corporate aspect of humanity. The image of God is not possessed by an isolated individual but is possessed by individuals in community.

Karl Barth pointed to the importance of verse 27 in the Genesis account. Human beings are created as male and female, and thus, Barth concluded, 'the image and likeness of being created by God signifies existence in confrontation, i.e., in this confrontation, in the juxtaposition and conjunction of man and man which is that of male and female'.[25]

God creates community in which we find our humanity. An African proverb reads, 'Man is man ... only among men.'[26] Genesis would agree, although it would broaden the proverb to male and female! The contemporary German theologian Jürgen Moltmann states, 'Likeness to God cannot be lived in isolation. It can only be lived in human community.'[27]

Indeed, the basis for this is a reflection of God's own nature. Emil Brunner pointed out that divine 'us' of verse 26 is linked to the human 'them' of verse 27. This may fall into the trap of reading the Trinity too much into this text, but the doctrinal point is sound. We 'are created for life in relationships that mirror or correspond to God's own life in relationship'.[28] God's own nature is love. Therefore, we are given the capacity to love and to find our humanity in community. Our fellow human beings are important to us for they are God given.

This gives a common identity and dignity to all human beings whatever their sex, age or ethnic origin. We share the image of God and we need one another. This should affect our attitudes. Calvin stated, 'remember not to consider men's evil intention but to look upon the image of God in them, which cancels and effaces their transgressions, and with its beauty and dignity allures us to love and embrace them'.[29]

The world often is a place of dehumanization and alienation for many people. Indeed, this is also true of the church. Racism in terms of power structures working against those who have a different colour of skin is not just represented by fascist groups but is often embodied within institutions. Apartheid, bolstered by some churches in South Africa, was once justified by arguing that there is

[25] K. Barth, *Church Dogmatics* III/1.195, ed. G. W. Bromiley and T. F. Torrance, 4 vols. (T. & T. Clark, 1936–75).

[26] A. Boesak, *Black and Reformed* (Orbis, 1984), p. 51.

[27] J. Moltmann, *God in Creation* (Harper & Row, 1985), pp. 222–223.

[28] D. Migliore, *Faith Seeking Understanding* (Eerdmans, 1991), p. 122.

[29] Calvin, *Institutes*, 3.7.6.

in Scripture an order of creation that differentiates between black and white. This however is not represented in the Genesis text. The corporate nature of being the image of God means that ethnic diversity is a reflection of God's joy in creation, but such diversity is on the basis of common humanity before God.

The same can be said of sexism. Once again the Genesis text has been used by some to justify the oppression of women in hierarchical power structures. We shall return to this issue in Chapters 3 and 4 but it is worth emphasizing that the overall context of creation represented in verse 27 is of equality of both male and female in the image of God.[30]

The Genesis text gives no justification for a denial of equality of opportunity. God creates with diversity and intends community. We should thank God for the differences in background, language and culture that enrich our community, rather than allowing them to divide us. Such divisions in the church deny not only the doctrine of creation but also the doctrine of redemption where 'There is neither Jew nor Greek, slave nor free, male nor female, for you are all one in Christ Jesus' (Gal. 3:28).

## 3. A God who gives responsibility

If the dominant metaphor of Genesis 1 is the creation as kingdom, then within this kingdom human beings reflect their representative or ambassadorial function in the responsibility to have stewardship over the earth.

In the recent concern for environmental issues some have accused the Christian understanding of being part of the cause of our environmental abuse. The historian Lynn White at the American Association for the Advancement of Science in 1967 argued that our ability to harness natural resources was marred by the deep-rooted assumption that

> we are superior to nature, contemptuous of it, willing to use it for our slightest whim ... We shall continue to have a worsening ecological crisis until we reject the Christian axiom that nature has no reason for existence but to serve man ... Both our present science and our present technology are so tinctured with orthodox Christian arrogance towards nature that no solution for our ecological crisis can be expected from them alone.[31]

---

[30] M. Hayter, *The New Eve in Christ* (SPCK, 1987), pp. 87–92. See also A. Brown, *Apology to Women* (IVP, 1991), pp. 74–97.

[31] L. White, 'The Historical Roots of our Ecological Crisis', *Science* 155 (1967), p. 1203.

Thus Christianity bears 'a huge burden of guilt' for the environmental crisis. His analysis rests on what he claims is the orthodox interpretation of Genesis 1:26–29, which leads to the view that human beings have total sovereignty over the natural world.

Now it must be admitted that within Western culture dominion has quickly led to domination. However, the reasons for this are not due to the Genesis text itself. It comes from taking the command to 'rule over' without its correct context. It stems from seeing ourselves as the kings and queens of creation. If the context is of a world viewed as a machine, with human beings in sole authority, then domination and exploitation quickly follow.

Yet the context in Genesis 1 is very different. As we have seen, this is not about the Universe as a machine with humans as the sole authority. Human beings are given authority under their Creator God. Made in God's image they are given a unique status in creation and are capable of exercising authority, but as royal stewards. They are always accountable to the King for the exercise of that authority. This gives dominion a moral dimension. Scientific imperialism that exploits nature for human greed has no place here.

Often the motive for looking after the environment is selfish. We want to protect our children and ourselves in the future. To a large extent this view is held by our materialist consumer Western society, implicitly if not explicitly. The Bible goes beyond this motive. We care for the environment because God gives us this responsibility.

In addition, we have noted the strong link of being made in the image and the giving of responsibility. If we are to reflect the image of God, then we must exercise responsibility in a way that reflects the way he exercises authority. God values diversity, fruitfulness and creativity. In the New Testament we see him as the Servant King. We shall be called to account in the way we have managed the natural world in this perspective.

A great deal of contemporary debate has focused on the exact meaning of 'rule' and 'subdue'. Some prefer the term 'dominion', while others prefer 'stewardship'. Others fearful of the legacy of domination and environmental abuse even question whether stewardship is a helpful word. Much of this debate can be solved if the context is remembered.

God gives human beings unique responsibility over fish, birds, land animals and over all the earth. The command to rule over is repeated twice (vv. 26, 28). In addition, human beings are commanded to fill the earth (v. 28) and are given plants and fruit for food (v. 29).

Christians have understood these commands as God's encouragement to develop science and technology for the good of all. Those views of human beings as no different from the rest of nature, and indeed, of science and technology as being inherently evil, again have no place. Rather than being banned from 'interfering with nature' we are encouraged to do good. The American theologian Philip Hefner coins the term 'created co-creators' to describe human beings made in the image of God.[32] God gives us responsibility and ability not only to care, but also to innovate within the context of his creation and his will.

Science and technology should not be seen as selfish domination and exploitation of creation, but as given to us to grow in relationship. Whether it be by fulfilling our God-given curiosity about the world, or by using our God-given abilities to be partners with him in creation, science therefore has a moral content. Pollution of the environment, selfish exploitation of natural resources, animals and other human beings, or spiralling technology for war and destruction bear testimony to what can happen when science is separated from this dimension of relationship.

Lynn White attacked the Christian heritage but also concluded that 'since the roots of our trouble are so largely religious, the remedy must be essentially religious whether we call it that or not'. He called for 'refocused Christianity, not a wholesale repudiation of it . . . what we do about ecology depends on our ideas of the man–nature relationship'.

Genesis 1 gives us an environmentally healthy view of the human–nature relationship. The challenge is whether we are prepared to repent of our environmental sin and indifference, and work as individuals, churches, communities and nations so that God can rejoice in his world being 'very good'.[33]

## 4. A God who gives rest

The creation of human beings in intimate relationship with God, in community with each other and with God-given responsibility may be the high point of the week of creation, but it is not the end. The seventh day acts as a completion to the week of creation, both in terms of the structure of the narrative and in its theological significance. Verses 1 to 3 of chapter 2 echo the opening verses of the first chapter, acting as a conclusion.

[32] P. Hefner, *The Human Factor: Evolution, Culture and Religion* (Fortress, 1993).
[33] R. J. Berry (ed.), *The Care of Creation* (IVP, 2000); G. Prance, *The Earth Under Threat: A Christian Perspective* (Wild Goose, 1996); C. A. Russell, *The Earth, Humanity and God* (UCL Press, 1994); L. Osborne, *Stewards of Creation: Environmentalism in the Light of Biblical Teaching* (Latimer House, 1990).

The word *work* occurs three times (2:2–3), and it is a word used for human work. Some commentators have suggested that it is used to draw parallels with the need to stop human work for a period of rest. On the seventh day God rested, giving rise to the Sabbath principle.

It is somewhat surprising that God 'blesses' the seventh day, because God normally blesses living things. Wenham suggests that the meaning here is that God's blessing gives fruitfulness and that those who observe the divine command to rest will enjoy God's blessing and fruitfulness.

If this is the case, it is interesting that the day when God rested from his divine creativity is associated with fruitfulness. Western society does not encourage a link between fruitfulness and rest. Work bears fruit, and rest is often seen as merely a way of recovering for the work to begin again. Yet here is something quite profound about being human. Created in the image of God we are created both for responsibility and rest. Time and space for worship, leisure activities, play, developing relationships with family and friends are not optional extras but at the heart of being human. It is interesting that in the natural world fruitfulness is also associated with rest. A field cannot be farmed constantly, but needs a period of lying fallow to ensure continuing fruitfulness. Written into God's creation is the necessity of rest.

Christians have rightly been at the forefront of defending the importance of Sabbath rest within the week. The making of Sunday into 'just another day' not only impacts people's opportunity for worship, but also limits opportunities for communal rest. However, those in the leadership within the Christian church need to look at themselves too. How many Christian leaders have good Sabbath rest?

In addition, God makes the seventh day 'holy'. God chooses it for his purposes for human beings. Some suggest that the 'Sabbath' was created for human beings and this is correct. However, there is still a very strong sense that rest is important for God. Why should this be? Surely it is not because God becomes tired and weary. In the context of these verses, reflecting their literary structure, the seventh day becomes the time of appreciation of all that God has achieved, delighting in that which is *very good* (v. 31). Here again is the picture of a great artist, who delights not only in the process but also the accomplishment of that which is beautiful.

What does this mean for human beings made in the image of God? It says that at the heart of our humanity is the need to be involved in creativity, and the space and time to enjoy the accomplishments of that creativity. We need to ask whether our work reflects this. We also need to affirm the importance of participation in and appreciation of human creativity in music, drama, dance, painting, art, sport, sculpture, film and humour. It is in this that we find what it means to be human.

# 3. Genesis 2:4–25
# The Creator provides

The Bible, as most Christians know, is a peculiar book. It is a complex collection of books, letters, poetry, history, wise saying, worship songs, prayer and theology. It is at times difficult to understand and has kept professional biblical scholars in work for centuries in the attempt to trace its sources and interpret its meaning. Yet, at the same time, it speaks of a God who challenges and encourages. It tells of a God who is recognizably the same God who speaks and is experienced in different centuries and cultures. The Christian who may struggle with a passage, also finds it comes alive in personal reading, a group Bible study or a sermon. God speaks through it and lives are changed.

## The written Word God has provided

That has been my experience with these early chapters of Genesis. Difficult questions still remain that lie beyond my wish of simplifying. Yet the God I encounter in these chapters is the same God at work in my world. I find myself in Adam and Eve, experiencing the God who provides for all my needs, and I share with them the shame of sin.

We must try to do justice to the reality of Scripture. We cannot gloss over the difficult questions and just opt for the spiritual meaning. At the same time we cannot get so wrapped up with some of the unanswerable questions that we miss God's word for us.

We find these issues in sharp focus in Genesis chapter 2. We must begin once again with questions that have divided evangelical Christians. The first is the relation of Genesis 1:1 – 2:3 to 2:4–25. Since the work of Wellhausen at the end of the nineteenth century, a majority of Old Testament scholars have held to the view that these two sections come from different sources, the P source that gives us

Genesis 1:1 – 2:3 written around the sixth/fifth century BC, and the J source of Genesis 2:4–25, written much earlier, around the tenth/ninth century BC. Indeed, it is suggested that these sources in addition to E and D sources compose the Pentateuch, which was put together in the fifth century BC.

The argument for the different sources rested on distinguishing features in the following sections:

|  | **Genesis 1:1 – 2:3** | **Genesis 2:4–25** |
| --- | --- | --- |
| Name of God | Elohim, God | Yahweh, the LORD |
| Duplicate accounts | Creation of human beings | Creation of human beings |
| Style | Repetition, logical structure | Vivid narrative |

In addition, different vocabulary can be detected in the P and J sources throughout the Pentateuch.

However, this basic picture does not reflect the complexity of current scholarly debate.[34] Some argue that P itself consists of two sources. Further debate concerns the mechanics of how the final text was put together. Did the sources exist as discrete documents that were then put together by an editor using ancient cut and paste? Or was there one main source that was added to over many years? Or even, were there a large number of relatively short sections or retold stories that were combined as a long process or in a relatively short time? Each of these scenarios raises questions about dating. Even if one accepts that the present form of the text was finalized in the fifth century, the accounts contained within it could date from much earlier. Indeed, there are strong suggestions that because of parallels to stories in Mesopotamia many of the Genesis passages could come from before 1600 BC.

While these debates continue, other scholars have approached the text as a present literary whole, looking at themes that run throughout the Pentateuch, or the structure of the narratives in scenes, repetitions and key words.[35] They stress the importance of taking the text as we have it now, rather than trying to trace its sources.

These are important questions that Christians need to engage with at different levels. An understanding of the sources of biblical texts can help with an understanding of the meaning of the text. At the

---

[34] See in particular C. Westermann, *Genesis 1–11*, tr. J. J. Scullion (SPCK, 1984); G. J. Wenham, *Genesis 1–15*, Word Biblical Commentary (Word, 1987).
[35] D. J. A. Clines, *The Theme of the Pentateuch, Journal for the Study of the Old Testament*, Supplement Series 10 (JSOT Press, 1979).

same time, we need to grapple with the text as a whole. Both kinds of approaches are important. For example, is the duplication of accounts of the creation of human beings due to two separate sources being joined together, or the skill of a writer who uses repetition and differences to stress different points? At least we must admit that the final form of the text places Genesis 1:1 – 2:3 and 2:4–24 beside each other because there are connections between the two.

The second difficult question for biblical Christians is the question of whether Genesis 2:4–24 is history, as we would understand the use of the term in our modern culture. Some scholars have talked about it in terms of myth. This is an unfortunate term because in popular usage a myth is used often of that which is untrue. However, its technical meaning is symbolic story that describes the present situation in terms of a primeval event. In this sense, Genesis 2:4–25 can be described as myth, for the writer is not simply wanting to record history for its own sake. Here we are being told important truths about God, human beings and their relationship.

Yet is it more than that? Some Christians will want to maintain that this narrative is the history of human origins. Other Christians maintain that although the primary literary form is story, there are historical references, for example that Adam and Eve were real historical human beings. In this, we must be careful of imposing our Western intellectual tradition of what we mean by history on to the text.[36]

It is interesting that most recent commentators move away from the term 'myth'. Westermann and von Rad call it 'narrative'. Wenham helpfully calls it 'proto-historical', suggesting that it is a story with divine inspiration working through the author's creative imagination.

This is a helpful way of looking at the text. It is a reminder that what we are dealing with is something that does not easily fall into the neat categories that we have made. At the same time, we need to maintain that Genesis 2:4–25 is more than myth in the sense that it is written under and through God's inspiration. This is not simply a creative fiction on a par with *Alice in Wonderland*. This is the written Word of God given to us. We affirm this because of the witness of

[36] For more detail on how Adam and Eve relate to biology and anthropology see R. J. Berry, *God and the Biologist* (Apollos, 1996); J. P. Hurd, 'Hominids in the Garden', in K. Miller, *The Evolving Creation* (Eerdmans, forthcoming); R. G. Klein, 'The Archeology of Modern Human Origins', *Evolutionary Anthropology* 1.1 (1992), pp. 5–14; D. Young, 'The Antiquity and the Unity of the Human Race Revisited', *Christian Scholars Review* 24.4 (1995), pp. 380–396; G. R. Morton, 'Dating Adam', *Perspectives on Science and Christian Faith* 51.2 (1999), pp. 87–97.

Jesus as recorded in the Gospels (Matt. 19:4–6) and then subsequently the witness of the Spirit through the church.

However, does this view raise problems? Some would ask whether Adam has to be a historical character in order for Paul's contrast of Adam and Christ in Romans 5:12 to work. The question has some merit but we need to remember that even in a story about Adam and Eve, Adam and Eve could be historical people even if the nature of the account is highly stylized. We have many examples in our own culture of literature, theatre and cinema where real historical people are communicated in story form. In addition, many New Testament scholars do not feel that a historical Adam is necessary for Paul's understanding.

A second question is also posed. If we say that the early chapters of Genesis are not history in the way that we term history, then where do we stop? This is the so-called 'slippery slope' argument. Where in Genesis do we draw the line between proto-history and history? Are we simply opening the door to saying that the whole of the Old Testament and indeed the Bible is a purely human creation with no history in it at all?

This is not a good argument, although it sways a good many people. The Bible is a collection of a diverse range of different kinds of literature. Even within books that bear the name of one author there exist different literary forms. Luke's Gospel provides us with careful historical detail (Luke 1:1–4) but this does not mean that he does not include parables in the Gospel or write it for a specific purpose. A great deal of the Bible is easy to distinguish in terms of different literary types and we often do it automatically. For example we are not worried whether or not the parable of the prodigal son is about a real historical family. Its point is to teach us about the Father's love for all, including those who are perceived to be far away from him.

Yet when we come to certain passages of the Bible, distinguishing different literary types is not as automatic or as easy. Christians have disagreed over the literary form of the early chapters of Genesis. They do not easily fall into categories either of today's literature or indeed even into the categories of much of ancient literature.

If we are to take the Word of God in written form seriously, we need to look at each passage in its own setting and literary form. This does not mean that we make an artificial distinction at Genesis 3 or Genesis 11, in order to simplify our biblical study. We must look at each passage on its own merits. If we do this we shall find that far from subverting the Bible we find it ever more powerful. God has given us a book full of variety for a purpose. We do him a disservice if we try to mould the book into our own expectations.

## The written Word about God the provider

We now turn to what we need to learn about God in Genesis 2:4–25. Remember, the Bible never describes creation as an intellectual exercise. Here we are presented with the story of the creation of Adam and Eve for a purpose. That purpose is to see how God relates to men and women, who are his creation.

A great deal of scientific work has been done in the attempt to work out the difference between human beings and animals. At a purely scientific level the difference is not easy to specify. For example our genetic code differs by less than 2% from that of a chimp. Sensitivity to pain and capacity for intelligent behaviour are often mentioned, but animal studies show that these are differences of degree rather than kind.[37] Other differences are claimed, such as

- the ability to learn, plan, and conceptualize
- the use of developed tools, language and counting
- an artistic sense
- the ability to integrate a wide range of different areas of knowledge
- ability to make intuitive acts of judgment (which is often seen in science)
- moral sense
- the ability to recognize one's self in a mirror (which is also shared by chimps and blue whales)
- the capacity for language and abstract thought brings with it power to reflect on pain and death
- the ability to understand abstract mathematics and then use such mathematics to ask fundamental questions, such as the origin of the Universe
- altruism
- self-consciousness
- soul

However, as we saw in the last chapter, the core difference in biblical terms is our intimate relationship with God. Here in chapter 2 we have a beautiful description of such intimacy.

*⁴This is the account of the heavens and the earth when they were created.*

[37] W. H. Thorpe, *Animal Nature and Human Nature* (Methuen, 1974); D. R. Griffin, *Animal Minds* (University of Chicago Press, 1992).

When the LORD God made the earth and the heavens – ⁵and no shrub of the field had yet appeared on the earth and no plant of the field had yet sprung up, for the LORD God had not sent rain on the earth and there was no-one to work the ground, ⁶but streams came up from the earth and watered the whole surface of the ground – ⁷the LORD God formed a man from the dust of the ground and breathed into his nostrils the breath of life, and the man became a living being.

⁸Now the LORD God had planted a garden in the east, in Eden; and there he put the man he had formed. ⁹And the LORD God made all kinds of trees grow out of the ground – trees that were pleasing to the eye and good for food. In the middle of the garden were the tree of life and the tree of knowledge of good and evil.

¹⁰A river watering the garden flowed from Eden; from there it was separated into four headwaters. ¹¹The name of the first is the Pishon; it winds through the entire land of Havilah, where there is gold. ¹²(The gold of that land is good; aromatic resin and onyx are also there.) The name of the second river is the Gihon; it winds through the entire land of Cush. ¹⁴The name of the third river is the Tigris; it runs along the east side of Asshur. And the fourth river is the Euphrates.

¹⁵The LORD God took the man and put him in the Garden of Eden to work it and take care of it. ¹⁶And the LORD God commanded the man, 'You are free to eat from any tree in the garden; ¹⁷but you must not eat from the tree of the knowledge of good and evil, for when you eat of it you will surely die.'

¹⁸The LORD God said, 'It is not good for the man to be alone. I will make a helper suitable for him.'

¹⁹Now the LORD God had formed out of the ground all the beasts of the field and all the birds of the air. He brought them to the man to see what he would name them; and whatever the man called each living creature, that was its name. ²⁰So the man gave names to all the livestock, the birds of the air and all the beasts of the field.

But for Adam no suitable helper was found. ²¹So the LORD God caused the man to fall into a deep sleep; and while he was sleeping, he took one of the man's ribs and closed up the place with flesh. ²²Then the LORD God made a woman from the rib he had taken out of the man, and he brought her to the man. ²³The man said,

> 'This is now bone of my bones
> and flesh of my flesh;

> *she shall be called "woman",*
> *for she was taken out of man.'*

²⁴*For this reason a man will leave his father and mother and be*
*united to his wife, and they will become one flesh.*
²⁵*The man and his wife were both naked, and they felt no shame.*
(Gen. 2:4–25)

On a BBC Radio 4 *Any Questions* programme the panel of experts
was asked how they viewed getting old. One panelist, to much laughter and applause, suggested that as he got older he wanted to become
angrier and more objectionable. However, the next panelist, the former
Archbishop of York, Dr John Habgood, took a very different line. He
said that growing old was an important experience as it provided a time
of recognition that all of life was a gift from God. Early in life, a good
memory or the ability to run up stairs was often just taken for granted.
As you grew old these things were less taken for granted. Indeed,
Habgood went on, it becomes a time when you hand back to God
those gifts and abilities that you will not need in the life to come.

It is a prophetic word both for our culture and for many of us in
church. Our materialist culture sees life as a right rather than a gift.
We deserve this and that, and we despair if we do not get it. Rather
than thankfulness, there is demand.

Genesis 2:4–25 makes this point powerfully. Here we are introduced to life as a gift from a loving provider. Genesis 3 will show us
what happens if we forget this.

The opening phrase of verse 4b links this account with what has
gone before. *When the LORD God made* points us back to Genesis 1
and introduces an account that will amplify it. Some commentators
have claimed parallels to the opening line of the Babylonian epic
*Enuma Elish*. However, the much stronger reference is back to
Genesis 1:26–27. This is also seen in the use of *LORD God*. Yahweh,
the Lord, is the name of God unique to Israel. He is the personal provider and deliverer. 'Yahweh Elohim' only occurs once outside
Genesis 2 – 3 in the Pentateuch (Exod. 9:30). It is used here as part
of the link to Genesis 1. The same God, who is creator of the heavens
and the earth, now reveals himself as personal provider. The God of
all creation is the covenant partner of human beings. He is the one
who provides many gifts.

## 1. The gift of life

God is the source of all life in the natural world (v. 5) but within that
world he gives a special gift of life. The creation of the first human

being is described quite simply, *the LORD God formed the man from the dust of the ground* (v. 7a).

We notice first that we are part of the same creation and creative process as the rest of life on this planet. The creation accounts do stress the continuity between human beings and the rest of creation. We are created as part of the same week of creation, and both the animals and humans are created on the same day (Gen. 1:24–31). In addition, the first human being is created out of material God has already created: the dust of the ground.

Therefore, we must not force the distinction between the natural world and ourselves too far. We may have been given dominion over the earth and the animals, but we are all linked within God's creative work. The environment and the animal world have enabled the creation of human life as well as being valuable as God's creation. In addition, our continuity with the rest of creation means that we share much in terms of our physics, biochemistry and some of our behaviour patterns with animals. Indeed, it is because we are an integral part of the natural world that we can do science on ourselves in research or medicine!

However, Genesis 2 does not say that we are 'nothing but' dust. When Carl Sagan in his TV series *Cosmos*, or the actor Sam Neil in the BBC series *Space*, stated that we are made of stardust, they were referring to the atoms in our bodies being created in the furnaces of dying stars. However, they were wrong to give the impression that this is enough to explain human beings. Life is so much more than the reductionist fallacy of reducing us to our constituent atoms.

God is in the process of forming us from the dust. The image here is of a potter shaping clay. It is an image that communicates an artistic, inventive and intimate act, an act that requires skill and planning. God is not detached from the processes of the emergence of human beings. He is the choreographer of the DNA, the author of our genetic code, the sculptor of the human organs, the director of language, and the provider of life in all its fullness.

This is emphasized by the second half of verse 7, *the LORD God ... breathed into his nostrils the breath of life, and the man became a living being*. God blew into our nostrils the breath of life. The image is again of startling intimacy. God makes us breathe in a very personal way. Although the phrase 'living creature' is a phrase also used of sea creatures (1:20), and land animals and birds (2:19), human beings are distinct in the intimacy of creation.

We need to recapture this sense of human life as a special gift from God. If we do we will begin to be thankful for all that he has given us. We will also reflect his concern for those who are used and abused in society. In addition, we will gain a different perspective on death.

When our daughter was 7 months old she became very ill and over Christmas we spent a worried few days in hospital with her. I was angry with God as to why this young life seemed to be in danger of ending so soon. Yet at the same time my wife and I were thankful for this bundle of joy who was a gift to us, even if it was going to be only for 7 months. As it happened, she recovered, but I still try to view my children, my wife and my own life as gifts.

Of course, some applications of this are not so easy. Death involves grief that varies in different circumstances. There are unanswered questions when a gift seems to be snatched away before it can be received. The miscarriage of a pregnancy or the stillborn child at the end of pregnancy are difficult if not impossible to explain. At that point anger, sadness and grief are extreme in knowing that we come from dust and will ultimately return to dust. In addition, many people live in circumstances where life is not seen as a gift. Those who are ill with depression, or who suffer in frustration and pain, find it difficult to see life as a gift. We need to understand that and be sensitive to it as individuals and as a church. A glib celebration of 'family worship' or 'Mothers Day' can be very painful to those who do not seem to be able to receive the gift of children.

Yet those who see human life as a gift are able to get a perspective on both the joys and pains of life. This may not come overnight and those of us outside the situation do not have the right to expect it to come overnight for others. Such a perspective often comes through many tears and a great struggle with the Lord. However, with this perspective thankfulness replaces bitterness, and a valuing of all human life from the very young to the very old provides the basis for care and justice.

## 2. The gift of the world

This gift of life is placed in a context of beauty and fruitfulness, that is the *garden* in Eden (v. 8). Historically there has been much debate about where geographically Eden may have been. While the mention of certain rivers may suggest a location within the Persian Gulf, that is not the primary concern of the writer.

More important than where Eden is, is what it represents. Here is another gift provided by this generous God. Eden represents a closed and fertile area for cultivation. In other parts of Scripture it is described as an oasis with large trees (cf. Is. 51:3; Ezek. 31:9). This world that God provides for human beings is abundant in its provision. The trees show diversity, beauty and are good for food (v. 9). The world God has made provides for the everyday needs of human beings, but is also aesthetically amazing in its beauty and diversity.

Furthermore, it is a place of moral growth and challenge. At the centre of the garden are two trees (v. 9). Trees were associated with life, and within Scripture are often symbolic of the life of God (Ps. 1:3; Jer. 17:8). It is interesting that human beings are allowed to eat of the tree of life. Only one tree is forbidden within this abundant diversity. The *tree of the knowledge of good and evil* is not permitted to be eaten of and the consequences of such eating will be death (vv. 16–17).

Wenham lists five possibilities that have been suggested for understanding what this tree represents:

- A description of what happens when you follow the commandments; that is, a knowledge of evil follows as a consequence of disobedience
- Moral discernment
- Sexual knowledge
- Omniscience
- Wisdom

Most modern commentators, including Wenham, Cassuto and Westermann, take the last interpretation. Although human beings are encouraged to pursue wisdom, there is a wisdom that belongs only to God. The pursuit of wisdom without reference to God is the temptation here. It will be a hard lesson for Adam and Eve, as it is for all of us. Do we make moral decisions without reference to the Lord, or are we prepared to seek and follow his guidance?

God has provided a world that is full of moral choices – from the way we treat our friends and neighbours to our vast power in shaping the world through science and technology. As we shall see in the next chapter, our rebellion against God affects our ability to do the right thing. Nevertheless, even sinful humanity can see the moral questions and have the opportunity of gaining wisdom. God's ideal is for the world to be a place of exploration and growth for human beings.

Yet this is a world where we are not left alone. This is not some sort of cosmic experiment where God stands outside and tests human beings as if they are laboratory rats. The mention of gold, aromatic resin and onyx (vv. 11–12; cf. Ezek. 28:13) partly refers to the richness of natural resources given by God, but may also be suggestive of the presence of God. This is because of the link with jewels used in decorating the tabernacle. Here is a picture of the God who is concerned for the welfare of Adam and Eve, who provides a garden of rich resources, but who is also in the midst of their lives. The one who is the Creator of heaven and earth is also the one who dwells with them in the garden, offering companionship and help. Christians have constantly stressed both the transcendence and immanence of God. He is both greater than and is present in this creation, so that in the words of Bishop David Jenkins he is 'transcendence in the midst'.

The sense of God providing a world infused with his presence has important consequences. Work done by David Hay at the University of Nottingham continuing the work of the biologist Sir Alistair Hardy suggests that at least two-thirds of the British population have had some kind of experience that they identify with transcendence.[38] As we shall see in chapter 16, part of Paul's confidence in evangelism comes from the fact that God is at work in his creation and is not far from each one of us (Acts 17:27).

It also means that we need to care for creation. Sir John Houghton, one of the world's leading environmental scientists, uses the analogy of a garden to speak of how we need to care for creation. First, a garden provides resources, whether food to eat, wood to burn as fuel, flowers for decoration or space to relax. Second, a garden is to be maintained as a thing of beauty. It is meant to be enjoyed and when taken care of properly gives joy not just to those who work it. Third, a garden is a place where humans can be creative – by working with the natural processes beauty can be enhanced and artistic statements can be made. Fourth, a garden is to be kept for future generations. If a garden is overly exploited or spoiled it is in danger of becoming unusable by the next generation.

If that is not enough to question our exploitation of the world, we can add that this passage sees the owner and creator of the garden as a constant visitor. As a minister I once moved into a church house that had a big garden in beautiful condition, planted and kept by the previous minister. My wife and I did not look after it and it became a complete mess. What was worse was that the previous minister had moved only two miles down the road, and passing the house often would see the mess!

God is not just the judge of how we have messed up the world. He is also the present helper, ready to work with us in the stewardship of his creation. He is ready to guide and empower, if we are prepared to follow his way. As we saw in chapters 1 and 2 this again is a mandate for Christians to be at the forefront of environmental issues both locally and internationally. We need to join with others in caring for the world, while prophetically pointing to the God who provides and the God who desires to be followed.

[38] D. Hay and R. Nye, *The Spirit of the Child* (Fount, 1998).

## 3. The gift of work

The gift of the garden comes with the gift of work. Many of us would be happy with a garden where we simply put our feet up and enjoy, but God knows better! The gift of the world comes with the gift of responsibility and creativity.

Verse 5 may refer to agricultural land where flood waters bring fertility; but what is interesting is that the fertility of the ground is linked to the presence of someone to *work the ground*. Human presence and work is essential to the fruitfulness of the world. There is no sense in the biblical account that nature is better off without human beings. The reaction against human exploitation of creation, which suggests that human beings have no right to be managers of the natural world, has no warrant within the Christian faith.

Human beings are provided with responsible work by God himself. God put human beings into the garden (v. 8) in order to work it and take care of it (v. 15). This is the initiative and gift of God. To work the garden uses a word commonly used in a religious sense of serving God (Deut. 4:19) and in tabernacle duties (Num. 3:7–8). To cultivate the soil is to serve God. To take care of the garden has the sense of guarding it from harm. The word used has the sense of taking care of observing God's commands, or guarding the tabernacle from desecration.

Here we see the nature of the dominion referred to in Genesis 1:26–28. Rather than ruling in an arrogant and exploitative way, human beings are given the work of 'to serve and keep it'. We are given responsibility for wise stewardship and use of the creation, but at the same time we must humbly take care of it: we must keep it.

Human beings are given the opportunity for responsibility in work, which is intrinsic to human life. In Mesopotamian thought, human beings worked for the gods. Here God works until all of our needs as human beings are provided for. Yet we are given the gift of work, to cooperate with God's purposes. What does this mean for society? It means that work is to be valued and enjoyed as much as possible. Work is sometimes seen as a necessary evil to gain money for leisure, holidays and a bigger house. Sometimes Christians see work as a lesser activity to their ministry within the Christian community.

Here Genesis reminds us of the gift of work that is to be valued. Caring for the resources of the world, using the resources creatively in science or technology, managing the resources in finance, and serving the needs of others are all Christian ministries. We are also reminded of the need for society to give people work that involves creativity and responsibility. Many jobs within society are badly paid and the tasks and relationships within the workplace are dehumanizing. The early origins of the Trade Union movement in Britain recognized the Christian view of work and argued for work and conditions that valued human beings. Christians today, whether in unions or in positions of influence in industry or public services, need to continue to argue for work that fulfils our human potential.

It may be taking the text too far, but I am impressed by just how much responsibility God gives to human beings who have no experience, no references and no academic qualifications! God gives responsibility to those who have potential. Perhaps that is a lesson for church leaders. Too often young people are denied leadership responsibility because they are perceived to be too young and inexperienced. The question however is whether they are called by God and have potential.

### 4. The gift of sex

The theme of goodness and diversity is picked up again from chapter 1. God's view of the creation of male and female as very good is alluded to in his observation of verse 18, *It is not good for the man to be alone.*

This account of the creation of male and female stresses the importance of diversity, complementarity, companionship and fellowship. That God provides a *helper* has often been taken as signifying that women are subordinate or weaker. This is not justified by the text. Indeed, God himself is often referred to in other parts of Scripture as a helper or as giving help, which does not make him a subordinate! It simply means that the helped is not sufficient alone. Human beings cannot exist as male or female only: we need gender diversity, mutual support and companionship.

Having said that, the account is quite surprising. Why does God go through the process of bringing all the animals in front of Adam? No doubt it heightens the suspense of the story, but the real reason is probably in the sense of importance it gives the creation of Eve. The naming of the animals again reflects the dominion gift of Genesis 1.

The creation of Eve is a delightful poetic picture (vv. 21–25). We lose its importance immediately if we start counting the numbers of ribs that men and women possess! Here is the differentiation between men and women that will unite again in the intimacy of sex. This is something completely different from God's way of creating the animals. The significance of sleep may indicate that God's ways are mysterious (v. 21). What is clear however is the key role God has in all of this. He gives to human beings the gift of gender and the gift of sex. The differentiation and then bringing together of Adam and Eve gives a pattern for marriage. Harmony and intimacy exist within the recognition of diversity and mutual support.

Does the fact that Adam is created first and then names Eve suggest subordination of the female to the male (v. 23)? This has been the interpretation of some Christians who see this text as a warrant for the man being the ultimate authority for decisions in marriage and the primacy of male leadership within the church. Other Christians have pointed out that the text does not support such an interpretation. First, we need to remember that when it comes to the order of creation that the animals were created before Adam and fortunately that does not mean that we have to ask our dog for guidance. Second, in terms of naming, within the story of creation there is a qualitative difference between the creation of animals and humans. Indeed, verse 23 is more of an exclamation of joy in the creation of woman than the naming signifying authority. More importantly, the mutuality between Adam and Eve runs throughout the whole account. They are of the same flesh and bone. Hartley further points out that *called* is in the passive and lacks the term 'name'.[39] This is not a 'naming' that symbolizes authority. Trible suggests that man was not naming the woman but identifying their commonness in difference.[40]

Before we move on to marriage, it is worth pausing for a moment. Men and women are created equal before God and their diversity enriches God's world. A denial of equality in terms of the valuing of men and women, or injustice concerning opportunities in society or in the church is a denial of God's gift in creation. At the same time ignoring the differences between men and women is a denial of God's gift of diversity. Of course the differences between women and men represent a spectrum of different styles of learning, leadership, relating and expectations that will vary from person to person, rather than the traditional stereotypes of men and women. We celebrate God's gift by maintaining diversity in equality.

We also need to reflect this equality in diversity in issues of singleness and marriage. The Genesis text does not view single people as somehow subhuman. Single women and men, whether single by circumstances, choice or calling, are part of the diversity that characterizes the human community. We still need the mutual support of both men and women outside the marriage relationship. In terms of human society the Genesis text however poses the question of how

---

[39] J. E. Hartley, *Genesis*, New International Biblical Commentary on the Old Testament (Paternoster, 2000), p. 63.
[40] P. Trible, *God and the Rhetoric of Sexuality* (Fortress, 1978), pp. 99–102.

effectively men and women relate and work together. Single people need friendship and love not only of their own gender but of the other gender too if they are going to fulfil their humanity. The church provides God's new corporate context where that can happen. It is therefore a shame that single people feel so isolated in church life, and church leaders must be sensitive to it.

The context of marriage can be characterized in terms of priorities, passion and permanence (v. 24). The priorities of the man are no longer directed to parents but to his wife. The image of one flesh, fulfilled in sexual intercourse, symbolizes a deeper emotional, spiritual, psychological as well as physical union. The permanence of this union stems from the gift of God in bringing it about.

Such a picture is important today. We are bombarded with various pictures of sex and relationships. It is often said that young people are especially susceptible and that is obviously the case, but we do well to remember that whoever we are, we need to come back to the biblical understanding. Our understanding of sex may be deeply ingrained in us from peer pressure and furtive conversations at school, parents, teaching from authority whether it be from school or church, experiences of abuse, media dreams and pictures, what we dream about for the future, pornography, or sexual experiences and experimentation. Some of these will be positive about sex; others will be very negative. As we try to understand ourselves or search for love, we can experience joy and excitement, or fear, guilt, anger and addiction.

Although the Genesis account says clearly that sex is good, for it is a gift from God, some Christians subtly communicate a different message. Afraid of the abuse of sex, they constantly warn of its dangers, leaving fellow Christians with a deep-down belief that it is dirty and disapproved of by God. I talked with one student who had been to a church that advocated the 3-foot rule – which was how far you had to stay apart until you had been going out a few months. He said, 'It makes sex sound more dangerous than radioactivity!'

In contrast, the Bible views our physicality as good. Lewis Smedes sums this up when he says, 'to be wildly irrational, splendidly spontaneous and beautifully sensuous . . . is a gift'.[41] The Greek view, often taken into Christian tradition, that the body is less important than the spirit finds no support from the Bible.

Neither does the view that sex is purely for procreation. Once again we find an interesting dynamic between Genesis 1 and Genesis 2. The command to be *fruitful and increase in number* (Gen. 1:28) is to be seen in the light of this picture of sex as intimacy. Procreation

---

[41] L. B. Smedes, *Sex For Christians* (Eerdmans, 1977), p. 30.

and intimacy are to be held together in our understanding of sex. When Louis Armstrong was given an audience with the Pope, the Pope asked him, 'Do you have any children?' Armstrong replied, 'No, but we're having a lot of fun trying.' The possibility of sex without procreation is gift! This understanding encourages responsible contraception, and the importance of sex being practised for mutual delight.

Alongside the celebration of the goodness of sex, it is clear that God gives a certain context to this becoming of one flesh. In fact the goodness cannot be separated from the context. This involves the recognition that relationship is a gift from God that brings with it responsibility to use it in his way.

His way is that one flesh is about one man and one woman, in a relationship that has both a public act and a transfer of primary commitment. The traditional understanding of Christian marriage traces its origin back to this passage. It attempts to embody these principles for one flesh given in creation. The result of one flesh in this context is peace and intimacy, without shame or embarrassment (v. 25).

Rather than dishing out condemnation on those who do not follow God's plan, Christians are called to embody the joy of this gift of sexuality and gender. The quality of Christian marriage and the valuing of gender diversity within the church will communicate God's gift far more effectively than condemnation. Sadly, the oppression of women within the church and the pain of dehumanizing marriage both deny the goodness of God's rich gifts in creation.

God has provided us with the gift of sex, the gift of work, the gift of the world and the gift of life itself. He has also provided us with the gift of his Word to help us understand these things from his perspective. There is great responsibility in such gifts. The challenge is whether we value the gifts and use them wisely. In the next chapter we see what happens when such gifts are abused.

# 4. Genesis 3:1–24
# The Creator rejected

## Ground Zero

On 11 September 2001 I was trying to rid a computer of a frustrating but rather weak virus. Then my wife called me to the television. For some minutes I stood transfixed, not sure what I was seeing. Was this some movie that had been made or was this real? The television pictures were graphic and unbelievable. I was watching video clips of people flying aircraft into the Twin Towers and thousands of people being killed through the explosions and subsequent collapses.

For the rest of the day we were transfixed by the television. Eyewitness accounts were interlaced with speculation about why this had happened. For the next week I read the papers and listened to the news as I had never done before. The scale of this was so overwhelming. I wanted to know why it had happened and who was responsible? As evidence emerged, I listened to analysts and debates as to the background of the terrorists who had committed such an act, and what their possible motivation was. I struggled to reconcile my understanding of Islam with what they seemed to believe in order to justify their actions. I sympathized with those who argued that there was no justification at all, and also with those who spoke of the deep hatred of the West caused by our policies in the Middle East.

A few weeks later I flew in and out of New York. Suddenly the reality hit me afresh. I realized that I had moved from the horror of the act to an attempt to rationalize it. My need to find motives, mechanisms and solutions to stop this happening again were a way of coping with the pain and grief of the situation. I wept for the families involved and was frightened for what it meant for the vulnerability of my own life and my family and friends.

This was a horrific picture of the rejection of a God who creates the Universe and life. It was a denial of the goodness of creation. I might not have easy answers about why it happened, but I know that it demonstrated the reality of sin in all of its ugly complexity. It also showed starkly the consequences of sin. The world is a different place after 11 September. The effects of an act by a small number of human beings has led from the death of firefighters in New York to the death of Taliban fighters in Mazar-i Sharif. But the consequences will reach much wider than that.

I approach this passage with those thoughts in mind. Here is an account of the reality and consequences of sin. Here is the story of the rejection of the Creator God and all that he has provided. Within Western culture it is easy to avoid the gravity of this passage by asking numerous questions about the origin of sin. Yet we can often do this in order to avoid the full horror that this is *our* sin and that we are affected by its consequences.

Mark Twain once said that the human being 'is the only animal that blushes, or needs to'. This passage is not meant to be read in the abstract, putting us above the text by asking purely the intellectual questions. As one commentator puts it, 'The sin depicted is not simply the first sin; it is all human sin; it is my sin. And I who hear the tale am forced to acknowledge that my sin too has cosmic dimensions; my sin too is an attack on creation and an establishment of moral chaos.'[42]

*Now the serpent was more crafty than any of the wild animals the* LORD *God had made. He said to the woman, 'Did God really say, "You must not eat from any tree in the garden"?'*

*[2]The woman said to the serpent, 'We may eat fruit from the trees in the garden, [3]but God did say, "You must not eat fruit from the tree that is in the middle of the garden, and you must not touch it, or you will die."'*

*[4]'You will not surely die,' the serpent said to the woman. [5]'For God knows that when you eat of it your eyes will be opened, and you will be like God, knowing good and evil.'*

*[6]When the woman saw that the fruit of the tree was good for food and pleasing to the eye, and also desirable for gaining wisdom, she took some and ate it. She also gave some to her husband, who was with her, and he ate it. [7]Then the eyes of both of them were opened, and they realized that they were naked; so they sewed fig leaves together and made coverings for themselves.*

*[8]Then the man and his wife heard the sound of the* LORD *God*

[42] J. Walsh, 'Genesis 2:4b – 3:24: A Synchronic Approach', *Journal of Biblical Literature* 96 (1977), p. 177.

*as he was walking in the garden in the cool of the day, and they hid from the* LORD *God among the trees of the garden.* ⁹*But the* LORD *God called to the man, 'Where are you?'*

¹⁰*He answered, 'I heard you in the garden, and I was afraid because I was naked; so I hid.'*

¹¹*And he said, 'Who told you that you were naked? Have you eaten from the tree from which I commanded you not to eat?'*

¹²*The man said, 'The woman you put here with me – she gave me some fruit from the tree, and I ate it.'*

¹³*Then the* LORD *God said to the woman, 'What is this you have done?'*

*The woman said, 'The serpent deceived me, and I ate.'*

¹⁴*So the* LORD *God said to the serpent, 'Because you have done this,*

> *'Cursed are you above all the livestock*
> *and all the wild animals!*
> *You will crawl on your belly*
> *and you will eat dust*
> *all the days of your life.*
> ¹⁵*And I will put enmity*
> *between you and the woman,*
> *and between your offspring and hers;*
> *he will crush your head,*
> *and you will strike his heel.'*

¹⁶*To the woman he said,*

> *'I will greatly increase your pains in childbearing;*
> *with pain you will give birth to children.*
> *Your desire will be for your husband,*
> *and he will rule over you.'*

¹⁷*To Adam he said, 'Because you listened to your wife and ate from the tree about which I commanded you, "You must not eat of it,"*

> *'Cursed is the ground because of you;*
> *through painful toil you will eat of it*
> *all the days of your life.*
> ¹⁸*It will produce thorns and thistles for you,*
> *and you will eat the plants of the field.*
> ¹⁹*By the sweat of your brow*
> *you will eat your food*
> *until you return to the ground,*
> *since from it you were taken;*

*for dust you are
and to dust you will return.'*

*[20]Adam named his wife Eve, because she would become the mother of all the living.
[21]The LORD God made garments of skin for Adam and his wife and clothed them. [22]And the LORD God said, 'The man has now become like one of us, knowing good and evil. He must not be allowed to reach out his hand and take also from the tree of life and eat, and live for ever.' [23]So the LORD God banished him from the Garden of Eden to work the ground from which he had been taken. [24]After he drove the man out, he placed on the east side of the Garden of Eden cherubim and a flaming sword flashing back and forth to guard the way to the tree of life.*

(Gen. 3:1–24)

This is an account of both the origin and the reality of sin. It is a simple narrative account that communicates its main points clearly. It is also a skilfully constructed, subtle account of the reality and consequences of sin. As we have noted above Christians have disagreed on the historicity of these passages, but all have agreed on the need to see ourselves in Adam and Eve.

Wenham reviews the options that different commentators have taken and suggests that this passage is a 'proto-historical' story or tale. Perhaps what we have here is divine inspiration working through the author's creative imagination. He comments:

> It is suggested that under the guidance of the Spirit the author of these chapters identified the origin of the problems that beset all mankind – sin, death, suffering – with a primeval act of disobedience of the first human couple. Whereas a modern writer might have been happy to spell this out in abstract theological terminology – God created the world good, but man spoiled it by disobedience – Genesis puts these truths in vivid and memorable form in an absorbing yet highly symbolic story . . . The validity of this hypothesis, like most critical suggestions, remains open to debate, but its validity or otherwise in no way impairs the inspired truth of the present narrative.[43]

We need to be careful in terms of what we mean by 'origins'. Does Genesis give us a full historical description of the origin of sin, in such terms as today we describe the origin of say the Internet? We

---

[43] G. J. Wenham, *Genesis 1–15*, Word Biblical Commentary (Word, 1987), p. 55.

need to note first that this text is used very sparingly in the rest of the Old Testament. In most of the Old Testament the reality of sin is understood without much reference to its origin. Certainly in the New Testament Paul locates the origin of sin in this account in order to show the act of redemption in Jesus Christ: 'Therefore, just as sin entered the world through one man, and death through sin, and in this way death came to all people, because all sinned' (Rom. 5:12). Yet, as we shall see, this is a highly symbolic account. Lucas wisely does not deny that there is history in this passage but cautions that because of its symbolic nature we should be extremely cautious about addressing historical questions to it.[44] There may remain a degree of mystery about the origin of sin, but there is clarity about the reality and consequences of sin.

It is to these two points that we now turn.

## 1. The reality of sin

As we have seen so far, creation is never discussed in the Bible purely out of abstract and academic interest. We therefore need to read this story asking how it relates to practical questions of life. The first six verses paint a picture of the nature and reality of sin in human life. With great subtlety, the passage illustrates how easy it is to reject the Creator who made us.

### a. Subtle temptation

The section begins with introducing us to the *serpent* (v. 1). Immediately, the writer warns us to treat this animal with suspicion because he is *crafty*. The inference is that we need to discern carefully what this animal says. The questions of why a serpent and what the serpent symbolizes are difficult. A great deal of Christian tradition has identified the serpent with the devil. While this may be a helpful way to read back later Christian theology into the story for the purposes of teaching, it is difficult to justify in terms of the mind of the author. The serpent is referred to as one of the *wild animals* and the concept of a personal devil does not appear early in the Old Testament.[45]

In attempting to see what the author saw in the serpent image, some commentators have suggested that it is the symbol of the Canaanite fertility cults, or the ancient oriental symbol of life,

---

[44] E. Lucas, *Can we Believe in Genesis Today?* (IVP, 2001), p. 91.
[45] 'Satan', in L. Ryken, J. C. Wilhoit and T. Longman III (eds.), *Dictionary of Biblical Imagery* (IVP, 1998), pp. 759–762.

wisdom and chaos. Wenham suggests the possibility of a transformation of the story in the Epic of Gilgamish which also has a combination of snakes, plants and immortality.[46] However, he follows most contemporary commentators in seeing the serpent simply as a symbol of that which opposes God. The serpent would be seen as an unclean animal (cf. Lev. 11; Deut. 14); indeed, probably the most unclean. The reason why the serpent should be involved in this rejecting of God and tempting of humans is never explained, which adds to the mystery of the origin of sin.

It is part of the Christian experience to recognize the existence of something outside us that encourages us into sin. This can take many forms. The temptation of an image, the power of peer pressure, the structures of life and culture that seem to lull us into sin, often before we fully realize what is happening. Behind such temptation there often seems to be an intelligence and a power that knows our weaknesses. This is the devil at work frustrating God's purposes for his creatures.

However, rather than giving a picture of a fiery creature with horns and three-pronged spear, the serpent is gentle and seductive. The path into sin is to misrepresent God and to misrepresent what God has said – but to do it with great subtlety. Up to this point the author has used LORD God to refer to the Creator. As we have seen, this is to express the conviction that the Creator of all creation is also the personal covenant partner. However, the serpent avoids this term, referring simply to God (v. 1b). The woman's understanding of the Creator changes, for she follows this lead and uses the same term (vv. 1–5). It is a very small change but it is moving God from the personal covenant partner to a remote creator. The second strategy the serpent uses is to question what God has said and why he said it. In this is also a small but significant change made by the serpent. He questions whether God said not to eat from *any tree in the garden*. This is a twisting of Genesis 2:16, *You are free to eat from any tree in the garden*. The God of abundant provision is being misrepresented as a god who wants to restrict rather than give. This god cannot be trusted because his motives are not good.

Sin often begins in such a small and subtle way. It may be a misrepresentation of God we have picked up from others, or a corrupted view of his purposes owing to our circumstances. It is a doubting that God's way is the best way for us to go. It begins in small ways but then builds up quickly.

---

[46] Wenham, *Genesis 1–15*, p. 72.

## b. Distorting our understanding

Yet sin is much more than that. It is an owning for ourselves of those lies about God. Those influences that affect us, whether spiritual, psychological or sociological we cannot do anything about. They are powerful but not responsible for sin. Sin is when we ourselves reject God.

Again this begins in a very small and subtle way. In verses 2–3 the woman corrects the serpent but in a corrupted way. First, she follows the serpent's name for the Creator, calling him *God* rather than LORD *God* (v. 3). Almost imperceptibly she is moving to view the Lord God as remote. Second, she quotes Genesis 2:16 but drops the sense of 'any trees' (v. 2). God's abundant provision is questioned. Third, she adds her own interpretation to God's words. In Genesis 2:17 God says *you must not eat*. The woman reports this as *You must not eat . . . and you must not touch it* (v. 3).

The passage is giving a profound insight into the dynamics of spiritual life and sin in particular. The woman has now distorted her understanding of God in a small way, but in a way that denies who God is, denies his generosity, and misrepresents his words.

Many of us within the church have an overly simplistic view of sin. We view it as certain sexual acts, or major errors of doctrine. We blame Satan for our sin, or think that as long as we have not committed certain acts we have not sinned. Sin is far more subtle and therefore far more dangerous than many of us imagine. We may make a public stand against pornography or the occult, but live a life of materialism that denies God's gracious provision for all. In our churches we may be proud of our orthodox doctrine but deny God's love for those who get it wrong. We may call the sinner to repentance but so add to God's words that we turn the Christian life into drudgery and guilt.

## c. The art of seduction

The woman has opened the door to temptation and, once she has stepped through, it is very difficult to get back. Now the serpent disputes God's words and challenges his motivation (vv. 4–5). Although there is some uncertainty as to the translation of *You will not surely die* the NIV sees it as a contradiction of God's warning of *when you eat of it you will surely die* (Gen. 2:17). The serpent then tells the woman what will happen. In his prediction he is reasonably accurate; that is, their eyes will be opened and they will know good and evil (cf. vv. 7, 22). However, the context turns it from a warning to a questioning of the nature and purpose of God. He is telling them the truth but its context is misleading. The serpent does not directly tell the human beings to eat; he lures them.

Such is the power of seduction. The questioning of motivation can sour a good act or situation. The impression of a good sermon can be destroyed by one sentence said in a conversation over coffee that questions the preacher's lifestyle or motivation. The truth that God wants us to enjoy the goodness of creation, once separated from his concern for all human beings, can be a justification for selfishness. We enjoy the goodness at the expense of others, as many of our sisters and brothers in the developing world know only too well. As C. S. Lewis pictured in *The Screwtape Letters* the work of Satan is rarely outright attack, but subtle luring and corrupting.

### d. Desire and act

Yet still that is not the whole of sin. Desire and action are also involved in this rejection of God. The gentle, small initial steps of verses 1–5 are now replaced by actions reported in a way to communicate their seriousness and significance. Here sin is represented by *saw, took, ate, gave* and *ate* again (v. 6). One leads almost inevitably to another in rapid succession.

The author parallels the woman's actions in order to make the point that her sin is an attempt to become like God. Verse 6, *the woman saw . . . good*, echoes the refrain from Genesis 1 of God seeing that his creation was good. The Creator is rejected and replaced. Human beings become their own lord and provider.

Some blame the woman for sin, but such a reading does not reflect the creativity of the text. The author is clear that her husband *was with her* (v. 6) and was equally responsible for this rejection of the Lord God. Indeed, those who apportion blame to the woman on the basis of this story or Paul's comment on the story in 1 Timothy 2:13–14, should at the same time remember that Paul also comments that 'sin entered the world through one man' (Rom. 5:12)!

Rather than pointing the finger at the man and the woman, the story turns the finger back at me. I live in a world of temptation that is both bold and subtle. I can easily and very gradually misrepresent God and then let desire for autonomy lead into actions that go against his will. There is a complexity to sin but also a reality. Ultimately it is to deny that I am a creature, who has received everything as gift and whose life depends totally on my good Creator.

69

## 2. The consequences of sin

If the nature and reality is skilfully represented in a way that we see ourselves in the story, we now encounter in the same skilful representation the consequences of sin. This is presented primarily in terms of broken relationships. The harmony of the created order is disrupted. Human beings disrupt their relationship with God, with themselves, with one another and with creation itself.

### a. Broken community

Their eating of the fruit is the central point around which we see how their hopes are unfulfilled. The promised pleasure and wisdom turned out to lead to shame and guilt. Indeed, their eyes are opened but what they see is something of a let-down. Wenham even comments that in their desperate attempt to provide coverings for themselves they use fig leaves, which are not the most comfortable things against the skin (v. 7)!

The dynamics of sin are pictured here so well. Sin that seems so attractive never ultimately delivers. It may be pleasurable and indeed give one short-term success, but the story illustrates how self-defeating and self-destructive it is to go against the Maker's instructions.

Verse 7 is a dramatic picture of the way that, owing to our rebellion against God, God's ideal plan in creation becomes distorted. The relaxed intimacy of the man and the woman (Gen. 2:25) becomes dominated by shame. That which is meant to be good in one context can often become the source of pain, guilt, embarrassment, disease and abuse in an inappropriate context.

The picture of the shame of nakedness is a comment on how the consequences of sin affect human sexuality, and indeed more broadly human interpersonal relationships. Our rejection of the Lord makes us fearful of one another and corrupts a good gift. The joy of our sexual nature can be corrupted either by our own sin, or by the sin of others. The sin of the child abuser or the adulterer has consequences far beyond their own lives.

### b. Broken intimacy

The lovely picture of God walking in the garden shows us what sin does to our relationship with the Lord (v. 8). Instead of the ease of communication, full of shared responsibility and celebration of chapter 2, the man and the woman hide from him. The trees that were pleasing to the eye and good for food (Gen. 2:9) are now turned into a hiding place to avoid the one who created them.

The Lord God's questioning of the man and woman further illustrates how sad they have become (vv. 9–13). The author possibly uses the description LORD God in contrast to the woman's earlier God to remind us that, even in this situation, the Lord God is still the powerful provider and covenant partner of the man and the woman (vv. 8–9). Some commentators also see in the question *Where are you?* (v. 9) an indication of the Lord being the one who seeks out the lost. The man and the woman are presented no longer as God's covenant partners who are given responsibility but as pathetic, childish humans who can no longer take responsibility.

Sin breaks the intimacy of our relationship with God. The man is now afraid of God and full of shame (v. 10). However, he is also unable to be honest about what has happened. He begins by referring to his nakedness rather than what caused his nakedness. So the Lord makes the connection for him (v. 11). Christians have long recognized that both theologically and pastorally the recognition and repentance of our sin is an essential part of the healing process. Here God tries to help the man to do that.

Nevertheless, the man cannot see it and directs the implication away from himself to the woman (v. 12). Indeed, it is not just the woman he blames but also the Lord himself for putting the woman with him. We see in this our own experience of sin – perhaps more if we are men! We want to blame someone else, or we want to justify ourselves with reference to someone else. We may not say it publicly but sometimes we think, 'Lord, you made me with this sexual desire I find so hard to control – it's not my fault.' Or 'If you want to see a sinner, Lord, then look at him, not at me!'

This pushes both God and other human beings further away. Our relationships are further disrupted as sin works its way out. The woman in turn blames the serpent (v. 13). Some commentators see this as a symbol of how sin shatters our relationship with animals. While this point may be true within the overall biblical vision, it may be going too far to see it in the mind of the author in this passage.

Perhaps we just need to pause at this moment and ask ourselves the question of whether we are honest in our relationship with God and indeed with one another. The small-group meetings devised by John Wesley, which were foundational to the growth of Methodism, had an element of corporate confessing of sins. The honesty this encouraged led to deeper fellowship. The act of confession in corporate worship is another important aspect of being honest. Do we have that honesty in personal relationships? Do we let the sun go down on our anger? And do we have the humility to acknowledge to others how we have hurt them?

Part of the role of the Holy Spirit is to seek the lost and to make the connection between the consequences of sin and the reality of sin (John 16:8–9). This may happen through the ministry of someone else, as we read the Scriptures, or as we pray. The Lord in this story of the man and the woman is very specific in his questioning. This seems to be one of the marks of the Holy Spirit's work of conviction of sin in the life of the believer. Many of us struggle with guilt, partly because of our childhood or background. We have been taught to be perfectionists and when that does not happen we feel we fall short of the expectations of others. At the same time, part of the attack of Satan is as the accuser of the followers of Christ (Rev. 12:10). How do we differentiate between the convicting work of the Holy Spirit and other sources of guilt that drag us down? The Anglican preacher and evangelist David Watson used to make the helpful distinction that the Holy Spirit is always specific in bringing the reality of sin to light, whereas the accusation of Satan that we are not good enough is always in a non-specific sense.[47] That is, the Holy Spirit wants to bring specific attitudes and actions to light so that they can be confessed and the relationship with God healed and strengthened. God is the one who seeks the man and the woman and brings them back into intimate conversation, as this is what he desires.

At the same time God is real about the consequences of sin. Verses 14 to 21 clarify all too painfully the consequences of rejection. Some commentators have suggested that these verses are a later addition to the narrative. If this is the case, which is debatable, at least we can say that they are extremely well integrated into the text as we have it at present.

First, God describes a curse on the serpent (vv. 14–15). The causal link is emphasized by *Because you have done this*. Indeed, the present nature of the serpent is meant to be a symbol of the consequences of sin. Verse 15 is a little more difficult to understand. What is the reason for the hostility between serpents and humans? (Other translations go for 'snake' rather than *serpent*.) Some commentators see an image of those who were in sin together now being driven into hostility. This may be so. But is something more profound being communicated? Wenham suggests that the image is of a lifelong battle between human beings and sin, death and evil, seeing the serpent as the symbol of that which is against God. This is an advantage in the NIV translation as *serpent*, as 'snake' immediately leads people's minds to think of a purely biological hostility.

This fits with the complex view of sin being developed in this chapter. Sin will be a reality not just for this man and woman but also

---

[47] D. Watson, *Hidden Warfare* (Send the Light Trust, 1980).

for their offspring; and indeed, the consequences of sin are not confined to one generation. Sin will always have power in this battle. It
is interesting in the light of this to see how the New Testament uses
this verse to speak about Jesus. So Romans 16:20, 'The God of peace
will soon crush Satan under your feet,' is a reference to this verse
seeing Jesus as the one who will crush the head of the serpent. Sin
may be real in all generations but there is one who is coming who is
more powerful.

### c. Broken mutuality

The Lord then speaks to the woman (v. 16). Some commentators
point to the disruption of the woman's appointed roles of 'helper and
mother'. It is interesting that while helper is clearly central to
Genesis 2, mother is not. In fact, apart from the command to *Be
fruitful and increase in number* (Gen. 1:28), which is given to male
and female together, the role of mother has not been mentioned at all
so far in the narrative. However, it is clear that sin corrupts that
which is good, and the pain in childbearing is a symbol of the way
that sin affects even the God-given and joyous mandate to be fruitful.

The next part of the verse has often been misunderstood, both in
terms of what *desire* signifies and in terms of the man's rule. Kidner
comments that '"To love and to cherish" becomes "To desire and
dominate."'[48] However, we need to ask what that really means. Is
sexual desire being referred to here and does that mean that sexual
desire is part of the consequences of sin for a woman? That seems
ludicrous in the light of the earlier celebration of human sexuality in
the image of becoming one flesh (Gen. 2:24). Other commentators
point out that the literal meaning is 'Your urge will be to your
husband' and see in this the woman's desire to dominate the man or
to achieve independence from the man.

This links in to what is the significance of *he will rule over you*.
Some have seen here a pattern for the relationship of men and
women. However, Brueggemann rightly reminds us:

> Like so much other disservice drawn from this text, the narrative
> has been used to justify the subordination of women, first because
> the woman is created derivatively (it is argued) and second,
> because she is the temptress of man (it is argued). Such exegesis
> betrays the text and is a good example of the ways our values and
> presuppositions control our exegesis . . . In God's garden, as God

[48] D. Kidner, *Genesis*, Tyndale Old Testament Commentaries (IVP, 1967), p. 71.

wills it, there is mutuality and equity. In God's garden now, permeated by distrust, there is control and distortion. But that distortion is not for one moment accepted as the will of the Creator.[49]

The reality of the consequences of sin is disrupted relationships between the sexes. Sin leads to the oppression of one gender by another. While this may be our experience, it is not as God wants it, and within his new community of the church it should have no place.

In the Lord speaking to Adam (v. 17), he reminds Adam that he was the one who received the word about not eating of the tree of the knowledge of good and evil (Gen. 2:16–17). The sense of this is 'Do not blame the woman for this because she was not around when I commanded you personally!' Adam's sin was in listening to his wife rather than to the Lord, who is asking, 'Whom did you trust in this?'

### d. Broken world

The result of Adam rejecting his Creator means that that which was good is now tinged with difficulty. The fertility and ease of gathering food to eat in the garden is now replaced by the need for painful, difficult and tiring work (vv. 17b–19). Human sin has led to the land being cursed, which means it does not fulfil its potential for beauty and usefulness. This is because its chief steward is not in harmony with God and therefore does not care for it in the way it should be cared for.

The mention of thorns and thistles (v. 18) raises some interesting questions about the consequences of sin for the natural world. Traditionally Christians have struggled to describe the effects of the 'fall' on the natural world. Is it simply that the natural world is out of sorts because we can no longer till and serve creation in a way that makes it live up to its beauty and usefulness, or is there a fundamental change in nature? The difficulty that Christians have had in trying to answer the question is that Genesis 2 and 3 contain very little data to make a judgment on this. Rather than things like earthquakes and storms being a result of the fall, perhaps in our disrupted relationships we no longer have the strength to cope with such things.

Even without final answers to such questions, we are pointed to the fact that the nature of sin is to have consequences far beyond just the individuals involved. This cosmic description of the consequences of sin is a reminder of the way sin affects the whole creation.

[49] W. Brueggemann, *Genesis*, Interpretation (John Knox, 1982), pp. 50–51.

## e. Broken life

The second part of verse 19 picks up the important issue of death. It has already been stated by both God and the serpent (Gen. 2:17; 3:4) and has been hinted at in terms of the references the Lord has made to the man and the woman in terms of *days of your life* (vv. 14, 17).

Is human death simply due to the consequences of sin? The link between sin and death seems to be evident in the passage, but we must ask the question of what is meant by 'death'? The interesting thing about the passage is that it clearly states that *when you eat of it*, that is 'on the day' then you will die (Gen. 2:17). However, Adam lives on through the expulsion from the garden, being father to Cain, Abel, Seth and other sons and daughters. The narrator then says, 'Altogether, Adam lived 930 years, and then he died' (Gen. 5:5). That is a very long time after he was supposed to die!

What then is the text saying to us? Lucas argues powerfully that death is not seen simply as the end of physical existence but as a 'spiritual power . . . which weakens and diminishes life, eventually leading to its end'.[50] He offers biblical support for this in terms of the way that a person is seen to fall into the power of death when cut off from God, the source of life (Deut. 30:15–20). In addition, Saul 'died' when he rejected the word of the Lord at Gilgal and Samuel mourned for him (1 Sam. 15:35 – 16:1). Further, no physical meaning of death is clearly meant in John 8:51, 'I tell you the truth, if anyone keeps my word, he will never see death.'

Thus the death caused by sin is to be cut off from God, which is symbolized by the expulsion from the garden and the tree of life (v. 24). The garden uses the symbols of the holy of holies, in terms of jewels and gold, to express that this is where the full life and presence of God are to be found. Adam and Eve therefore experience death as soon as they are expelled from Eden, although it takes many more years for Adam to die physically.

Would Adam and Eve therefore have died if they had not sinned? If they had carried on walking with God in the garden, would they have been translated like Enoch without dying physically (Gen. 5:24)? Or is physical death without the negative effects of disrupted relationship with God simply part of being a creature on the Earth in this creation?

One might try to address these questions intellectually by asking, 'If there was no death either in the human or animal world, how could the Earth support such a massive growing population?' The

---

[50] Lucas, *Can we Believe?* p. 143.

other aspect is to look at the question from the point of view of pastoral theology. Those who have prayed and sat with those facing death know that there is often a clear distinction between a 'good' death and a 'bad' death. I have been with a number of Christian people close to their death and for some there is a joy and peace that this life is over and they are going to be with their Lord. For others however death is a time of fear and guilt. All deaths are not the same, and it may be that sin causes the overlaying of spiritual death with physical death. The overlaying of the life of the Spirit in the follower of Christ with physical death is a different matter entirely.

Some readers will object that too much of this is speculation, and they will be right in this objection! The fear of death and the sense of alienation from God is however undeniable to the author's view of the consequences of sin.

### f. Broken hope?

Is this passage therefore without hope? Sin seems to have an inevitability to it and its consequences are far-reaching, seriously disrupting our self-image, relationships with others, with the creation itself and, most importantly, with God.

Yet there are clear pointers to hope in such a desperate situation. Verse 21 gives us such a pointer. The Lord God replaces the feeble and uncomfortable attempt of clothing that Adam and Eve have made with garments of skin. Wenham sees in this a reminder of their sinfulness because before they were naked and unashamed. Yet at the same time it is a tender act of grace and a reassertion of the providing role of the Creator. There may be a breakdown of relationship but God's care and power will go on.

The Christian cannot but help to think of the New Testament images of being clothed in the righteousness of Christ. This speaks of the seriousness of our sinfulness, a reality so grim that Jesus went to the cross for each of us. At the same time we see the depth of love of God who dies for the unrighteous.

The story of Genesis 3 is a contrast to the provision of Genesis 2. There the Lord provides life, the world, free choice, work and sex. All are messed up by the rejection of the Creator who provides. We no longer guard the garden (Gen. 2:15; cf. 3:15). No longer do we walk with God in the garden, for our sin is about our alienation from him.

However, for the Christian this story needs to be read in the light of the gospel. We rediscover the depth of our sin in the light of the cross of Christ and through the work of the Holy Spirit within us. We may have a serpent tempting us, but we have a risen Lord who stands beside us, ready to help in times of trouble and taking our rejection into himself. He is the one who has crushed evil in the cross and resurrection. As Paul will write in Colossians, when we were dead in our sins God has made us alive with Christ, forgiving us all our sins and triumphing over evil by the cross (Col. 2:13–15).

In the rubble of Ground Zero there was only one symbol that could stand in the face of such evil and sin. That was the two pieces of metal that formed the shape of the cross.

# The songs of creation

One of the major themes of creation in the Bible is the call to praise this Creator God. These four passages are all hymns of praise. While sharing common themes, they give different windows into the Lord.

Proverbs 8:22–36 is at first glance a hymn of self-praise to wisdom, yet it draws us into seeing things as they really are. The three psalms teach us about the greatness of God, the value of human beings, the delight of his Word and the role of his people – and we are called to praise.

# 5. Proverbs 8:22–36
# The wisdom of God

## Welcome to the world of the real

'Welcome to the desert of the real,' says Morpheus to Neo in *The Matrix*, the hit movie of 1999. This Hollywood blockbuster achieved the unique status of teenage cult movie and subject of a University philosophy module. It was part of a number of movies that explored 'virtual reality' taking their inspiration from a media critique that sees the new information societies as having created and imposed on their populations a form of organization structured by mediated forms of experience. Movies such as *The Truman Show* and *Total Recall* suggest that there is both a 'real' life and an artificial one that we need to dismantle in order to see things as they really are.

*The Matrix*, written and directed by Andy and Larry Wachowski, tells the story of an office worker Neo, who as a computer hacker is trying to discover the meaning of the 'Matrix'. He is contacted by a group of fellow hackers who are led by Morpheus, who offers to reveal the secret of the Matrix. By accepting Morpheus's offer Neo suddenly awakens to find himself plugged into a tank along with thousands of other human beings. Freed from the tank, Morpheus takes him on board a ship and shows him the nature of the real world. Neo has been living his life in a collective virtual reality construction designed to subjugate his mind while his physical body has been used as a battery to support the artificial intelligence machines that now rule the Earth. The Earth far from the technological and safe world of the virtual reality is in fact a desert ruled by robots.

This is a multilayered movie with references to myth, philosophy and Christian theology. Along with the many allusions and subplots, central to the movie are two themes. First, the way that science can get out of control. Science and technology are ways that we control the world, but *The Matrix* paints a picture of a fearful future where experiments in artificial intelligence have got out of control. Human beings have therefore become oppressed by their own inventions. Science has always had that capacity. The knowledge pioneered in Einstein's $E = mc^2$ and the Manhattan Project led to the tyranny of the Cold War nuclear arms race. The second theme is, how do we know the world as it really is? How much of our perception of the world is true to reality? And how do we know what reality is?

Many thousands of years before *The Matrix* similar questions of life were being asked in collections of insights that became the book of Proverbs. These collections of poems, dialogues, instructions and sayings give instruction in wisdom, that is, knowledge of God, the world and human life that leads to a life of virtue and the construction of a world optimal for human living (Prov. 1:2–7). They most likely arose in a variety of settings, in particular, the court, royal and temple schools, and the family. Very little of the material makes any attempt to explain just what constitutes wisdom, and indeed there is complexity of what wisdom really means.[51] However, wisdom is integral to living life well, and entails a responsiveness to God.

The understanding and practice of wisdom keeps human beings from abusing the world. Further, as the Old Testament scholar Gerhard von Rad pointed out, wisdom was about an understanding of reality through contemplation.[52] The wisdom tradition of the Old Testament sees human beings in dynamic relationship with their environment; that is, the world of nature speaks about God's creation, the nature of God and nature of humanity.

Yet where does such wisdom come from? In chapter 8 of Proverbs, wisdom is personified and its relation to creation is pictured:

> [22]*'The LORD brought me forth as the first of his works,*
> *before his deeds of old;*
> [23]*I was appointed from eternity,*
> *from the beginning, before the world began.*
> [24]*When there were no oceans, I was given birth,*
> *when there were no springs abounding with water;*
> [25]*before the mountains were settled in place,*
> *before the hills, I was given birth,*
> [26]*before he made the earth or its fields*
> *or any of the dust of the world.*

[51] R. W. L. Moberly, 'Solomon and Job: Divine Wisdom in Human Life', in *Where Shall Wisdom Be Found?* ed. S. C. Barton (T. & T. Clark, 1999), pp. 3–17.

[52] G. von Rad, *Wisdom in Israel* (Abingdon, 1972). See also R. E. Murphy, *The Tree of Life: An Exploration of the Biblical Wisdom Literature* (Eerdmans, 1996).

*²⁷I was there when he set the heavens in place,*
  *when he marked out the horizon on the face of the deep,*
*²⁸when he established the clouds above*
  *and fixed securely the fountains of the deep,*
*²⁹when he gave the sea its boundary*
  *so the waters would not overstep his command,*
*and when he marked out the foundations of the earth.*
*³⁰ Then I was the master worker at his side.*
*I was filled with delight day after day,*
  *rejoicing always in his presence,*
*³¹rejoicing in his whole world*
  *and delighting in the human race.*


*³²Now then, my sons, listen to me;*
*blessed are those who keep my ways.*
*³³Listen to my instruction and be wise;*
  *do not ignore it.*
*³⁴Blessed are those who listen to me,*
  *watching daily at my doors,*
  *waiting at my doorway.*
*³⁵For those who find me find life*
  *and receive favour from the LORD.*
*³⁶But those who fail to find me harm themselves;*
  *all who hate me love death.'*

(Prov. 8:22–36)

To speak of God's presence in the world of wonder and order, wisdom is personified in the metaphor of Woman Wisdom. Here in this part of Proverbs she appeals to all, including the simple and the fools. Woman Wisdom and Woman Folly are locked in a battle for the possession of the youth and this is a matter of life and death (Prov. 8 – 9).[53]

Why such a personification? Some have suggested that it has its origins in Assyrian or Egyptian goddesses, but there is no general agreement on this. There is little to support the view that wisdom is seen here as a heavenly being, as Woman Folly in the next chapter has no existence (Prov. 9:13–18). Woman Wisdom is used as a poetic

---

[53] For questions of the book as a whole and greater detail on context and background of this passage see D. Atkinson, *The Message of Proverbs*, The Bible Speaks Today (IVP, 1996); D. Kidner, *Proverbs*, Tyndale Old Testament Commentaries (IVP, 1988); R. Murphy and E. Huwiler, *Proverbs, Ecclesiastes, Song of Songs*, New International Biblical Commentary on the Old Testament (Hendrickson, 1999); R. N. Whybray, *Proverbs*, New Century Bible Commentary (Eerdmans, 1994); L. G. Perdue, *Wisdom and Creation* (Abingdon, 1994); R. J. Clifford, *Proverbs* (John Knox, 1999); L. G. Perdue, *Proverbs* (John Knox, 2000).

image. But why such an image? Wisdom is a feminine noun, which may be part of the answer. Further, in ancient Israel wisdom was not the province of male teachers only. There seems to have been a significant tradition of female wisdom teachers. We read of the wise women of Tekoa (2 Sam. 14) and the wise women of Abel Beth-maacah (2 Sam. 20). Proverbs itself recognizes the teaching of mothers in the home or senior females in the wisdom schools and royal courts (e.g. 31:1–9).

Perdue goes on to ask whether this was part of the way that monotheistic Israel faced the question of how the feminine could be brought into the patriarchal religion. Rather than pagan religion, which solved this problem with divine pairs of male–female gods, here is a metaphor for some of the one God's characteristics. Whatever the origin of this metaphor, it is useful to recognize the rich variety of metaphors used in Scripture and to reflect that in our theological understanding. Alongside the dominant 'God as our Father' image of the Bible, God is also seen as shepherd and as a woman who has lost a coin (Luke 15:8–10). Jesus himself uses a feminine image to speak of God's love and care: 'O Jerusalem, Jerusalem, you who kill the prophets and stone those sent to you, how often I have longed to gather your children together, as a hen gathers her chicks under her wings, but you were not willing' (Matt. 23:37). Perdue comments on the image of Woman Wisdom: 'this element of Proverbs and the other wisdom literature equips the church for a more rounded, inclusive representation of God in faith and practice and theologically shatters the sexist portrayals of God so prominent in much Christian theology for two millennia and that remain embedded in much contemporary faith language'.[54]

The personification of wisdom is used to speak of providence (Prov. 8:12–21) and here of creation in a hymn of self-praise (vv. 22–31). What does this hymn tell us?

## 1. Wisdom is of first importance to the Creator

Verse 22 starts a new section by referring to the LORD. In God's view wisdom is seen as primary and indispensable. The argument is that if God has made and done nothing without wisdom, then we must do nothing without wisdom.

The verse has some difficulties in translation. The phrase *brought forth* can be translated as 'created' or 'possessed'. It literally means 'fathered' and this image of parenthood fits in with verses 24 and 25, *I was given birth*. This may speak of the Lord's intimate relationship

[54] Perdue, *Proverbs*, p. 51.

with wisdom, but more importantly is a reference to wisdom's importance. Likewise, the *first of his works* may be a reference back to Genesis 1:1, but is probably an image to convey that the first-born in Israelite society held a privileged rank, and was expected to become head of the family. In the light of the above reference to the importance of the feminine it is interesting that the combination of a female child with the priority of the first-born questions social convention.

Whether in terms of birth or in terms of having a royal appointment (v. 23), there is the clear sense of being the best and most valued of all the things God created.

## 2. Wisdom is fundamental to the Universe

Wisdom is before the Universe and fundamental to its creation (vv. 23–29). The argument here is that as the Universe exists by wisdom, therefore by wisdom the world is rightly used. The verb translated *appointed* (v. 23) is again difficult to translate. Indeed, the several verbs used to speak of the origin of wisdom suggest a mystery surrounding this. However her pre-existence is clear, not least in the repeated *when there were no* (v. 24) and *before* (vv. 25–26). Before the creation and from the beginning wisdom existed.

Then wisdom's relation to the creation is given in terms of an architect (vv. 27–29), a builder (v. 28) and a ruler (v. 29). Some have suggested that the images here are not of creation *ex nihilo*. While this is partly true, these images need to be seen against the background of the *when there was no* and *before* of the previous verses.

Wisdom is fundamental to the whole creative process, and in particular of ensuring the stability and continuation of the creation. Wisdom is key to the continuous process of fashioning creation into a world that is intelligible, orderly and good. The images of architect and builder give a picture of a well-structured creation. Further, Wisdom rules the chaos of the sea, setting boundaries for it. There is no suggestion of a primeval battle between the waters and God, but that simply the chaos of this world is contained by Wisdom.

There is an order in creation due to Wisdom. Indeed, within the rest of the book of Proverbs this order is found not only in the cosmos but also in the patterns of human life and human society. It is an order rooted in the character of God, and by following such wisdom, human beings keep chaos at bay.

## 3. Wisdom is the source of joy

The term translated *master worker* in the NIV (v. 30a) again provides difficulty. It may mean artisan or craftsman, which would fit with the above. However, an alternative translation would be 'little child',[55] which fits better with verses 30 and 31. In addition, the sense of verse 30b could be *I was his delight* rather than *I was filled with delight*. If these translations are preferred, then the image is of wisdom as a small child in whom the Lord takes daily delight.

The image of a small child in joyful play, both in God's presence and in the midst of human beings and the world, may be an imaginative way of speaking of wisdom as the linkage between the Creator and the Universe. Wisdom overcomes the distance between the transcendent Creator and the world of human beings. While God's transcendence may be thought of in terms of powerful Creator or perfect judge, his immanence is like the play of a small child, full of activity and joy.

We should not overlook the emphasis on joy and delight in these verses. The passage says that wisdom is the source of joy, and therefore joy in human life is to be found in Wisdom (v. 31). Human beings can share in this celebration of life through the joy and wonder derived from seeing the real nature of the cosmos and human beings' place in it. Far from the reality of creation being a desert or nightmare, it is a place of joy and delight.

## Now then

Wisdom now continues speaking and spells out the implications of this understanding of creation (vv. 32–36). People are *blessed* if they both listen to and keep the ways of Wisdom (vv. 32, 34). The instruction to listen occurs three times in these verses. This is not an understanding of creation that is simply for philosophical discussion, or indeed an exercise in imaginative thinking in terms of theological tradition. This is an understanding of creation that is meant to have practical implications. It is meant to encourage the pursuit of Wisdom, for Wisdom is of first importance to God, is fundamental to creation and is the source of joy.

This wisdom is to be desired and searched for (v. 34). This is what the Lord wants, and those who find wisdom find out what life is all about (v. 35). Indeed, through their embodiment of the teachings of the wise, human beings have the opportunity to experience the life-sustaining power of creation, and through their own behaviour contribute to maintaining the order of the cosmos and human society. However, those who reject the search for wisdom mess their own lives up and disrupt the goodness of creation (v. 36).

[55] Perdue, *Wisdom and Creation*, p. 91.

Where does such wisdom come from? In terms of Proverbs it comes from the inspection of the world and the teachings of those who are wise. But this poem of Woman Wisdom grabs our attention and turns it to a deeper perspective. Wisdom comes ultimately from God. It is a reflection of his character and this is communicated through the work of creation. The Lord's wisdom is before the Universe and still active within the Universe. To search for wisdom is not to search for intellectual knowledge, but primarily it is an openness, desire and enjoyment of God. Wisdom begins with a faith in God that seeks understanding.

The matrix of the patterns of the order of the world and human societies point us to a deeper reality. This reality is not a desert nor a nightmare, but is a world reflecting God's transcendence and immanence. Some people will see pointers to a deeper reality, but just as Neo has to take a step of faith in order to see reality as it is, we are encouraged to take a step of faith into a relationship of trust and obedience to God. In such a relationship we learn how to care for ourselves and the world rather than abuse it.

Thus science and technology are only rightly used when in reference to God. Without reference to God they become dangerous and ultimately self-defeating. This means that it is of prime importance that Christians are active at all levels of the scientific enterprise, whether as students, teachers, researchers or policymakers. They will not be able to give easy answers to ethical questions or predict the future perfectly, but they will want to act as salt and light in pointing people back to the God whose wisdom made the Universe and underlies its good use.

There is another level to *The Matrix* that is enlightening. Neo not only sees the nature of reality; he is also able to act in a transformative way. Neo is presented as a messianic figure who frees fellow humans from their oppression. The Matrix of virtual reality instructs us to accept the illusion of this world as fixed and unable to be changed. Yet Neo is able to transcend this set of rules to offer redemption.

The New Testament, as we shall see in chapters 10–12, uses this personification of Wisdom and applies to it to the Messiah, Jesus Christ. Jesus embodies this divine wisdom in his work of creation. Further, he is the one who through his own transformative actions generates possibilities of change for human beings and the world. At the heart of the work of creation and redemption is not just a poetic personification but a divine person. The wisdom tradition prepares the way for that understanding.

# 6. Psalm 8
# The majesty of God

## Into perspective

The parents of a university student in his final year were becoming worried about him because they had not heard from him for some time. Eventually they received a letter that went like this:

> Dear Mum and Dad, I know you haven't heard much from me in recent months, but let me tell you what happened. A few weeks back there was a fire in my flat and I lost all my possessions. I jumped out of my second floor window and broke my legs in four places. However, while in hospital I met a wonderful nurse. To cut a long story short we fell in love and got married a couple of weeks ago. I will send the photographs to you. Please do not be put off by the metal studs in her forehead or her pink hair. In order to support her and her eight children and two grandchildren, I stopped college and tried to rob a bank. Unfortunately I was caught and I am now in prison for four years, although the authorities say that I will be released in two due to my terminal illness.

The parents were understandably shocked until they saw a 'PTO' at the bottom of the page. They turned the letter over and found these words: 'Mum and Dad, by this time, I guess you are getting a little worried. So let me tell you straight that everything I have written in this letter up to now is completely untrue. The truth is that 2 weeks ago I heard that I had failed my final exams. I just wanted you to get this in proper perspective.'

How do you get things into proper perspective, because we as human beings regularly get things out of perspective? A teenager falls desperately in love with someone else and every waking moment is consumed with thoughts of the other person. A middle-aged person follows his favourite football team and his mood is decided for the rest of the weekend by whether the team wins or loses. A couple crippled by debt long for a solution through a win on the National Lottery and feel sick every time a bill drops through the letterbox. An older person has been hurt badly by something someone said carelessly and is now filled with bitterness. It could be the joy of getting David Beckham's autograph or the grief of failing an exam that leads us to get things out of perspective.

Part of this is understandable. In human life, relationships, sport, money and success are all important to us. They express something about what it means to be human. However, when we concentrate on one thing to the exclusion of everything else, we deny that humanity. Getting things out of perspective is often related to how we view ourselves. We may put ourselves at the centre of everything, and so pride takes over. It may also be pride in our nation or pride in our church that leads us to get things out of perspective.

We can also get things out of perspective when we see ourselves as unimportant. We doubt whether we are significant at all in school, in relationships, in our job or in our family. Instead of putting ourselves at the centre of everything we see ourselves as useless and irrelevant.

How then do we keep things, and particularly our view of ourselves, in proper perspective? The Bible consistently answers that by pointing at creation and its Creator. In the light of his majesty and the glory and honour he gives to us, we see ourselves in true perspective.

Perhaps one of the best examples of this is Psalm 8:

> *¹O LORD, our Lord,*
>  *how majestic is your name in all the earth!*
>
> *You have set your glory*
>  *above the heavens.*
> *²From the lips of children and infants*
>  *you have ordained praise*
> *because of your enemies,*
>  *to silence the foe and the avenger.*
>
> *³When I consider your heavens,*
>  *the work of your fingers,*
> *the moon and the stars,*
>  *which you have set in place,*
> *⁴what are mere mortals that you are mindful of them,*
>  *human beings that you care for them?*
> *⁵You made them a little lower than the heavenly beings*
>  *and crowned them with glory and honour.*

*⁶You made them rulers over the works of your hands;*
*  you put everything under their feet:*
*⁷all flocks and herds,*
*  and the beasts of the field,*
*⁸the birds of the air,*
*  and the fish of the sea,*
*  all that swim the paths of the seas.*

*⁹O LORD, our Lord,*
*  how majestic is your name in all the earth!*

(Ps. 8)

## 1. The majesty of God

Once again, we find creation discussed not as a scientific account of
the physics of the early Universe, but used within the context of a
song of worship! Psalm 8 is a hymn of praise, although it has proved
difficult for scholars to fit into a precise mould. Debate continues as
to its connection with wisdom material, similarities to the form of
the lament, its authorship, the era when it was written and how it was
used in worship.[56]

Some have argued that the title of the psalm indicates that the
psalm came to be used in regular worship in the temple. However,
this is dependent on understanding the Hebrew word *gittît* as a
musical instrument or a festival of some kind. This is far from clear.
However, such a setting in worship seems to be strengthened by the
use of both plural and singular references in the psalm such as *our
Lord* (v. 1) and *When I consider* (v. 3). These could reflect its communal use within worship. Whether or not that was its original
setting, it is certainly true that this psalm has been used regularly in
both individual and corporate worship of both Jewish and Christian
communities.

The refrain referring to how majestic the Lord's name is directs us
both at the beginning and end of the psalm to the one we are called
to worship (vv. 1, 9). Yet one might ask what is majestic about a name
of four letters! *Name* represents not only God but also God's revelation of himself. God has revealed the majesty of who he is and his
creation in the divine name and all that it implies in all the earth.

---

[56] See P. C. Craigie, *Psalms 1–50*, Word Biblical Commentary (Word, 1983), p.
105. For a fuller discussion of these issues see also D. Kidner, *Psalms 1–72*, Tyndale
Old Testament Commentaries (IVP, 1973); W. Brueggemann, *The Message of the
Psalms* (Fortress, 1984); M. Wilcock, *The Message of Psalms 1–72*, The Bible Speaks
Today (IVP, 2001).

God's majesty and glory are present throughout the earth and are greater than the heavens (v. 1). There is therefore no excuse for people who do not worship. His power is so great that our rightful response is to cry out in worship.

Verse 2 is difficult to translate. It is not clear whether *From the lips of children and infants* is a qualification to the previous verse or whether it is connected to the rest of verse 2. However, the contrast is clear between the apparent weakness of children and the apparent strength of God's enemies. The God whose name should be worshipped in all places has enemies, but the futility of this challenge is seen in the praise of God coming from children and infants. *You have ordained praise* can be alternatively translated 'you have established strength'. In this sense the strength of God even in infants is stronger than the force or power of the godless. Whatever the enemies of God do they will never suppress the praise of God. Indeed, they will themselves be silenced by that which the world considers weak. Such is the power of his name.

In the New Testament Jesus uses the psalm in this way. In Matthew 21:16, after the cleansing of the temple, he is criticized by the chief priests and scribes for accepting the praise of children. His reply uses Psalm 8:2, saying that the truth comes from infants rather than enemies.

So, from a picture of such majesty, the psalmist asks the obvious question 'What are human beings in relation to this?' Gazing at the Moon and stars, the vastness of the heavens emphasizes the majesty of this God. In a striking poetic picture the psalmist refers to creation as the *work of your fingers* (v. 3). It is as if God is so great that he did not even need to use his arm to form the vast array of billions of stars; he used only his fingers! One can imagine the psalmist looking up at the night sky, far away in time from all the light pollution of the industrialized West of today, and being struck by such a picture.

This is the first part of getting a proper perspective. 'Consider the majesty of God,' says the psalmist. The heavens are just the work of this Creator's fingers. His majesty is more powerful than the strongest of enemies. See yourself in this perspective. Within Western culture God is often relegated to the sidelines. He has become just a private belief on a par with the healing power of crystals or the 'you will meet a handsome stranger' of the astrology pages in the newspaper. He is occasionally wheeled out for national crises, as long as he does not upstage the politicians, or is enrolled for personal convenience in hatching, matching and dispatching, better known as baptisms, weddings and funerals. He is often used as a divine parachute, the object of a frantic prayer in a difficult situation.

Our pride exalts us and pushes God away. Yet it makes no sense. In the light of the Universe what are human beings? We are nothing compared to the size of the heavens, never mind the majesty of God. Such a perspective demolishes pride and invites us to get serious with God. He is not there simply to be used for our own benefit. Nor is he there to be ignored or discussed as simply an academic thesis. This majestic Creator God is worthy of our worship and praise.

You can get this perspective in part from looking at the Universe. Put it together with the experience of worship and you begin to see the whole perspective. Communal worship can remind us of the majesty of God in praise, thanksgiving and confession. The reading of such Scriptures as the psalms or the singing of hymns and songs can restore our perspective.

Christian worship often falls short of this. Some of our songs and hymns centre on us rather than on the Lord. Rarely do we reflect the grandeur and beauty of creation within our services. I have found in my own life great help in praying or worshipping out of doors, or with images of creation in displays or on video screens inside church buildings. On being helped to reflect on the greatness of God I have restored perspective to my life.

## 2. The special place of men and women

Yet there is another aspect to this proper perspective. The question of what human beings are in the light of this vast creation may suggest that human beings are small and insignificant (v. 4). Indeed, the question is phrased in such a way that the obvious answer is 'nothing'!

Science by itself has little to offer in answer to this question. The biologist Jacques Monod wrote, 'Man at last knows that he is alone in the unfeeling immensity of the universe,' and summed up the thoughts of a generation.[57] Greta Garbo once famously proclaimed, 'I want to be left alone,' but many in today's society want to look for another answer. The fascination with extraterrestrial life, the science fiction of *ET* or *Independence Day* and X-Files type phenomena show people wanting to know that we are not alone.[58]

Pascal wrote, 'The eternal silence of those infinite spaces strikes me with terror . . . When I consider the short extent of my life, swallowed up in the eternity before and after, the small space that I fill or even see, engulfed in the infinite immensity of spaces unknown to me and which know me not, I am terrified and astounded to find

[57] J. Monod, *Chance and Necessity* (Collins, 1972), p. 167.
[58] D. Wilkinson, *Alone in the Universe? The X-Files, Aliens and God* (Monarch, 1997); P. Davies, *Are we Alone?* (Penguin, 1995).

myself here and not there.'[59] Danah Zohar, the contemporary writer of popular philosophy, echoes this when she says that the vastness of the Universe fills her with fear and a sense of insignificance.[60]

If we are insignificant compared to the Universe, then the problem may seem even worse when we consider God. How can this God who brought into being the billions of stars in billions of galaxies ever be interested in a human being who lives for a short span of human history, in a house in Durham, who will never be world famous and who consistently ignores God and his will? Does God think or care about me? The obvious answer of human rationality is 'no'!

It is interesting to note the contrast here to Psalm 19. As we shall see in chapter 7, in Psalm 19 the psalmist says that the heavens declare the glory of God. Here in Psalm 8 the psalmist is not saying that nature reveals God, but in fact the very opposite. Creation by itself can lead to the despair of insignificance.

This mounting sense of despair in the human condition heightens the impact of what comes next. The role of human beings cannot be worked out by science and philosophy. However, human beings have significance in the light of God's revelation. The questions of verse 4 find an astonishing answer: the psalmist rejoices in the place given to human beings by God. In order to understand human beings in the context of creation we need God's revelation. This is an important caution to those who would try to prove God through science or logic, using the Universe alone. It is also an important point against those who exalt creation spirituality without any emphasis on incarnation and redemption in Jesus.

The real significance of human beings is not to be seen in anything inherent within human nature, but is to be seen in what God has done. Verses 5 to 8 stress the initiative of God, who

- *made* (v. 5)
- *crowned* (v. 5)
- *made* (v. 6)
- *put* (v. 6)

The tenses of these verbs are difficult, perhaps referring to what has been accomplished in the past, but also providing a contrast with what will be the future for human beings. Once again there is a clear resonance with Genesis 1, especially in the responsibility of steward-ship over the world.

[59] Quoted in M. Rowan-Robinson, 'Flying in the Face of God', the *Guardian*, 28 October 1993.
[60] D. Zohar, *The Quantum Self* (Bloomsbury, 1990).

Human beings are given a special place in the created order by God. We are made a little lower than *heavenly beings* (v. 5). Some traditional translations have used 'angels'. Craigie suggests that that this translation was prompted by modesty and argues that the better translation is 'God'.[61] Such is the high view of human beings. Human beings are *crowned with glory and honour* (v. 5). Sometimes we move quickly over such extraordinary words. We need to remember just how valuable we are to God.

A man was desperately ill in hospital. The church music group went into the ward to sing some of his favourite worship songs. They sang the following:

> Lord you are more precious than silver
> Lord you are more costly than gold
> Lord you are more beautiful than diamonds
> And nothing I desire compares with you.[62]

Then they changed the words slightly and sang it as if God were saying to this man:

> My child you are more precious than silver
> My child you are more costly than gold
> My child you are more beautiful than diamonds
> And nothing I desire compares with you.

In a world that often devalues people, we need to hear again God's value of human beings. People are often devalued because of gender, ethnic origin or age. In a culture of fame and fortune, if we lose our job, if our relationship breaks up, if we fail exams, if we are poor, or if we live in the wrong part of town, then people say that we are not special. But God says something different. To those who feel insignificant God says they are special and important. And for those in society whom we dismiss as unimportant, God tells us to think again and see people as he sees them.

Verses 6 to 8 fill out the Genesis command, setting the stewardship in terms of domestic and untamed animals, birds and fish. Verse 8 may be an allusion to great sea monsters. We are special in that God trusts his creation to us. The early church saw in these verses a description of Jesus, which also reminds us of the tension between our present and future roles. Hebrews 2:6–8 points to Jesus as the

---

[61] Craigie, *Psalms 1–50*, p. 108.
[62] Lyn Deshazo © 1982 Integrity's Hosanna Music / Sovereign Music, PO Box 356, Leighton Buzzard, LU7 3WP, UK. Reproduced by permission.

one crowned with glory and honour. Dominion is represented supremely in Jesus (cf. 1 Cor. 15:27; Eph. 1:22), while not all things are as yet subjected to human beings.

The final refrain of praise reminds us of how we can know this. We know of our place in God's creation not because we can read it from the Universe alone, but because God has revealed himself to us. O LORD, our Lord uses the name Yahweh, which was revealed to the Jewish people, the special name of the God who saved and delivered them from Egypt. This Creator God was also their covenant God, revealed in his actions in the space-time history of the Universe.

For Christians, our significance in the Universe is shown to us by the revelation of God in Jesus Christ, who dies on the cross for each one of us. That is the message that we can and must share in a culture that asks, 'What is a human being?' It is a message that calls us to worship afresh this great God who is compassionate towards and acts for us.

Kidner comments, 'This psalm is an unsurpassed example of what a hymn should be, celebrating as it does the glory and grace of God, rehearsing who He is and what He has done, and relating us and our world to Him; all with a masterly economy of words and in a spirit of mingled joy and awe.'[63]

In this hymn of praise we get a proper perspective.

---

[63] Kidner, *Psalms 1–72*, p. 66.

# 7. Psalm 19
# The glory of God

## Reading the books

What is your favourite book? Even in the televisual age books have seen a renaissance of popularity. The Harry Potter books of J. K. Rowling, biographies of celebrities from Victoria Beckham to Anne Robinson, cookery and history books, novels and even such a 'simple' book as the 10 million best-seller *A Brief History of Time* generate more than £25 million a week in UK high street bookshops.

However, the reasons for buying or liking a particular book are not simply the literary merits of the text. Some of my treasured books are because of relationships and context. *Jennings' Little Hut* is a story about a boy at a boarding school which is totally alien to my childhood. However, it was the first older children's book bought for me by a good friend. David Watson's book *Discipleship* was the first book I read after becoming a Christian. Even the stories of Alfie and Annie Rose have significance for me at the moment as they are the favourite bedtime reading for my children.

Books are far more than just written texts. They represent the imagination and person of the writer and resonate with the imagination and person of the reader. That fundamental aspect of relationship is key to understanding books. It is key to understanding both the Bible and God's creation. Francis Bacon (1561–1626), one of the founders of the modern scientific method, used the concept of God's two books. These two books were the book of his works and the book of his word. For Bacon, as for many of the early scientists, these books needed to be held together. Perhaps nowhere is this seen more beautifully than in Psalm 19:

> [1]*The heavens declare the glory of God;*
> *the skies proclaim the work of his hands.*

<sup>2</sup>*Day after day they pour forth speech;*
  *night after night they display knowledge.*
<sup>3</sup>*There is no speech or language*
  *where their voice is not heard.*
<sup>4</sup>*Their voice goes out into all the earth,*
  *their words to the ends of the world.*

*In the heavens he has pitched a tent for the sun,*
  <sup>5</sup>*which is like a bridegroom coming forth from his pavilion,*
  *like a champion rejoicing to run his course.*
<sup>6</sup>*It rises at one end of the heavens*
  *and makes its circuit to the other;*
  *nothing is hidden from its heat.*

<sup>7</sup>*The law of the LORD is perfect,*
  *reviving the soul.*
*The statutes of the LORD are trustworthy,*
  *making wise the simple.*
<sup>8</sup>*The precepts of the LORD are right,*
  *giving joy to the heart.*
*The commands of the LORD are radiant,*
  *giving light to the eyes.*
<sup>9</sup>*The fear of the LORD is pure,*
  *enduring forever.*
*The ordinances of the LORD are sure*
  *and altogether righteous.*
<sup>10</sup>*They are more precious than gold,*
  *than much pure gold;*
*they are sweeter than honey,*
  *than honey from the comb.*
<sup>11</sup>*By them is your servant warned;*
  *in keeping them there is great reward.*

<sup>12</sup>*Who can discern his errors?*
  *Forgive my hidden faults.*
<sup>13</sup>*Keep your servant also from wilful sins;*
  *may they not rule over me.*
*Then will I be blameless,*
  *innocent of great transgression.*

<sup>14</sup>*May the words of my mouth and the meditation of my heart*
  *be pleasing in your sight,*
*O LORD, my Rock and my Redeemer.*

(Ps. 19)

We have little knowledge concerning the origin in terms of date and context of this psalm.[64] It is clearly in two parts. Verses 1–6 and 7–14 form two distinctive units. They use *God* (v. 1) and *the LORD* (v. 7) respectively to refer to God. There is also a difference in style with verses 1–6 using longer lines. This obvious difference has brought a number of speculative suggestions. Some have suggested that two distinct psalms have been brought together. Others have argued that a hymn has been put together with wisdom poetry. Even others have suggested that the author took an already existing hymn fragment and then added a theological passage to balance it.

Whatever its origin, we encounter the psalm as a unity today. As we shall see, there are numerous points of contact between the two parts of the psalm, which are skilfully combined to make key theological points. Indeed, some see strong references back to Genesis 1 – 3 in the mind of the psalmist.[65]

## 1. The book of God's works

The two sections of this psalm represent Bacon's two books. In the first section (vv. 1–6) the overriding theme is the glory of God, that is, that which is worthy of honour and praise.

God's glory is declared by the heavens (v. 1). The reference here is not to heaven or heavenly beings but the creation itself in terms of the stars. This creation shouts, gossips and exclaims the glory of God in wordless revelation. The skies, including the Sun by day and the Moon and stars by night, are testimony to the work of his hands. The poetic imagery is rich. Like Psalm 8 it speaks of the care and the greatness of God in his work of creation.

The creation testifies by its very existence to the Creator. Kidner suggests that *pour forth* (v. 2) suggests the 'irrepressible bubbling up of a spring'.[66] Creation cannot help itself but be a continual witness to its Creator. It makes known knowledge about the Creator because it is the work of his hands. I once took the funeral service of the husband of a woman who was part of the church where I was one of the ministers. I had not met the man before he died, but when I

[64] For a more detailed discussion of issues of origin and context see P. C. Craigie, *Psalms 1–50*, Word Biblical Commentary (Word, 1983); D. Kidner, *Psalms 1–72*, Tyndale Old Testament Commentaries (IVP, 1973); W. Brueggemann, *The Message of the Psalms* (Fortress, 1984); M. Wilcock, *The Message of Psalms 1–72*, The Bible Speaks Today (IVP, 2001).
[65] D. J. A. Clines, 'The Tree of Knowledge and the Law of Yahweh (Psalm XIX)', *Vetus Testamentum* 24 (1974), pp. 8–14.
[66] Kidner, *Psalms 1–72*, p. 97.

visited their house every wall was full of the most beautiful paintings and drawings. I asked who the artist was and the woman said, 'It's all the work of his hands.' I saw in his paintings a person of perception, imagination, creativity and joy. The paintings spoke to me of him.

Yet the creation is more than just giving knowledge about the Creator. There is a strong sense here of creation itself giving praise to its Creator, a theme to which we shall return in chapter 8.

Verses 3 and 4 continue this theme of declaring the glory of God. Verse 3 can be translated in different ways, and so it has different senses. The NIV translation before us gives the sense that this knowledge of God is communicated to all different cultures and languages, which links to the sense of verse 4. Certainly that is a theme represented in other parts of Scripture. Paul in Romans 1:20 will even go as far as to say that all people are without excuse because of the way God reveals himself in creation.

Alternative translations put verse 3 as 'there is no speech or language: their voice is inaudible'. This translation focuses on the wordless speech of creation. There are no audible words or even sounds from the heavens. In this sense, the psalmist is saying that there is communication without words and the glory of God is so powerful that it can be carried without words. However, it may also mean that there is a subtlety to creation's praise of God. This voice is inaudible to those who are not sensitive to it.

My children often seem to have selective hearing. When we ask them to tidy their bedrooms it is as if they have both become profoundly deaf. However, barely whisper the fact that there are presents for them and their hearing is miraculously restored! We too can be very selective in hearing the voice of God. It may be something we want to hear or something we do not want to hear.

Creation can speak but we need to be ready to hear it. For some the Universe simply leads to despair and a sense of loneliness. Yet for others the beauty of a sunset, the birth of child, or the fundamental laws of physics speak of a Creator God. The voice of creation cannot be divorced from our relationship with the Creator.

For some, the Holy Spirit at work within them can use creation to begin to ask questions about the existence of a Creator. They may even be led to some belief in a Creator God. However, for others creation will be silent. I have met many people who have only heard the voice of creation after they have encountered the voice of Jesus saying, 'Come follow me.' As a new Christian I read a few books but found many of them very difficult. Then I heard Alan Redpath, the Baptist preacher, speak at our Christian Union. I was struck by his preaching and holiness and then found myself eager and able to read his many books. Knowing the author allowed me to hear his voice in his books.

We need to be careful here, and not limit God. The psalmist is saying that the glory of God is greater than we can imagine. Certainly, in evangelism and apologetics, the book of God's works is very powerful. Intellectual discussion is very useful concerning how science has revealed the way in which the Universe is carefully balanced to bring forth and sustain life, in addition to its intelligibility and order. This, for many scientists and others, is a pointer to God. The imaginative use of video, pictures, music and poetry, which reflect the beauty of creation, can also move people towards the gospel. All of this proclaims the glory of God, but we need to remember that this is not enough in itself, as the psalm itself makes clear in its second section.

Certainly, Christians should be at the forefront of discussion about the nature and origin of the Universe if at the very least able to object to false views. There is a sense of this in verses 4–6. The Sun is seen as the crowning achievement of God's work, but the real sense is how much greater God is, compared to the Sun. God has pitched a tent for the Sun (v. 4). The image here may simply refer to where the Sun goes at night, but it also speaks of a God so powerful that he is Lord of the Sun, whether you see it or not. The psalmist then uses two similes to describe the glory of a sunrise (v. 5). First, a human wedding with the bridegroom going to his bride, or perhaps emerging the following morning. Second, a warrior rejoicing to run and show strength. The psalmist may have drawn on existing poetry to describe the Sun, but the description is used to speak of God.

If the psalmist has borrowed imagery from elsewhere, then it is interesting to see how such imagery is used. Poetry describing the Sun is present in the Babylonian hymn to Shamash, and Egyptian hymns to various Sun gods. However, in these contexts nature itself is deified. Here nature is personified but not deified. Personified nature praises God, and in doing so the psalmist reinforces the belief in one true God. If the psalmist does use borrowed poetry, it is used in order to repudiate the theology behind it. As we have already seen, this device is also used in Genesis 1. The Sun is glorious but is not a god; indeed its glory points to the glory of God.

We need to ask the question of whether such engagement with culture could be done in our own world. There are many theological agendas associated with various views on creation. The scientific materialism of Richard Dawkins argues for a Universe without a creator. Astrology and New Age philosophies often deify various parts of the world. How might a Christian engage imaginatively with these views in order to oppose them?

The first step is that of understanding the views and what lies behind them. The second step is learning to connect the Christian faith in terms of the opportunities and challenges that such non-Christian views bring. The third step is to identify the right medium, whether in radio, television, music, art or the university lecture theatre, to point to the glory of God. Here the psalmist gives us a good lesson in the much-needed arena of apologetics.[67]

## 2. The book of God's Word

The second section of the psalm (vv. 7–14) emphasizes that in knowing God the book of his works is not enough. You may be able to think about God in the general sense (the word used once in v. 1), but you can know him personally as Yahweh the Lord, his more specific revealed name (used seven times).

The focus here is not on the glory of the heavens, but on the glory of the law or Torah (v. 7). This is God's written word to his covenant people. The transition between the two sections contrasts the role of the Sun with the divine law. Just as the Sun sheds forth light and heat (v. 6), the divine law enlightens the eyes and illumines the servant of the Lord (v. 8). And just as the Sun can give life and no-one is hidden from its heat, so the Word of God gives life and has a testing and purifying effect.

The section is carefully constructed, listing six aspects of God's Word. The words are interchangeable but give the sense of the diverse and all-embracing nature of God's Word.

| Aspect of Torah | Description | Role |
| --- | --- | --- |
| Law (v. 7) | Perfect | Reviving the soul |
| Statutes (v. 7) | Trustworthy | Making wise the simple |
| Precepts (v. 8) | Right | Giving joy to the heart |
| Commands (v. 8) | Radiant | Giving light to the eyes |
| Fear (v. 9) | Pure | Enduring forever |
| Ordinances (v. 9) | Sure | Altogether righteous |

Here is one of the best adverts of all time! Although referring specifically to the law contained in the Pentateuch of the Old Testament, Christians would want to apply these things to all of God's written Word, the Bible. Jokes abound about the difficulty of reading through certain parts of the Bible and the boredom of listening to preachers. However, here the psalmist is delighting in the book of God's words, as something essential, helpful and indeed exciting and

---

[67] See A. McGrath, *Bridge Building* (IVP, 1994).

beautiful. Verse 10 goes on to liken them to the delights of gold and honey.

Perhaps at this point it would be useful to spend a little time meditating on some of these words. We often read the Bible or commentaries and take things in purely at an intellectual level. But the Word of God speaks to both our head and heart. Take one or two of these verses, be quiet in the presence of God and let your imagination engage. For example, what does it mean for the law of the Lord to be described as perfect? Sometimes perfection can be very negative for us. If I do not get a perfect score in the exam of 100%, then I fail. Perfection often shows my imperfection. Is this what God's law does? But there is also a positive sense of perfection. If a recipe turns out well, if I hit a golf shot just right, if everything works out brilliantly on a first date, then we use the word 'perfect'. Perfection is something to be enjoyed! What does that say about God's Word?

The Bible is to be treasured and enjoyed. The story is told of Karl Barth who was asked at the end of a lecture what the greatest thought was that ever went through his mind. The audience was keen with anticipation about the answer from one of the greatest minds of the twentieth century. After a silence, Barth said, 'Jesus loves me this I know, because the Bible tells me so.' The book of God's Word can change lives. From Augustine to Wesley, an honest engagement with the Bible has inspired, challenged and encouraged the great saints.

Once again, this is important for us to hear in terms of apologetics and evangelism. The book of God's works can be interpreted in many ways. It does not lead inevitably to a knowledge of the nature of God as loving and good. Indeed, the suffering in the world may lead some to question whether the Creator is good at all. That is why any natural theology must be held together with God's special revelation of himself in Jesus and in the Bible which speaks about him. We need to be centred on the Bible in our entire ministry. While starting where people are at, perhaps in terms of their experience of creation, we need to able to encourage them to engage with the written Word of God. We need to be confidant that the Bible is trustworthy and that as people engage with Scripture they will hear God speak.

God's written Word is not just for our ministry; it is also for our lives. Think too of your own life today. Are you tired and thirsty, needing renewal or constant sustaining? At work, or in family or in Christian ministry have you been expending all your own strength so that you now feel drained? Or do you need wisdom to cope with difficult decisions and a confusing world? Or have you lost the sense of joy deep in your life? Has life become a drag, where a frown is the constant expression? Or is it difficult to see the way ahead? Is it as if you are walking in total darkness, unsure of direction and worried about dangers ahead? Or do you feel you need a permanent foundation to your life? Is life chaotic, the experience of being tossed around in a small boat in the midst of a storm? Or do you long for righteousness in your own life and the life of the world?

In answer to those kinds of questions the psalmist directs us to God's written Word. But we should be careful not to deify the written text just as some would deify creation. These things are 'of the Lord'. It is only the Lord who meets our deepest needs. Of course he is the inspiration and communicator of his written Word, but pure Bible knowledge will not by itself meet our needs. Some Christians and some churches fall into the trap of following the letter of the law and losing the relationship. This was true of some of the religious leaders of Jesus' own time. For them, the law had been interpreted simply as a legal code of what to do and what not to do, rather than God's living communication of his nature and purposes.

Such a tendency exists within evangelicalism today. We rightfully want to assert the importance of biblical truth, particularly in the face of criticism. We rightfully want to stand for orthodox doctrine. But we need to be careful that in desiring to be 'sound' we in fact do not turn out to be 'sound asleep'. The Torah was an expression of the will of a covenant God who had revealed himself in the exodus as Saviour and Lord. The Bible is the expression of the nature and will of the same covenant God who in Jesus reveals his love for us, his offer of salvation and the power of the Holy Spirit in our lives.

The Scriptures have their power and effect because they come from God through a variety of means and historical contexts. They always need to be seen in relationship to Him. Our prayer should not primarily be to be better Bible scholars but to know him more. In verses 11–13 the psalmist finds that the glory of God in creation and the law of the Lord lead to self-assessment. Here is a warning and the need to ask forgiveness for hidden faults and wilful sins. Alan Redpath would often say that it is a great experience as a preacher to look at a passage, think about it and then divide it up in order to preach it. However, even more important was when the passage took hold of him, examined his life as the preacher, divided it up and transformed it into a much more powerful message!

The conclusion sums up the psalm, the psalmist wanting to please God and join in the praise of his glory. The Lord is our Rock and Redeemer. We have moved through God's revelation of himself from a Creator God to a picture of intimate relationship, of a God who offers stability and help to those who trust in him (v. 14). This is the climax of the psalm.

Here we have laid out the two books of God. The psalm reminds us of the importance of keeping them together, but most of all of the importance of knowing the author. How we perceive a book depends on the context of relationships surrounding the book. I will hear God speaking to me clearly both in creation and in the Scriptures only if my desire is that my life is pleasing in his sight. C. S. Lewis once called this psalm 'one of the greatest lyrics in the world'[68] and that has to be true. However, it is great because of its witness to the glory of God and becomes great for those who love him.

---

[68] C. S. Lewis, *Reflections on the Psalms* (Geoffrey Bles, 1958), p. 56.

# 8. Psalm 148
# The universal praise of God

## One of those mornings

The worship leader came back to her home after the service. It had been a depressing morning. She should have known it was going to be a bad day when her two-year-old had decided to scoop out a jar of jam on to the new sofa. That was at 8am as she was trying to write down the link she was going to use between the two opening songs. If she had only been in the lounge at the time or had put away the jam last night! But she was so tired.

She had arrived late for the music rehearsal and the musicians were waiting for her. The photocopier had run out of toner, so the copies of the songs could barely be seen. Two of the singers did not turn up, as they had slept in. The hour before the service was not a time of prayerful preparation but of hassle, panic and strained relations. The person who was doing crèche that morning turned up half an hour late and so she had to contend with a two-year-old who made it his mission to collapse music stands.

The worship began and things did not improve. Her attempt to lead joyful songs was as effective as a cheerleader in a graveyard. The organist seemed to be from a different planet where clocks ran slower than those on Earth. No-one prayed during the time of praise, apart from one person who seemed overly concerned for his dog. The preacher fell into the old cliché of delivering a Rolls-Royce of a sermon: one concerned for image, almost inaudible and able to go on forever. The political situation did not help either. The news was so depressing and believers were such a small minority in society. What was this worship going to achieve when Christians had no influence on the culture?

Looking at the people, she was reminded of her friend's comment that most people on their way to the service looked as if they were going to the dentist and most people on their way home from the service looked as if they had been to the dentist. She heard two teenagers say 'boring again' on the way out of the service and she had to agree with them.

At home and with her two-year-old being entertained by the neighbours' children, she put her feet up and let her mind wander. How could worship be improved? Why was it always so rushed and badly prepared? Why was there so little joy. Even when they did have a good time of praise it still felt inadequate. How could a few prayers and a few songs ever give praise to such an amazing God. She knew how God had turned her life around and healed her of so many broken emotions. She marvelled at creation, whether on her way to work or on the television science documentaries. What would be fitting praise for such a God?

It would surely be more than an hour given by 100 people at her fellowship once a week. God is worthy of so much more. In her mind she began to wonder. What would it be like to lead in worship the whole Universe! Instead of inviting her fellowship to praise, what about all the angels in heaven. And then what about all that God had created. Her imagination was getting disturbingly close to a Disney animation with singing teapots, but such a great God was worthy of praise on the most universal basis. And then what about the governments of the world. It would be amazing and right if those in power in the world all praised the God who had given the capacity for power in the first place. Finally it would be great if everybody joined in together. She could see in her imagination the people who thought God could only be praised in the hymns of the eighteenth century worshipping alongside those doing the action choruses. Men and women were taking equal part, and teenagers and children were viewed as the church of today rather than the church of tomorrow.

That would be the kind of praise that would be worthy of such a God. The only question she could not work out was what then was the point of her local fellowship? She heard the neighbours with her child at the door, and realized that she had been sitting in strawberry jam!

*¹Praise the LORD.*
*Praise the LORD from the heavens,*
  *praise him in the heights above.*
*²Praise him, all his angels,*
  *praise him, all his heavenly hosts.*
*³Praise him, sun and moon,*
  *praise him, all you shining stars.*

⁴*Praise him, you highest heavens*
*and you waters above the skies.*
⁵*Let them praise the name of the* LORD,
*for he commanded and they were created.*
⁶*He set them in place for ever and ever;*
*he gave a decree that will never pass away.*

⁷*Praise the* LORD *from the earth,*
*you great sea creatures and all ocean depths,*
⁸*lightning and hail, snow and clouds,*
*stormy winds that do his bidding,*
⁹*you mountains and all hills,*
*fruit trees and all cedars,*
¹⁰*wild animals and all cattle,*
*small creatures and flying birds,*
¹¹*kings of the earth and all nations,*
*you princes and all rulers on earth,*
¹²*young men and women,*
*old men and children.*

¹³*Let them praise the name of the* LORD,
*for his name alone is exalted;*
*his splendour is above the earth and the heavens.*
¹⁴*He has raised up for his people a horn,*
*the praise of all his saints,*
*of Israel, the people close to his heart.*

*Praise the* LORD.                                                    (Ps. 148)

## Praise from creation

This hymn of praise is beautiful in its simplicity and urges us to expand our perspective.[69] There are two sections which encourage praise *from the heavens* (vv. 1–6) and *from the earth* (vv. 7–14). Each starts with *Praise the* LORD and is rounded off by *let them praise the name of the* LORD.

---

[69] For a discussion of the background and origin of this psalm see D. Kidner, *Psalms 73–150*, Tyndale Old Testament Commentaries (IVP, 1975); L. C. Allen, *Psalms 101–150*, Word Biblical Commentary (Word, 1983); J. W. Rogerson and J. W. McKay, *Psalms 101–150*, Cambridge Bible Commentary on the New English Bible (CUP, 1978); C. G. Broyles, *Psalms*, New International Biblical Commentary on the Old Testament (Hendrickson, 1999); M. Wilcock, *The Message of the Psalms 73–150*, The Bible Speaks Today (IVP, 2001).

First the call to praise is addressed to lists of heavenly creatures. From the spiritual beings (v. 2) the call goes out to objects in the sky (v. 3). The *waters above the skies* (v. 4) is probably a reference to rain clouds but is also an echo of Genesis 1:6–8. This call to praise points us to God's creative work on the widest canvas. It is based on the belief that just as a painting or sculpture brings attention and glory to its artist, so the created Universe glorifies the Lord by reflecting his power. It may also be a corrective to those tempted to worship created objects, whether they be angels, stars, the Sun or the Moon, which, as we saw in chapter 1, is the polemic of Genesis 1.

The second section is a call of praise *from the earth*. The reference to *great sea creatures* and *ocean depths* (v. 7) is interesting in terms of the mythology of those stories that saw God in conflict with the great sea monsters or ocean depths. Here God's supremacy and lordship are reflected in the call to praise. The inclusion of the weather (v. 8) in this section rather than the first section is possibly because it affects the Earth. There is inclusivity in the call to praise from land, vegetation, animals, political leaders, all ages and all genders. Indeed this is emphasized by the repeated call to *all*.

Throughout this call to praise there are numerous resonances with Genesis 1. Some have suggested that the psalm is a version of Genesis 1:1 – 2:4 suitable for use as a hymn.[70] This is an interesting suggestion particularly in view of the liturgical form of the Genesis text (see chapter 1). However, one of the difficulties of this view is the uncertainty of the dating and origins of the texts. Others argue that this view is an overstatement, but nevertheless acknowledge the partial influence of the Genesis text upon the psalmist.[71]

The theology is very similar to Genesis 1. The call to praise is based on a number of reasons. These are introduced by *for* in verses 5 and 13. God is seen as supreme Creator (v. 5), he establishes order in the Universe (v. 6), there is no-one like him (v. 13a) and his splendour is above the heavens (v. 13b).

The closing part of the psalm turns to the Lord's special relationship with his people (v. 14). Some commentators have suggested that the last part of verse 14 is misplaced and should have been the title of Psalm 149. Alternatively, Psalm 149 could have been written to enlarge on verse 14.

This special relationship to his people has a number of different aspects. The image of *a horn* symbolizes a strong one and could be a reference to God's provision of a king. However, it probably just refers to anyone's strength (Pss. 75:4–5, 10; 92:10; 112:9). In the New

---

[70] Rogerson and McKay, *Psalms 101–150*, pp.184–185.
[71] Allen, *Psalms 101–150*, p. 316.

Testament it is used to refer to Jesus as a strong deliverer (Luke 1:69). Broyles links this image with the praise of all the saints in terms of the following: 'Israel's power is now embodied in their worship of God. The liturgy of this hymn thus draws the congregation to exercise power not in a political or militaristic fashion but by means of praise.'[72] If this psalm was composed during the post-exilic period as some have argued, then this shows a reinterpretation of earlier psalms. These were composed when the Jewish people were enjoying military and economic success under the strength of the Davidic monarchy. Here in the powerlessness of their political circumstances they find power in praise.

Indeed, the worship of this insignificant people is seen as the centre of the praising Universe. God's people act as the worship leader commanding the choirs of the heavens and earth. The people who are *close to his heart* are the focus of the universal act of praise.

## Down-to-earth praise

What does this mean in our own time for worship in the local church? First, the praise of God's people is important in his sight. Whatever the inadequacies of music, participation, language, diversity and imagination, praise is at the core of who we are as created beings and indeed at the heart of the Universe.

Second, praise responds to the nature of God rather than our feelings or circumstances. This psalm is an expression of the praiseworthiness of the Lord whatever the circumstances. Often praise is reduced to thanks for what God has done specifically for me, and my feelings about this will change due to circumstances or psychology. The psalm points us back to the question of who God is.

Third, in praise we need the widest possible perspective and creation can help us to get this. Church architecture, especially in the Free Church tradition, has contained our praise in the square box of a building with windows that make it impossible to see both in and out. This often subtly reduces the greatness of God, the only exception being the annual Harvest Festival when God's extravagance, imagination and power in creation are seen. Now of course the cross, bread and wine, and the Scriptures are at the heart of worship for Christians. Yet how do we reflect also his greatness in creation? In churches with views of the natural world, then, clear glass in the windows can do wonders for worship. For those churches without natural views, the use of video images, banners,

---

[72] Broyles, *Psalms*, p. 516.

paintings or even flowers can enrich worship. People can also be encouraged to worship outside church buildings. Praise on an outdoor pilgrimage or under a starlit sky can help us recapture the amazing nature of God. As Kidner comments on this psalm, 'If any notion of a colourless and cloistered regime were associated with the name of God, this glimpse of His tireless creativity would be enough to dispel it.'[73]

Fourth, the psalm is a reminder of the subversive power of praise. The call to the angels, stars, Sun and Moon to praise is in part a subverting of those who believed in other gods. Praise has a subversive effect. In turning our minds and hearts to an attitude of thankfulness and focusing on the God who provides, we subvert the values of a society that seeks fame and power through greed and selfishness. In a consumerist and pluralistic culture praising the name of the Lord is a reminder of who we really are and who God is.

Fifth, we have a common bond in humanity, which is the praise of God. In John's vision in the book of Revelation he sees 'a great multitude that no one could count, from every nation, tribe, people and language, standing before the throne and in front of the Lamb' (Rev. 7:9–17). They are united in praise of the Lord. The psalmist desires such a time when different ages and different genders will praise God together. The church provides a foretaste of that heavenly reality. In different nations, cultures, languages and styles we praise the same God, Father, Son and Holy Spirit. Each of us will prefer a different style, but there should always be occasions when we get a sense of the universal praise of God. The large international or national worship celebration or all-age worship in the local church are essential occasions to remind us of this.

Sixth, praise is important in tough circumstances. We do not know for certain whether this psalm was written in the post-exilic period, but there are many illustrations in Scripture of the power of praise in difficult circumstances. When Paul and Silas are stripped, beaten, flogged, thrown into prison and fastened in stocks in Philippi, Luke records, 'About midnight Paul and Silas were praying and singing hymns to God' (Acts 16:25). Some of the most powerful praise I have ever witnessed has come from people who are in the most difficult of circumstances. Churches in the poor developing nations, or under oppressive regimes, have found an identity and power in praise. Individual Christians going through experiences of abuse, bereavement, illness or the breakdown of relationships have found in the midst of unanswered questions, strength in songs, hymns, psalms and poems of praise.

[73] Kidner, *Psalms 73–150*, p. 487.

Often our experience of praise in our local church can be dry and depressing. The dominance of a particular tradition or group of people within the church, the lack of creativity and preparation for worship, and even the physical environment can all be factors towards this. However, another important factor is our own expectation and sense of the presence of God. We have a crucial part to play, whoever we are. We can pray for those who lead worship, we can volunteer to use our gifts in worship and we can come ready to meet with the Lord.

A praising local church, for all its inadequacies, can give strength to people, can point forward to a common and redeemed humanity, can subvert the values of a secular society, and can give a wider perspective of God's nature and work. Most important of all, it is pleasing to God.

# The Lord of creation

We move now to the New Testament, where we see how the writers of both Gospels and letters spoke of Jesus using the Old Testament themes of creation.

Luke uses a story of the stilling of the storm to pose the question of the relationship of Jesus to the Creator God. John in his prologue, Paul in Colossians and the writer of the letter to the Hebrews give us amazing pictures of the cosmic significance of Christ.

All see in Jesus the Creator becoming human, to reveal his love to us and to deliver us from the ugliness of our sin. This is not a Creator God who stands apart from his fallen creation, but a God who gives himself for it.

# 9. Luke 8:22–25
# The wind and waves obey him

## Winds light to variable

Sir Harry Secombe was a Welsh singer, comedian and television presenter. He spanned a number of different worlds from *The Goon Show* to the religious programme *Songs of Praise*. At the tribute service following his death in 2001 a piece that he himself had written was read. He had been asked by a newspaper to sum up his life in 100 words and this is what he wrote: 'Records, books, telly, hymns, peritonitis, diabetes, knighthood, Songs of Praise, six grandchildren, devoted wife, prostrate cancer, stroke, malaria expected soon, winds light to variable!'[74]

It is an interesting challenge to be asked to sum up your life as it draws to an end. I guess most of us, if we were honest, would reflect Sir Harry's combination of that we want to give thanks for and that which we have struggled with. Most human lives deal with illness, grief and difficulty as well as faith, family and friends.

That is true of churches as well. If you were to sum up your church in 100 words, what would that consist of? Again, if it were a typical church then there would be a combination of things. You might want to give thanks for the building, but there would always be a property steward saying, 'Don't forget the dry rot.' You might want to give thanks for the generous giving, but the church treasurer would caution, 'We need more.' When it came to worship, one person's thanks might be another person's despair in terms of the style of worship or the kind of music. You might even want to say that the sermons were 'light to variable'!

The same type of combination would be there if we were asked to sum up the world. For every step forward in peace there seems to be

[74] *The Times*, 27 October 2001.

a terrorist round the bend. The astonishing beauty of nature is experienced alongside the ugliness of war, disease and famine. The same atmosphere that paints the colours of the sunset leads to the destructive power of hurricanes.

It is a fair question to ask God 'Why?' Some of the mess is obviously due to our own bad choices, abusing the freedom that God gives to us. But beyond that there seems to be a fragility to this world. Some of course say that little of this would happen if we only have enough faith. God's plan for our lives is for health and wealth, not illness and poverty. If you have enough faith, then you simply claim God's power and all will be well, including a parking space whenever you need it.

It is into this context that the following passage from Luke's Gospel speaks afresh. Against those who would oversimplify both the world and faith, it gives us a picture of real faith in a real world:

> [22]*One day Jesus said to his disciples, 'Let's go over to the other side of the lake.' So they got into a boat and set out.* [23]*As they sailed, he fell asleep. A squall came down on the lake, so that the boat was being swamped, and they were in great danger.*
>
> [24]*The disciples went and woke him, saying, 'Master, Master, we're going to drown!'*
>
> *He got up and rebuked the wind and the raging waters; the storm subsided, and all was calm.* [25]*'Where is your faith?' he asked his disciples.*
>
> *In fear and amazement they asked one another, 'Who is this? He commands even the winds and the water, and they obey him.'*
> (Luke 8:22–25)

This is a short passage but it is rich in meaning.[75] We can see something of the doctrine of creation in three key pieces of dialogue in Luke's account of this incident.

## 1. A plea for help

The disciples and Jesus begin to cross the Sea of Galilee, and Jesus after a tiring time of visiting and preaching falls asleep in the boat (v. 22). As someone has pointed out, he must have been exhausted, considering the uncomfortable nature and smell of fish characteristic of such boats!

---

[75] For a more detailed exposition of this passage and the background of the Gospel see I. H. Marshall, *Luke* (Paternoster, 1978); J. B. Green, *The Gospel of Luke*, New International Commentary on the New Testament (Eerdmans, 1997); J. Nolland, *Luke 1–9:20*, Word Biblical Commentary (Word, 1989).

The lake is surrounded by steep mountains down which the wind is funnelled so sudden squalls or storms can arise. One such storm arises, and the boat is in danger of being swamped (v. 23). If not quite on a par with George Clooney's plight in *The Perfect Storm*, no doubt the full range of emotions are also present. It is at times intriguing to imagine what was going on in the boat. Luke tells us little but our imagination might fill in some possibilities. I suspect that there were some in the boat who pointed the finger of blame, as that seems to be the usual thing for humans to do in a crisis. 'Well, it's obviously Jesus' fault that we are in this kind of mess. I could have told him a storm was coming. If only he had asked my advice, we could have waited until tomorrow!' Others might have felt that they should demonstrate confidence. 'Call this a storm? You should have seen the one we had two winters ago. Now that was a storm! Look, we've been fishermen here for years. We can handle this ourselves.' Nevertheless, it may have been that some of the other disciples reflected the characteristic line of Private Fraser in the BBC comedy *Dad's Army*, 'We're all doomed!' Such a range of reactions is often reflected within church meetings!

No doubt there was a debate about whether to wake Jesus. Some would argue that he had more important things on his mind to deal with. His recent extensive travelling and ministry is recorded by Luke to form the background to this account (Luke 8:1–2; 8:19–21). Others would feel embarrassed about waking Jesus. After all, he had trusted them to take the boat to the other side. This was their profession, their area of expertise, and they should be able to handle it alone. Perhaps others thought that being with Jesus in itself would automatically protect them from any real danger. Others no doubt demonstrated that peculiar male trait of stubbornly not asking for help. This 'testosterone poisoning', as the American singer Nanci Griffith calls it, lies behind the refusal of men to ask for directions from passers-by when they are utterly lost in their cars!

It was only as the storm grew worse that embarrassment, complacency and stubbornness were replaced by desperation. Luke's use of *Master, Master, we're going to drown!* (v. 24) is polite compared to Mark's more panicked, 'Teacher, don't you care if we drown?' (Mark 4:38). It was only when they got to this place of desperation, with nowhere else to go that they learned two important things.

### a. Vulnerability

The first was that being with Jesus would not remove them from the troubles of this world. So far the disciples had seen a lot of miracles. The driving out of evil spirits showed them that they were with someone with great authority and power (Luke 4:31–37). He had healed many (Luke 4:38–44) and had exceeded their natural expectations in the massive catch of fish (Luke 5:1–11). He had even claimed authority to forgive sins (Luke 5:17–26), which to those with an Old Testament background was a claim of God himself. Although the disciples were not yet sure of who Jesus really was, it was logical to believe that if you were a disciple of such a powerful man, then life was going to be plain sailing!

Many Christians today have a similar view. Come to Jesus and all will be well, they proclaim and want to believe. God does not want you to be poor or ill, so that wealth and health can be yours now. In fact, if you are not enjoying such blessing, then the fault lies with you not God. There must be unconfessed sin in your life or you must not have enough faith. Such teaching may not always be so brazen. In the consumer world of the West where life is comforted by medicine and the protection of wealth it is easy to believe subtly that to be a Christian is plain sailing.

The view is unbiblical and dangerous. When the storms of life come it is easy for a person's Christian commitment to wither and for the person to accuse God of being the cause of all the troubles. Yet here the disciples are being taught that being with Jesus will not guarantee them a life free from trials and tribulations.

It is interesting in terms of our modern understanding of science that they learn it in the midst of a storm. Newton's predictable view of the world, the so-called mechanistic Universe, was largely due to the fact that scientists began trying to understand fairly simple systems. This is entirely understandable, as we start with the problems that we think we can solve. It was only with the availability of the number-crunching power of computers that more complex systems could be studied. What was found was that the world is not as simple as the Newtonian view would suggest. Complex systems are inherently unpredictable, even if you understand the laws that underlie them. This phenomenon is called chaos and one such chaotic system is the weather system. It is a system where the flapping of a butterfly's wing in Rio can lead to a hurricane in New York.[76]

---

[76] The original work on this was presented in E. N. Lorenz, 'Deterministic Nonperiodic Flow', *Journal of the Atmospheric Sciences* 20 (1963), pp. 130–141. The scientific background to chaotic systems is presented in J. Gleick, *Chaos: Making a New Science* (Abacus, 1993); J. Crutchfield et al., 'Chaos', *Scientific American* 255.6 (December 1986), p. 38; I. Stewart, *Does God Play Dice? The Mathematics of Chaos* (Basil Blackwell, 1989). The theological implications are discussed in J. T. Houghton, 'New Ideas of Chaos in Physics', *Science and Christian Belief* 1 (1989), pp. 41–51; J. C. Polkinghorne, *Science and Providence* (SPCK, 1989).

We thus live in a world so complex that we are vulnerable to the flapping of a butterfly's wing. The faithfulness of God is demonstrated in the predictable systems and also in the laws of physics. However, we also live in a finely balanced and fragile world. It is not only unpredictable in terms of the atmosphere, but it is also fragile in terms of the affect of sin and evil. The greed of the West pollutes the atmosphere, and the sin of one individual can lead to the suffering and death of thousands of others.

The unpredictability of certain storms is an important part of an atmosphere that sustains human life. The disciples were learning that they were vulnerable to such a fragile system as much as anyone else. Indeed, as Michael Wilcock suggests, chapter 8 of Luke's Gospel illustrates through miracles the reality of evil and hardship in this world.[77] In contrast to the miracles so far recorded by Luke that have been in the full gaze of public view, these miracles are only done in the presence of the disciples. Here in chapter 8 the disciples encounter unpredictable nature, demonic possession, mental and physical illness and bereavement. If Wilcock is correct to suggest that Luke is presenting a new community being formed by Jesus in the disciples with a new Sabbath (6:1–11), new leadership (6:12–16) and new law (6:17–49), then this section emphasizes that troubles will be real for this new community.

Christians are as vulnerable as anyone else and are not isolated from the fragility of nature, evil, mental illness, physical illness and bereavement. When I first became a Christian I remember being asked to give my testimony at the church youth group. My testimony was that life had been up and down before I met Jesus and now life was very smooth. I felt that was what Christians had to say! In fact, twenty years on, my Christian life has been more like a roller coaster. There have been great moments of blessing and great depths of struggle. Yet my experience pails into insignificance in the light of some of my Christian sisters and brothers, who have been persecuted, afflicted with serious illness, and lost children at a young age. These have been Christians of great faith. I do not understand why some of these things happen but I know that they do.

### b. Honesty

However, there is a second lesson for the disciples in this: in the midst of a crisis they need to ask for help. The world may be a fragile and evil reality, but Jesus is with us. His help is not automatic on all occasions, for as we recognize our need and turn to him, so relationship

[77] M. Wilcock, *The Message of Luke*, The Bible Speaks Today (IVP, 1979), p. 99.

grows. Does pride hold us back, especially in areas where we think we have it all sorted out? Does lack of self-worth and confidence hold us back when we think we are not important enough for God to help? The plea of the disciples was one of desperation. God does not mind how we ask. Sometimes it will be a shout in the midst of anger and despair. Sometimes it will be in the quiet confident prayer. But it is only if we confess our need that Jesus will respond.

A preacher once said that if you have come to church this morning feeling as low as you can get, then first of all you have come to the right place; and second, if you are in that place of desperation, the only way with Jesus is up.

## 2. A plea for trust

Jesus wakes and brings calm in the most dramatic way (v. 24). However, he is not in the business of leaving an opportunity for teaching the disciples about what it means to be in relationship with him. He asks them, *Where is your faith?* (v. 25).

In contrast to Mark's telling of the story Jesus does not reproach the disciples directly. He does however question them about faith. The phrasing of the question in the NIV translation is very helpful. It directs us, and indeed the disciples, to where our faith is located.

In one sense we all have faith. It is not important whether some have a lot and others have little. What is important is not me as the subject but what the object of my faith is. Everyone has faith. What varies is what we put our trust in. Jesus is asking the disciples, 'Is it located in me or something else?' Indeed, by implication he is saying that if it were located in me then you would not have got so worked up.

It seems to me that we Christians find it difficult to live through crises when our faith is put in other things apart from Jesus. We trust in our abilities, our church, money or even our own holiness. We therefore tell ourselves that we shall be fine in the storms of life. Yet none of these things has power over the wind and the waves.

Jesus is the one who asks *Where is your faith?* He asks it to a world that in the Western context has often put its faith in the dream of human progress. The twentieth century was dominated by the belief that science, technology and education would deliver us into some kind of perfect society where all our problems would be solved. After all, science gives us trustworthy knowledge of the world, and technology can solve any problem presented to us. Gene Roddenberry, the creator of *Star Trek*, bought into this dream, seeing the human species in space with only the odd Klingon to worry about. The trouble is that the dream has not delivered. In fact, it has become a nightmare.

Hollywood demonstrates this. *Saving Private Ryan* and *The Killing Fields* show that whatever our progress in civilization our inhumanity towards one another also progresses. The arrogance of the unsinkable *Titanic* cannot cope with the icebergs of this world. Even movies of the future such as *The Matrix* or *The Terminator* movies of James Cameron look forward with pessimism when science in the form of artificial intelligence is out of control.

The technological and economic power of the West can easily become the object of our faith. But such faith cannot deliver us. Jesus asks, *Where is your faith?*

He also asks, *Where is your faith?* to his church. Within Western countries this has been a time of deep and serious decline in the traditional churches. Part of that decline is in part due to the shifting nature of culture around us. However, part of it is due to the putting of faith in other things rather than in the living Head of the church. Some churches put their faith in tradition, in the sense of 'We have always done it like this.' Others put their faith in their ministers or in charismatic leaders. Others put their faith in whichever new programme or movement of the Spirit is famous in the Christian world at the time. Others will put their faith in money, the number who attend their church, or their reputation. A story is told of Thomas Aquinas, who was given a tour of the treasures of the Vatican. The person who showed him the treasures said, 'No longer can we say, "Silver and gold have we none."' Aquinas responded, 'No longer can we say, "Rise up and walk."'

While the church always needs reformation in terms of training leaders, new forms of worship, improved buildings, and imaginative forms of evangelism, the core of the church's life is whether we put our faith in Jesus. It is so easy to locate our faith elsewhere. A good test for any church of where faith is located is how important prayer is in the life of the congregation.

When I was invited to look after a church in Liverpool I was the thirteenth person to be asked. Twelve others had turned down the appointment and I was the only one left! It was not a successful evangelical church, but was a church that admitted it needed to grow. When in a church council meeting the church treasurer proclaimed, 'Either we change or we are a car park in ten years,' it summed up where we were. Yet as we prayed together, read God's Word together and worshipped together we began to locate our faith again in Jesus. Growth came often in unpredictable ways.

Jesus also asks us individually, 'Where is your faith?' We often play an 'if only' game in life. We think to ourselves, if only certain things were different, then life would be fine. If only I won the national lottery and had no money worries, then life would be fine.

If only I had a better job, or things were better at work. If only family and friends would help me more. If only I had a more supportive and lively church, then my faith would grow. In all of this Jesus challenges us with *Where is your faith?*

### 3. A plea for understanding

In response to Jesus asking them about faith, the disciples respond with another question, *Who is this?* This is not a bad response. At least they are beginning to recognize that at the heart of faith and discipleship is the question of who Jesus is.

This is part of a sequence of stories that Luke tells in the lead up to the great confession of Peter (Luke 9:18–27). Here Jesus' power, compassion and willingness to save are demonstrated. The fact that he commands the elements and they obey him is not just a demonstration of his power; it is a clue to his identity. Power over the elements is possessed only by God. Indeed, he is described in the Old Testament in terms of his power over the elements (Pss. 89:8–9; 93:3–4; 108:6–7; 107:23–30; Is. 51:9–10), and this is now applied to Jesus. The disciples are beginning to address the fundamental question of whether this human being who is tired enough to fall asleep is at the same time more than a human being.

We should not underestimate the length of the process involved for the disciples. The disciples have to think things through and it is clear just how unclear they are at times, wondering if he is John the Baptist, Elijah or one of the prophets (Luke 9:19). Even when Peter makes his breakthrough of seeing that Jesus is the Christ, the other Gospels remind us of how difficult Peter found the concept of a suffering Messiah (Luke 9:20–22; cf. Mark 8:31–33). The insight of the transfiguration led to Peter wanting to build shelters and Luke defending his stupidity by recording, 'He did not know what he was saying' (Luke 9:33). The disciples still do not understand (Luke 9:43–45), at times they are so wrong they have to be rebuked (Luke 9:55), and judging by some of Jesus' teaching to the disciples they were worried (Luke 12:22), afraid (Luke 12:32) and tempted to give up (Luke 18:1). Answering the question *Who is this?* is a lifelong process.

Even with the knowledge of his death and resurrection, the disciples still have to learn many things about him, including the nature of the kingdom (Acts 1:6–8) and the fact that the gospel is for the Gentiles as well as the Jews (Acts 15:1–35).

In the plea of the disciples for understanding, Luke provides us with one of the key questions of discipleship. There may be moments prompted and empowered by the Spirit when we see Jesus in a new and life-transforming way. At other times we will grow in our knowledge of him over time and in the midst of both joy and difficulty.

We need to be constantly reminded in our discipleship that at the heart of the physical Universe is not a mechanism, nor an impersonal set of laws, but a personal God. In the light of the answer to the question that Jesus is God himself in human form with God's freedom to exercise his power over the wind and the waves, miracles are entirely reasonable. The laws of physics are God's usual way of working, and their consistency speaks of his faithfulness and gives us a space and time to grow in different circumstances. However, alongside this are God's occasional acts of grace when he goes beyond his usual ways of working, for his own specific purposes.[78]

The process of understanding for the disciples will lead them to transfer their faith away from self and direct it to the Lord. As they see Jesus as God with the power and compassion to save, they will trust more and more of their lives to him. As the great missionary C. T. Studd once said, 'If Jesus Christ be God and died for me, then no sacrifice is too great for him.'

The lessons for the church of today are clear. First, is Jesus the centre of our evangelism? Do we present the fringe benefits of salvation rather than the question of *Who is this?* Second, do we recognize that being a Christian is not a one-off event but a process that needs nurture and support? The prolific evangelistic success of the founder of Methodism, John Wesley, was due to a strategy that took this seriously. Wesley preached to many, but did not believe that the work stopped there. He created small-group structures where those who began to think about Jesus could be helped and supported. Such small-group nurture is key to the evangelistic success today of Alpha, Emmaus and Cell-church programmes. Within such programmes we see a range of people exploring in different ways and at different rates the answer to the question *Who is this?* They will need space and understanding to be able to express fear, misunderstanding, worry and faith. Third, this plea for understanding needs to be at the heart of those of us who have been Christians for some time. There is always more to know about Jesus and more to be experienced of him. When the going is tough as Wilcock comments, 'perhaps the church does need reminding, especially when it has become established and organized, and has set up its machinery for

---

[78] D. Wilkinson and R. Frost, *Thinking Clearly about God and Science* (Monarch, 2000). See also C. Brown, *That you May Believe* (Eerdmans, 1985); C. S. Lewis, *Miracles: A Preliminary Study* (Fontana, 1967).

coping with trouble, that it is Jesus who puts forward his power in the conquest of evil'.[79]

When the winds of life are variable to hurricane force, there is one in whom we trust who commands even the winds and the water.

[79] Wilcock, *Message of Luke*, p. 101

# 10. John 1:1–18
# The Word became flesh

## How can human beings ever know God?

What actually is going on within a black hole? This is one of those impossible questions. The trouble is that these objects formed by the collapse of massive stars have intense gravitational fields so that everything including light cannot escape from the black hole. Information therefore can never reach those of us who stand outside a certain distance from its centre. The same would be true of course with astronauts who wanted to find out what was going on inside. It would be easy enough to get in but once you saw what has happening you would never get out to tell anyone. Perhaps it is this kind of mystery that fascinates the public and allows scientists to devise all kinds of exotic theories about black holes.

To use the cliché, some people think knowledge about God is a bit like that. How can we ever know the nature of God? Even if you claim some personal experience of God, it is argued, then no-one else can really share or understand that experience. Some years ago the British mathematician John Taylor published a book entitled *Black Holes*.[80] It was good popular science but alongside the properties of black holes surprisingly came an argument against the existence of God. Taylor suggested that any Creator who created such a vast Universe must be greater than the Universe, in fact it would be reasonable to suggest that such a Creator is infinite. However, we have small and finite minds. The question then is how a finite mind can ever understand an infinite God. Indeed, we have great trouble in just understanding some of the finite Universe. Taylor concluded that we could never understand such a Creator. In the light of that there was little point talking about God and therefore it would be

[80] J. Taylor, *Black Holes* (Sovereign, 1998).

simpler to say God did not exist. As we can know nothing about this subject, why speculate about it?

Before we object too strongly to this it is worth recognizing the force of such an argument. For many centuries, some Christians laid a great deal of emphasis on logical arguments that would prove the existence of God. The cosmological argument tried to prove that the Universe needed a first cause and that first cause was God. The design argument pointed to apparent design in the natural world and argued that such design needed a designer. The ontological argument considered the existence of a perfect being and attempted to prove that the existence of such a being was logically necessary.

These arguments became key to theology and evangelism up to the nineteenth century. The trouble was that they did not work. Philosophers such as Immanuel Kant and David Hume pointed out the flaws in the logic and Charles Darwin demolished the design argument by showing that the design in the biological world was the result of natural selection.[81] Yet there was an even more important problem with these attempted proofs of God. That was, what kind of God do you end up with at the end of the process? At most you could claim the existence of some sort of cosmic architect, but nothing more than that. A God who is personal and whose nature is one of love and justice was a long way beyond such proofs, for the reason that Taylor highlighted. A finite mind starting with a finite Universe can never get to an infinite God.

Such arguments are around today in trying to provide a 'surer path to God'. Paul Davies, the cosmologist and popularizer of science who uses that very phrase has been struck by the anthropic balances that make possible life in the Universe.[82] These sensitive balances for Davies and others point to a deeper purpose to the Universe. If this echoes the design argument, the cosmological argument has been resurrected by some in relationship to the origin of the Universe. The Big Bang far from disproving the existence of God for some scientists points the way to God. Edward Milne, Professor of Mathematics at Oxford, concluded his work on the expansion of the Universe by saying, 'The First Cause of the Universe is left for the reader to insert. But our picture is incomplete without Him.'[83]

If a consideration of the origin of the Universe points some to God, then its rationality is a pointer for others. As Davies comments:

We who are children of the universe – animated stardust – can nevertheless reflect on the nature of the same universe, even to the

[81] See J. R. Moore, *The Post Darwinian Controversies* (CUP, 1979).
[82] P. Davies, *God and the New Physics* (Pelican, 1983).
[83] E. A. Milne, *Kinematic Relativity* (Clarendon, 1948), p. 233.

extent of glimpsing the rules on which it runs ... What is Man that we may be party to such privilege? I cannot believe that our existence in this Universe is a mere quirk of fate, an accident of fate, an incidental blip in the great cosmic drama. Our involvement is just too intimate. The physical species Homo may count for nothing, but the existence of mind in some organism on some planet in the universe is surely a fact of fundamental significance ... This can be no trivial detail, no minor byproduct of mindless purposeless forces. We are truly meant to be here.[84]

Outside science, other arguments are used to encourage belief or to provide proof of the existence of a Creator. Some speak of signals within the goodness of human life, such as the birth of a child or enjoyment of scenery as being religious experiences.[85] Others point to our human faith that good will triumph in the end. Many Hollywood movies reflect this belief.[86] Where does this faith come from when our experience of the real world is that, certainly in the short term, evil is dominant? Is this a pointer to a God who is in control? Yet others point to the testimony of women and men down the centuries who have experienced, taught and preached about the nature of God. This they claim is how we might know that God exists. Finally, there are those who speak about their own personal experience and how their lives have changed. The implication is that a loving Creator must exist because I have experienced him.

All these arguments have some merit to them. They may be pointers of one kind or another to a Creator. However, we are still left with the question of how we would know that Creator's nature? This is particularly difficult in a world of pluralism where many answers are being offered to the question 'What is God like?' For those outside the church spiritual hunger is real. The response in Britain to the death of Diana, Princess of Wales, showed the need for prayer, pilgrimage and symbol.[87] The actress Shirley Maclaine is one of many who have pursued New Age thought as a way of saying that there is more to life than just materialism.[88] The existence of different faith communities in a geographical locality shows the centrality of spirituality even in the so-called secular West as well as posing the question of whether all faiths lead to the same God. These things heighten the importance of the question of what God is like.

Such questions and different approaches are not unique to the

---

[84] P. Davies, *The Mind of God* (Simon & Schuster, 1992), p. 173.
[85] M. Fox, *Original Blessing: A Primer in Creation Spirituality* (Bear, 1983).
[86] R. K. Johnston, *Reel Spirituality: Theology and Film in Dialogue* (Baker, 2000).
[87] J. Drane, *Cultural Change and Biblical Faith* (Paternoster, 2000), pp. 78–103.
[88] S. Maclaine, *The Camino* (Pocket, 2001).

world of the twenty-first century. They are approaches that have a long history in human thought and would have been reflected in the culture as John composed his Gospel about Jesus. In my imagination I see a group of people listening to John's prologue to the Gospel and finding things in it that fitted in with their own approach:

> [1]In the beginning was the Word, and the Word was with God, and the Word was God. [2]He was with God in the beginning.
>
> [3]Through him all things were made; without him nothing was made that has been made. [4]In him was life, and that life was the light of all people. [5]The light shines in the darkness, but the darkness has not understood it.
>
> [6]There came a man who was sent from God; his name was John. [7]He came as a witness to testify concerning that light, so that through him all might believe. [8]He himself was not the light; he came only as a witness to the light. [9]The true light that gives light to everyone was coming into the world.
>
> [10]He was in the world, and though the world was made through him, the world did not recognize him. [11]He came to that which was his own, but his own did not receive him. [12]Yet to all who received him, to those who believed in his name, he gave the right to become children of God – [13]children born not of natural descent, nor of human decision or a husband's will, but born of God.
>
> [14]The Word became flesh and made his dwelling among us. We have seen his glory, the glory of the One and Only, who came from the Father, full of grace and truth.
>
> [15]John testifies concerning him. He cries out, saying, 'This was he of whom I said, "He who comes after me has surpassed me because he was before me."' [16]From the fulness of his grace we have all received one blessing after another. [17]For the law was given through Moses; grace and truth came through Jesus Christ. [18]No-one has ever seen God, but God the One and Only, who is at the Father's side, has made him known.
>
> (John 1:1–18)

John reflects many of these approaches in his prologue. The prologue of course introduces the Gospel. It highlights, as an overture to a composer's work would do, themes of the Gospel such as glory (John 1:14; 12:41), life, light (John 1:4), witness (John 1:7), truth (John 1:9) and world (John 1:10). The central focus of the Gospel, and indeed the prologue, are these themes as they relate to Jesus.[89]

---

[89] For a fuller discussion of the prologue and John's Gospel see B. Milne, *The Message of John*, The Bible Speaks Today (IVP, 1993); D. A. Carson, *The Gospel*

However, John picks up subtly many strands of human thought. Those from a Hebrew background would be excited by the reference to Genesis 1:1, *In the beginning* (v. 1). The first cause of creation was God's personal creative activity through his self-expression, his word. Thus in Genesis 1, God speaks and things come into existence. However, in a creative synthesis those from a Greek background would also be inwardly cheering because they would recognize the word *logos*, which in Greek represents the rationality behind and inherent in the Universe.[90] Those who put emphasis on life (v. 4), the symbol of light (v. 4) or the eventual triumph of light over darkness would find something that resonated with their thought (v. 5). In addition, those who saw the importance of the witness of others (vv. 6–9) or spiritual experience (vv. 12–13) would feel affirmed by John.

However, along the way John is beginning to work out the central theme. It is about a man who underlies all of this and is greater than all of these approaches. If the listener does not pick up the clues, John offers it boldly and dramatically in verse 14, *The Word became flesh*.

In my imagination I see a sharp intake of breath from those listening who were not Christians. 'John was doing ever so well until he introduced this bombshell,' they might have said! What is this about God's word having become flesh? Yet John is unapologetic. Although rationalism or mysticism may provide pointers to God, we cannot know the true nature of God simply through these means. Even the witness of John the Baptist or of the Old Testament Scriptures is not enough (Heb. 1:1–2). All these things have to be understood in relation to Jesus Christ.

So just as one can fully see a mountain from its peak, the best way to interpret this passage is to interpret it in the light of this key verse, *The Word became flesh*.

### 1. Jesus the Word shows us what the Creator God is like

How can we as human beings know what the God who created the Universe is like? John's answer is that he has become a human being in Jesus and lived amongst us. An evangelist tells the story of when he was a child seeing his parents about to destroy an ant-nest with a pan of boiling water. He ran down the garden to the nest and tried to warn the ants. He shouted, explained what was going to happen and motioned with his arms. It was of course no good and the ants

*According to John* (IVP, 1991); G. R. Beasley-Murray, *John*, Word Biblical Commentary (Word, 1987); C. K. Barrett, *The Gospel According to St John* (SPCK, 1978); R. V. G. Tasker, *John*, Tyndale New Testament Commentaries (IVP, 1983).
[90] Beasley-Murray, *John*, p. 9.

did not see their warm bath coming and take avoiding action. He came to the conclusion that the only way he could have saved the ants was if he had become an ant. That was the only way that he could have communicated in a way that would have been understood.

How could God communicate with human beings in a way that would be understood? The supreme way would be by becoming a human being. In response to the argument that the finite mind could never understand an infinite God, the Christian points out the possibility that the infinite God could decide to reveal himself to the finite mind in a way that would be understandable to the finite mind. That is a logical possibility and indeed is central to what John is saying about Jesus. This revelation needs to be in a form that does not overwhelm human understanding or freedom. At the same time it can be true without being exhaustive.

The word became flesh and lived among us (v. 14) in a way that human beings can relate to and understand. This is John's own experience of seeing Jesus at first hand, *We have seen his glory . . . who came from the Father*. Here is the manifestation of God through his one and only or only-begotten Son (vv. 14, 18). No-one has seen God, but the Word has made him known (v. 18).

This image of God living among us has many references in the Old Testament (Zech. 2:10; Joel 3:17; Ezek. 37:27–28). These passages may at first glance refer to the longer term of eschatological hope, but John uses the image to express the reality of God in Christ.

### a. Seeing the image

The relevance of this is clear. In answer to the question of what God is like, Christians respond that he is like Jesus. Creation, and indeed our experience in this world, can lead to different conclusions as to the nature of God. One might see the wonder of the heavens as the creation of a good, loving and extravagant God, but what about suffering caused by natural events such as earthquakes or diseases such as leukemia? These things might lead you to another conclusion all together. In the same way spiritual experience is not always a reliable guide to rely solely upon. There may be times of joy and forgiveness and answered prayer, but in most Christian lives there are also times when God seems a long way away and many things happen that we cannot easily explain.

When Philip asks Jesus the fundamental question 'Lord, show us the Father and that will be enough for us,' Jesus answers, 'Don't you know me, Philip, even after I have been among you such a long time? Anyone who has seen me has seen the Father' (John 14:8–9). In a fallen Universe of mixed messages, Jesus is the plumb line who allows us to test our claims about God.

This has a pastoral application for those who are struggling with faith, but it also has something important to say in terms of what we put at the centre of Christian faith. We have already noted that some Christians put a great deal of faith on the design argument to prove the existence of God. When Darwin's theory came along such an argument was exposed as folly, and such faith was undermined. However, those who based their knowledge of God on his revelation in Christ were much more relaxed towards Darwin's theory, taking time to assess it both scientifically and theologically.[91] An emphasis on the centrality of the Word made flesh allows Christians to be less threatened by the various and changing scientific discoveries. In the same way, the work of Stephen Hawking on quantum gravity undermines those who argue for God as a first cause or as a 'god of the gaps'. However, for those whose primary knowledge of the existence and nature of God comes through Christ, Hawking may be simply filling in more of the scientific story of how God created the Universe.[92]

In the light of this we can go back and listen to what John is saying again about this Word. For some might say that Jesus can tell us about God by simply being a good prophet. Perhaps he brought a message about God to us; that is, he brought God's word to us.

However, John will not allow that. His experience of Jesus of Nazareth is not that he brought God's word: he *is* God's Word. He starts the story even further back than John the Baptist or even the birth narratives of the other Gospels. Mark begins his Gospel 'The beginning of the gospel about Jesus Christ' (Mark 1:1). We do not know whether John knew Mark's Gospel in its final form. But it is interesting that John uses the concept of beginning, although he links it back to Genesis 1:1. This is to make clear that Jesus was not just a human being or a good prophet.

He was *in the beginning* (v. 1), that is, already in existence and always having been in existence. He was *with God*, which conveys the picture of a person distinguishable from God, but enjoying an intimate relationship with him.[93] However, he was also more than that, in that *the Word was God*. Tasker comments, 'The Word does not by Himself make up the entire Godhead; nevertheless the divinity that belongs to the rest of the Godhead belongs also to Him.'[94]

[91] D. N. Livingstone, *Darwin's Forgotten Defenders* (Scottish Academic Press, 1987).

[92] D. Wilkinson, *God, Time and Stephen Hawking* (Monarch, 2001), p. 120.

[93] Carson, *John*, p. 116.

[94] Tasker, *John*, p. 45.

Verse 2 re-emphasizes verse 1, in case we have not fully understood the significance of this amazing claim. Jesus Christ is the agent of creation (v. 3) with an emphasis on *all things*. He is the source of all life and light (vv. 4–5). Here there is a reference back to Genesis 1:2, 3 but at the same time a reference forward to a theme in the rest of the Gospel, that is, the battle between light and darkness (John 3:19; 8:12; 12:35, 46). These universal religious symbols can only be understood in their relation to the Word.

For the person seeking the nature of God, John urges them to see Jesus Christ.

### b. Sharing the image

John is building bridges to those around him in order that they might go on and read about this man Jesus, and eventually that they might believe and have life in his name (John 20:31). This means a number of things for us today. First, for the person honestly searching, we as Christians need to present Jesus. This may seem obvious, but Jesus is often obscured by clever arguments or by questions of the style of evangelism. Any apologetic approaches must lead to Christ and indeed be dependent upon him, and the core of evangelism is to proclaim him. As John Stott has often said, although many people do not like the institutional church, very few do not find Jesus both appealing and intriguing. A preacher once challenged a congregation by saying simply, 'When was the last time you mentioned the word Jesus in conversation with anyone?'

Second, we need to hold the doctrinal point that at the core of Christian belief is that the Word became flesh. Today it is important to be in dialogue with other faith communities. We need to be humble to listen and learn from their insights. We need to find whatever common ground we can in order to break down divisions that would be exploited by many in the world. At the same time, true dialogue requires us to bear witness clearly to what we believe. In this dialogue, the revelation of God in Jesus Christ is not negotiable. Christians cannot accept that Jesus is one of many, even though some suggest that such a concept makes the dialogue easier. He is more than just a good human being, and more than just a prophet. The Word who became flesh was God, and to that we must testify.[95]

Third, John gives us a challenge as to how we build bridges in our own context. John uses lots of different images to speak of

[95] D. A. Carson, *The Gagging of God* (Apollos, 1995).

Christ. Why does he use the term the *Word*? We have suggested that he uses it because of the many different contexts in which the term resonated. For the Greeks it resonated with their thought. The Stoics used *logos* to describe the rational principle by which everything exists. It encompassed ideas of reason, science, speech and message. John uses these themes but goes further to suggest that this *logos* is personal. At the same time the Word in an Old Testament background would suggest God's powerful activity in creation (Gen. 1:3ff.), revelation (Jer. 1:4) and deliverance (Is. 55:11).

Whatever people had understood about it in the past, John was giving them an entirely new way of thinking. He was using words and images to communicate to others what he already knew to be true of Jesus. What are the images that can be used or subverted to speak of Jesus in our generation? Perhaps it may be the messianic images of movies such as *The Matrix*. Perhaps it is images of self-sacrifice or heroism? Sometimes youth workers and children's workers in the church are far better at this than preachers. We can learn much from kids' songs that speak of Jesus as greater than the greatest hero, or imaginative retelling of the stories of Jesus in the cartoons of *The Storykeepers* or *Veggie Tales* or holiday clubs where discipleship is presented in the context of *Going Bananas*! While we recognize the importance of this for children, we sometimes do not see it as important for adults.

How do we build bridges today? Alistair McGrath has suggested that bridge building is the work of apologetics. He suggests that this form of ministry is to create an imaginative and intellectual climate conducive to the birth and nurture of faith. Perhaps we might also add (keeping the alliteration) the importance of integrity to the images of Scripture, and indeed to the images of the world. Apologetics has traditionally stressed the intellectual side of this challenge. This is important but has often led to the dangers of intellectualism and depersonalizing God. John is an imaginative bridge builder to his culture, making connections, creating new images and then being able to tell the story dramatically.

Fourth, we see that the Creator God himself wants people to know him and is in the business of bridge building. God speaks of himself in a way that we can understand and therefore we need to be involved in his mission in this way. In a beautiful phrase John speaks of Jesus as *full of grace and truth* (v. 14). This is the nature of God and we must compare our own ministry and mission against this. Sometimes we are so full of truth that we lack grace. Sometimes we lack truth. Yet we must strive to embody both grace and truth.

## 2. Jesus the Word shows us what the creation means to God

A philosopher would have had some problems with John's prologue. The problem is crystallized in the *Word became flesh*. The problem is, how on earth does that happen, the Creator God becoming a human being? I can imagine a philosopher trying to suggest that John might have put it differently. If John had said the 'eternal entered the world', then that might have been easier to understand. If Jesus was not really human, just a human apparition used by God, then we could keep the dualist distinction between God and this world.

Yet John will not allow that. Verse 14 would have been shocking to the ancient world and is still shocking today to many people, in linking the Word with *flesh*. The image of *made his dwelling among us* expands on its meaning. The phrase literally means 'pitched his tent with us'. In the Old Testament God gave the Jews the 'tent of meeting' (Exod. 33:7 – 34:35), where Moses would speak to God face to face. Here John says that God pitches his tent with us in a way that affirms our human nature and the nature of this world.

Campers are selective about who they pitch their tent beside. At a recent conference where many of those attending were camping, although the conference did not start until the Saturday, people began arriving by the Thursday in order to get a 'prime pitch' for their tent or caravan on the site. This world and human nature is a prime pitch for God. He takes the initiative and comes into our world because it and we are important to him.

The revelation of the Creator God in Jesus is not simply a divine escape plan from this world once we know the nature of God, but is God saying that this world is important. We see this in two important areas.

### a. Value your history

First, history is important to God. John makes two references to John the Baptist (vv. 6–8, 15). This shares the common starting point to all Christian traditions in their story of Jesus, but more than that entwines the Word becoming flesh in a way that Carson notes, 'rises to the level of historical particularity'.[96] John was not writing against those who believed that John the Baptist was God's final revelation (*He himself was not the light* v. 8), but about the witness to the Word being a human being in history. God uses history and human beings in his work of revelation. It is a revelation embedded in history and

---

[96] Carson, *John*, p. 113.

embedded in human experience. This gives it a sense of particularity; that is, God's supreme revelation was in a particular person, in a particular place, at a particular time, in a particular history and culture. Why did he choose to do it this way? The answer is in part that this unfolding history of creation is important to God, and human experience within it is important.

### b. Value your world

Second, the world itself is important. Verses 9–10 can be translated in two different ways depending on who was coming into the world and the NIV reflects this in its marginal notes. Is it the *true light* or *everyone* who was coming into the world? It would be more in line with John's overall themes in the Gospel to see it as the true light. This prepares us for the entry of the Word into human existence in verse 14. While there may be many others claiming to show the way, the real or genuine light gives us God's revelation of himself. The phrase *coming into the world* we later see means 'becoming flesh'.

Here is an affirmation of the physical creation, as God becomes flesh in it. At one Christian conference held for many years in what became a very muddied field, many of the speakers did not sleep under canvas like those attending the conference but were bussed in from a rather nice hotel. This did not speak of the value of the conference field! But God pitches his tent with us.

As Carson and others have pointed out *the world* may simply refer to the created order but is often used by John with a negative sense.[97] For example *the world did not recognize him* (v. 10). It can be used by John to mean the created order in its rebellion against God (cf. John 14:17). If this is its sense here, which is likely, then it is even more amazing that God becomes flesh in our world. He does not come to pitch his tent with those who are already his friends but comes into a world that rejects him. Imagine arriving at a campsite and seeing a space beside some people you recognize. You know that they do not like you and have verbally abused you in the past. They will ignore your concerns, playing music loud into the night and throwing their waste over your plot. In such a situation we see how important human beings and this creation are to God. Paul puts it in Romans 5:8, 'But God demonstrates his own love for us in this: While we were still sinners, Christ died for us.'

So great is the love of God for you and me. The eternal Word of God became human for us. If human beings are special, so is the world. It is a heresy to deny the physicality of Jesus and just view

[97] Ibid., p. 122.

him as a spiritual being. Equally it is a heresy to suggest that Christianity is just about the spiritual. The Greek influence on Christian tradition has led to a view for many Christians that the physical was less important than the spiritual, or indeed was evil. Sex was bad, work was to be tolerated, this life was not to be enjoyed: only heaven was to be enjoyed. Religion was about the spiritual and we should separate politics from religion. God becoming flesh is an affirmation of the physicality of creation, and Christian faith is about the physical as well as the spiritual. For the son of a carpenter, work is a part of the stewardship of knowledge and resources; it is not simply there to support us financially so that we can exercise Christian ministry at the weekends, but is to be enjoyed and done to the glory of God. Likewise, sex in the right context is good, leisure time matters, this life as well as the next has value and meaning, and we must care for God's environment. Justice and politics are as much a part of the kingdom as forgiveness and baptism in the Spirit. The Word becoming flesh is both an affirmation of this creation and a claim of lordship over it. That means that the whole of life must be brought under the lordship of Christ. Indeed, this is the heart of the biblical doctrine of holiness.[98]

### c. Sharing God's way

What might this mean for the sharing of our Christian faith? It means first that the mission of God needs to reflect God's concern for body, mind and soul. Mission involves not just evangelism but also social caring and the struggle for justice. In such a holistic view of mission, evangelism goes beyond empty words to become a reflection of the incarnation. Jesus' concern for physical and mental healing is held together with his proclamation of the good news of the kingdom, even to the extent of worrying about the physical needs of those listening to him (John 6:5ff.).

We also need to follow this pattern in pitching our tent with those who need the gospel most and those who might reject us. I am reminded of a young Christian couple working in a church as community workers in an area of a city of extreme danger, persecution and violence. Yet most of the congregation and the minister of the church lived elsewhere in the city and commuted in to the church for meetings and services. This young couple spoke to me of the Word becoming flesh. They bore a high cost but this was incarnational evangelism. In twenty-first century Britain there are parts of cities that will only be reached by Christians pitching their tents in that

[98] D. Wilkinson, A Holiness of the Heart (Monarch, 2000).

neighbourhood. Not only does it point to where Christians need to live and work, but the Word becoming flesh is about us understanding the culture and world of our neighbours.[99] The neighbour of the cricketer David Shepherd, who became Bishop of Liverpool, led him to Christ by learning as much as possible about cricket. Do we reflect God's love for our neighbours in a way that means we are prepared to enter their world in order that they may be redeemed?

### 3. Jesus the Word shows us what creation is meant to be

Alongside this affirmation of creation is an important theme to hold with it. That is the theme that something has gone wrong with the world. The reference of verse 1 reminds us of God's pronouncement that what was created was good. That which is good is created by the Word. Yet something has happened, because the world he created is unable to recognize him and has rejected him (vv. 10–11).

It is into this situation, that Jesus not only shows us what God is like but also comes to give us the opportunity and power to be redeemed. Jesus not only gives us a picture of what human beings are meant to be like, but is the avenue through which we can reach our full humanity.

The Word is God's own and only Son (vv. 14, 18) and comes to enable us to be children of God (v. 12). John is very clear that this is totally a gift from God. To become a child of God is not part of normal human experience (v. 13). It is not something that comes through our genetic inheritance, nor is it because of our human decision: it is something that God gives the right to become (v. 12). This is done in relationship with those who receive him and believe in his name (v. 12); that is, those who trust in the character of his person, recognizing him and accepting him for who he is. Jesus will speak of such a new birth with Nicodemus (John 3).

The image of a child is a picture of both intimacy and privilege. Through God's Word he has restored us into this relationship. Some may not be able to understand fully how amazing this relationship is, because of their own life experience with difficult parents. Even those who have had a good childhood sometimes do not know just what God promises. When I was a small boy the 'big lads' came along and stole our football. My friend who was a six-year-old went up to these teenagers and said, 'Give our ball back.' The teenagers declined the invitation. He asked again and the teenagers asked why he thought they should give it back. My friend's answer was, 'Because my dad is a policeman and we live in that house just there.'

[99] See G. Hunter, *How to Reach Secular People* (Abingdon, 1992).

The ball was given back very quickly. It does not matter who you are, but it matters to whom you are related!

Verse 16 points us back to the initiative and grace of God in all of this. It is given to us as a gift through his gracious action. But what does it mean to receive *one blessing after another*? This may refer to the extravagance of the gifts God gives in terms of life in all its fullness, both in this life and in eternity. However, Carson sees the verse better translated as 'grace instead of grace'.[100] That is, the law is seen as a gift of grace, but this is now replaced by the grace and truth of Jesus. One grace replaces another, which fits with the sense of verse 17. Whether this interpretation is right or not, the main theme of these verses is the primacy and extravagance of grace.

This emphasis on grace should lead us to confidence and optimism in what God can do in the life of the believer and in his world. We see in Jesus what creation is meant to be. Indeed, as he is the one who brought this creation into being, we should have a joy in advocating the Jesus way. It is not as if we are forcing the world into a mould that does not fit. The values of Jesus embodied in following his way of living is how we become fully human and creation is healed.

It is often the case, however, that we cannot see the thing that is best for us. An elderly couple lived in a cold area of the country. Their house was badly heated with individual heaters in each room. During the winter they existed in just two rooms and woke in the morning to scrape the frost off the inside of their windows. They were afraid of changing to central heating because of the cost and the disruption this would cause. It took a long time, and the constant encouragement of family and friends, before they finally had central heating installed and found out what they had been missing all those years. Although it was expensive and there was some disruption, the longer-term benefits were far more important.

John wants us to receive this free gift from God, to become children of God. There is a cost, as we have to admit that going our own way has been wrong; and there will be disruption of some of the values we have cherished. Those of us who have *seen his glory* need to share with others that in Jesus we see what we are meant to be.

The grace of God at work in this world, working with us, gives us confidence and optimism. In John's Gospel some extraordinary people, from the proud religious teacher Nicodemus (John 3) to the serial bride of dubious lifestyle by a well in Sychar (John 4), will see the glory of Jesus. The lesson is never to underestimate the grace of God. At the same time, John acknowledges that many people do not see: those who will not recognize nor receive him. After teaching

[100] Carson, *John*, p. 132. Note that this is in opposition to Barrett, *St John*, p. 168.

about how he is the bread of life, some of his disciples grumble that the teaching is too hard. John records that at this time 'many of his disciples turned back and no longer followed him' (John 6:66). Jesus turns to the twelve and asks them whether they want to leave too. Simon Peter answers, 'Lord, to whom shall we go? You have the words of eternal life. We believe and know that you are the Holy One of God' (John 6:68–69).

We began this chapter with the problem of how we could ever know an infinite God? The question is not a black hole, in the sense of never knowing the answer. John has answered our question by pointing to Jesus. However, for John, as with the other biblical writers, this is not a question confined to philosophical or indeed scientific explanation. It is a question that is personal and life changing. Have we seen his glory and received him? If we have, are we prepared to go with him? The Jesus of history needs a response in our experience and commitment to him in order for us to know fully the nature of the Creator God.

# 11. Colossians 1:15–20
# Supreme in all things

## What's the question?

Bill Gowland was a British Methodist evangelist and a pioneer of industrial mission in the twentieth century. He used to object strongly to people using the phrase 'Jesus is the answer'. Then, in response to those fellow Christians who were shocked by such an objection, he would explain. His point was simply that the phrase did not make sense unless you defined the question. 'What is he the answer to?' We may proclaim Jesus Christ as the all-embracing answer in terms of Lord, Saviour, Mediator, and even Creator, but unless we hear the questions we shall not understand just how all-embracing it is.

The Christian church in the developed world is good at posing questions to the world. Yet sometimes we are slow in our ministry to hear the questions the world itself is asking. Indeed, it is only when faith in Jesus Christ is brought into honest engagement with the world that knowledge of him grows. A Christian faith that is insular and focused on self never touches the riches of God.

So what are some of the questions of today? Let us take two that have a connection to the passage we shall look at. First, the question 'How can we make the world a better place?' If everyone agrees on the question, there are many different solutions. The millennium of 2000, in terms of optimism, was very different from the turn of the century 100 years ago. In 1900 science and technology were triumphant. Evolution had explained the diversity of the natural world and virtually all the questions of physics seemed to be answered. The Eiffel Tower, cinema, comics, the popular press, radio and the first modern Olympics in Athens represented a time of romance, passion, art and technology. Western culture was to be exported as God's way of salvation. The provision of universal education and the power of reason would make the world a better place, and there would be no more war or suffering. Utopia of the twentieth century lay ahead and it was only a matter of years before it was achieved.

However, this dream of human progress quickly turned into a nightmare. The diversity of life was eroded by abuse of the environment, human value was mocked in the gas chambers of Auschwitz, technology continues to be used to kill millions in the horror of war, and a 'reasonable' economic system leads to hunger, debt and poverty for a large proportion of the world's population.

The power of reason, for all its achievements, has not led inevitably to Utopia. Perhaps our vision is not big enough. We often want to make the world a better place for 'me', 'my church', 'my community' and 'my nation', when the world does not operate like that. And we often feel we can make the world a better place by ourselves. The trouble is, we need help.

The second question is 'What is God like?' Perhaps this is even more important than the question of whether God exists. Even in secularized Western nations, surveys suggest that up to 70% of people have some experience that they identify as experience of transcendence. This is such a universal question that it is not limited to faith communities or academic discussion, and surfaces time and again in popular culture. The *Star Wars* films of George Lucas, for example, have grossed over $8 billion worldwide. Why the popularity? The stories' heroes, evil, hope and self-sacrifice seem to strike a chord with people. In particular, Lucas raises the question of God in his concept of the 'Force'. He comments, 'It's designed primarily to make young people think about mystery. Not to say, "here's the answer". It's to say "Think about this for a second. Is there a God? What does God look like? What does God sound like? What does God feel like? How do we relate to God?"'[101]

In a world where the media makes the global village into the global living room, pluralism reinforces the question. In a world of so many different claims and diverse religions, what is God like? A young man once had a pile of books on his bedside table. He had a Bible, a copy of the Koran, a Watchtower magazine from the Jehovah's Witnesses, a book on New Age, a book by Karl Marx, a book on astrology, and on the top a book entitled *How to Stop Worrying*. In a confusing world how can we know what God is like?

One of the tasks of Christian leadership is to listen humbly to the questions. Then it is easier to see how the Christian message relates to the contemporary world.

[101] B. Moyers and G. Lucas, 'Of Myth and Men', *Time*, 26 April 1999.

## Questions from Colosse

Paul's letter to the Colossian Christians is such an exercise. We do not know a great deal about the church in Colosse, a town on the river Lycus in modern Turkey. It is possible that the church began during Paul's prolific evangelistic ministry in Ephesus (Acts 19:9–10). Using the lecture hall of Tyrannus, Paul argued for the gospel every day for two years. Yet, so effective was his ministry that Luke claims all the residents of Asia 'heard the word of the Lord' (Acts 19:10). Possibly some from nearby Colosse also heard the word of the Lord and went back and planted a church.

In the first chapter of Colossians the letter records the visit to Paul of a worker from that church, Epaphras. It is important to note that there is considerable argument amongst New Testament scholars over the authorship of this letter. The debate centres around the language and style of the writing, and the theology in terms of the exposition of Christ, the church, hope and tradition. Some argue that on these considerations the letter may have been written by one of Paul's followers, as it is different from Paul's other letters. Others however counter by saying that the situation at Colosse provoked Paul to new ways of stating the gospel. In addition, the section 4:7–18 is very personal both in terms of greeting and in its claim to be written by Paul. The argument is complex, especially if Paul used other sources in his composition of the letter. My own view is that the evidence is strong enough to sustain the view of Pauline authorship and this will be the view taken in this chapter.[102]

Epraphras brings with him both good and bad news. The good news is that the church has 'love in the Spirit' (Col. 1:8). Here is the distinguishing mark of the Christian community. The church was planted and growing. Yet there was also cause for concern. The bad news is termed by some New Testament scholars 'the Colossian heresy' and its nature and existence have been the subject of many scholarly debates.

First, there are those who ask whether there really was something as structured and defined as 'heresy' amongst the Colossian

[102] For a summary of the issues surrounding authorship and for a general introduction to the letter and more detailed commentary see J. D. G. Dunn, *The Epistles to the Colossians and to Philemon* (Paternoster, 1996); N. T. Wright, *Colossians and Philemon*, Tyndale New Testament Commentaries (IVP, 1986); F. F. Bruce, *The Epistles to the Colossians, to Philemon and to the Ephesians*, New International Commentary on the New Testament (Eerdmans, 1984); A. G. Patzia, *Ephesians, Colossians, Philemon*, New International Biblical Commentary on the New Testament (Paternoster, 1995); P. T. O'Brien, *Colossians, Philemon*, Word Biblical Commentary (Word, 1982).

142

Christians. While today we can easily define heresy against some generally accepted orthodoxy, could that be done so early in the growth of the Christian church? Dunn follows this line and also points out that the mood of the letter is relaxed rather than aggressive towards one identifiable position. He suggests therefore that the response of this letter is to a more diffuse series of groups and ideas rather than one heretical stance.[103] There is much to commend this, not least stemming from the recognition that commentators have disagreed on the exact nature of the Colossian heresy. Some have suggested that the problem in the church was Gnosticizing syncretism where beliefs in intermediate cosmic powers and mystery-cult initiation rites were being grafted into Christian faith. Others have argued that the problem stemmed from Jewish synagogues as the source of influences that threatened the church, which attempted to force Christian converts to 'complete' their faith by becoming Jews.[104]

The truth may be that both elements and others were at work. There do seem to be clear Jewish influences, for instance in the reference to circumcision (2:11), while at the same time there are references to things more pagan than Jewish, such as the worship of angels (2:18), and ascetic practices that deny the goodness of creation (2:20ff.).

While no-one is certain of the details, Paul's response to these influences is clear. He identifies a common theme within all of these tendencies, the message that 'Jesus is not that special!' False teachers were saying to the Christians that they needed more than Jesus, whether this be Jewish or secret rites, or to receive secret knowledge to be Christians. The absence of polemic in Paul's response may indicate a more fundamental danger facing the Colossian Christians than obvious theological heresy: that Christ's status and significance were being devalued rather than attacked, and an alternative religious system was being subtly exalted. Paul saw great danger in this because it misunderstood who Jesus was and what faith in him implied.

Such dangers are around today. Some will say, 'What's the relevance of Jesus to today's world? He is simply one of many religious teachers. Religion is important, spirituality is important, justice is important, tolerance is important, but why focus on Jesus? In fact, if you focus on Jesus you will divide people rather than bring them together.' In a pluralistic culture, space and tolerance is created for Christians, as long as Jesus is just one of many. The temptation for

[103] Dunn, *Epistles*, p. 76.
[104] See e.g. Wright, *Colossians and Philemon*, pp. 21–30.

Christians is therefore to retreat into a privatized faith or Christian subculture that says Jesus is only special to my religious experience or my church community. Other tendencies also subvert the importance of Jesus in Christian faith. In the 1960s and 1970s, for example, the welcomed rediscovery of the Spirit within the charismatic movement sometimes exalted gifts such as that of tongues to central importance in the Christian faith – without such a gift you were not a true Christian. Other tendencies have exalted particular theological understandings, certain experiences or membership of certain types of churches as the mark of true Christian faith. I always feel this when walking around a Christian bookshop. The claims of some publishers in promoting their books makes me feel that unless I have read a particular book, my Christian life is defective and unfulfilled!

Paul's response to this is to remind his sisters and brothers in Christ of who Jesus Christ really is. In answering the types of questions that Epaphras brought him, he says to consider again the supremacy of Christ:

*[15]He is the image of the invisible God, the firstborn over all creation. [16]For by him all things were created: things in heaven and on earth, visible and invisible, whether thrones or powers or rulers or authorities; all things were created by him and for him. [17]He is before all things, and in him all things hold together. [18]And he is the head of the body, the church; he is the beginning and the firstborn from among the dead, so that in everything he might have the supremacy. [19]For God was pleased to have all his fulness dwell in him, [20]and through him to reconcile to himself all things, whether things on earth or things in heaven, by making peace through his blood, shed on the cross.*

(Col. 1:15–20)

It has long been recognized that this passage is carefully worded and rhythmically balanced with a number of significant repetitions and parallels. Some scholars have suggested that it is a Christian poem, or it could even be an early hymn. Since the work of Eduard Norden in 1923 scholars have suggested that Paul borrowed an already existing piece of a hymn or liturgy. Some scholars have even argued that he misunderstood or misapplied the hymn. There is not enough information for us to be sure of its original purpose and setting, but we can be clear about how Paul used this passage.

Paul's argument is simply that because Jesus is supreme in all things he is also sufficient for all things. The parallels within the passage stress the supremacy of Christ in both creation and new creation. Norden,[105] Robinson[106] and Hay[107] are amongst many who helpfully point out the parallels that emphasize the Son's role in creation and new creation:

- 'who is' the image of the invisible God (v. 15a) and the beginning (v. 18b)
- 'he is the first-born' of all creation (v. 15b) and from the dead (v. 18c)
- 'he is pre-eminent' as he is before all things (v. 17a) and that he might be pre-eminent in all things (v. 18d)
- the Son unifies as in him all things hold together (v. 17b) and he reconciles all things (v. 20a)
- everything is related to him in creation (v. 16b) and in new creation (v. 20c)

In addition the sequence of 'in him . . . through him . . . to him' is paralleled in both verse 16 and verses 19–20a. The significance of parallels is that the same agent accomplishes both creation and new creation. Jesus is not seen simply as a human being of history or even as a mediator of present religious experience. Here he is both Lord of creation and new creation.

Our daughter Hannah is only five years old and not so long ago she wanted to take a photograph of the rest of the family. She stood so close that when we asked her what she saw in the viewfinder, she said, 'Daddy's nose!' We had to tell her to step back. Next she said, 'Daddy's tummy!' Time after time we had to say, 'Step back' until she got all of us in focus.

Paul is asking us to take a step back to see the bigger picture. Whatever the immediate questions and influences upon you, take a step back and look again at Jesus. Two thousand years later in a very different context, the message has relevance to us. In the questions that people ask, the supremacy of Jesus means that he is the sufficient answer. Let's pick out the two areas where Paul details the supremacy of Jesus and how they relate to our own contemporary questions.

## 1. Who is Jesus?

There are some questions where the answer is always bigger than we expect. Things like, what's my hotel bill, or are there any clothes to

[105] E. Norden, *Agnostos Theos: Untersuchungen zur Formengeschichte Religiöser Rede* (1923; Wissenschaftliche Buchgesellschaft, repr. 1956).

[106] J. M. Robinson, 'A Formal Analysis of Colossians 1:15–20', *Journal of Biblical Literature* 76 (1957), pp. 270–287.

[107] D. M. Hay, *Colossians*, Abingdon New Testament Commentaries (Abingdon, 2000).

wash! 'Who is Jesus' is one of those questions. As we keep on asking it, the answer is always bigger than we expect.

### a. Supreme in revelation

Paul says that first he is the *image of the invisible God* (v. 15). The *he* of verse 15 refers back to 'God's beloved Son' (v. 13). In this is the answer to the question 'What is God like?' The idea that God cannot be seen is fundamental to the Bible. He is an invisible God, transcendent and surpassing human comprehension. No idols are to be made of God, because any such attempt will belittle his majesty. Yet in answer to the question 'What is God like?' Paul replies, 'He is like Jesus.' Jesus is the *image of the invisible God* (v. 15), the projection of God himself into the dimensions of space-time in a way that reveals his true nature. If we want to see what God is like, we look at the image. Here is a reminder of Genesis 1:26–27, where God created male and female in his own image. That image defaced by the rebellion of sin is now seen clearly in Jesus. Dunn also suggests a reference to divine Wisdom as the image of God, that is, God's outreaching and interaction with the world 'speaking of God's immanence' while safeguarding his transcendence'.[108]

As Bishop Peter Storey says, 'God became local in Jesus Christ.' As we have seen, John in his Gospel would put it as, 'No one has ever seen God, the only Son he has made him known' (John 1:18). Here is not just another holy person, another good teacher, or another radical leader. Nor is this just another god. Jesus has not replaced God; he has made him known.

Yet images by themselves can be quite misleading. I was speaking at a conference recently and someone came up to me and said, 'You look far more spiritual in your photograph!' Paul does not say that Jesus is simply a representation of God. As we shall see in the next chapter the letter to the Hebrews says that 'the Son is the radiance of God's glory and the exact representation of his being' (Heb. 1:3). Here Paul goes even further, as later in the passage he claims that all the fullness of God dwelt in Jesus (v. 19). Jesus is more than just an image: he is God in all his fullness walking amongst us. How can this be? The philosophical questions at this point are huge. I wonder if Paul realized the number of theological books that would be written on this statement; but he will not allow anything less than full divinity and full humanity in Jesus.

Wright suggests the translation 'God in all his fullness was pleased to take up permanent residence in him.'[109] Paul re-emphasizes such

---

[108] Dunn, *Epistles*, p. 88.
[109] Wright, *Colossians and Philemon*, p. 75.

an understanding in Colossians 2:9: 'in Christ all the fulness of the Deity lives in bodily form'. There were those who could cope with Jesus as a human being who was chosen by God for a specific purpose of revealing his will. Philosophically that is easier to understand. However, Paul will not allow that. Others can cope with Jesus as fully God but not really human, as if God came to earth just with the outward appearance of humanity. Again, Paul will not allow that. Notice the reference to physical body (v. 22) and 'bodily form' (Col. 2:9). Full humanity and full divinity, nothing less.

For Paul, Christ is not just a historical figure, but is also present reality. Christ *is* the image of the invisible God. This is present tense. God reveals his nature in Christ within the space-time history of the Universe, but that revelation is accessible to all peoples at all times. This same Jesus is alive, reigning as head of the body, his church. So the nature of God can be encountered by reading the history, experiencing his risen presence and seeing him present in the church.

What is God like? Are you asking that question today? Never mind the questions of the world. It is perhaps your question. My father died at Christmas at the grand old age of ninety-one. He had been a Christian for many years, but as illness and his fragile body became a source of mounting frustration, depression and pain to this very active man, he found himself asking the question 'What is this God like who seems to be doing this to me?' I asked him in hospital how he coped with such a question. He replied that each night in hospital he would recite the words of the hymn by John Newton:

How sweet the name of Jesus sounds in a believer's ear!
It soothes his sorrows, heals his wounds and drives away his fear.

As he stepped back and saw Jesus afresh he saw what God was really like. The experiences of this world, especially those of suffering and evil, may question our faith, even if we have held it for many years. At such times we need to refocus on Jesus.

This also leads us to the question of what in our ministries we are communicating. We may be evangelists, theologians, pastors or teachers. We may have many concerns to do with church, justice, growth, dialogue, leadership and education. At the heart of all of this, do we have a big enough picture of Jesus? Although God reveals himself in many and various ways, he does do supremely in the man born 2,000 years ago in a stable in Bethlehem.

One of the new songs that I find continually challenges me in my own ministry has the simple lyrics

Jesus, be the centre, be the source, be my light, Jesus
Jesus be my vision, be my path, be my guide, Jesus.[110]

## b. Supreme in creation

Yet that is not the only thing Paul gives us in answering the question
'Who is Jesus?' In case, in the words of J. B. Phillips, 'Your God is
too small' Paul goes on to tell us more about the supremacy of Jesus.
He is not only supreme in showing us what God is like; he is also
supreme in creation.

Paul's cosmic description of Jesus echoes the understanding of
'wisdom' in some of the Old Testament. There God creates the world
through wisdom. In 1925 C. F. Burney[111] suggested that this hymn in
Colossians applies to Jesus everything that could be said of the figure
'Wisdom'. Burney argued that Paul combines Genesis 1:1 with Proverbs
8:22 to suggest that the divine Wisdom has been fully embodied in
human form. Here the creative work of God is expressed not through a
concept or personification of a divine attribute or holy law but through
a person. At the heart of God's creative work is Jesus Christ.

The scale of this is staggering. He is *firstborn* (v. 15) signifying priority of both time and rank. Perhaps a better way of translation is
'firstborn before all creation'.[112] There is no sense of Christ being
created. Notice the way Paul describes it. *In him* – he is the foundation of creation of all things whether spiritual or earthly powers (v.
16). *By him* – he is the agent of creation (v. 16). *For him* – he is the
goal to which creation tends, its eschatological purpose (v. 16). And
if we haven't already got it, Paul reinforces the picture. He is *before
all things* (v. 17) and *in him all things hold together* (v. 17). He is both
the origin and sustainer of creation. The verb is in the perfect tense
indicating everything held together in him, which continues to do so.

Get the bigger picture, says Paul, stressing *all things* time after
time. These often can be only words on the page, so let me for a
moment take you on a journey, as you reflect on this picture of Jesus.
The journey from the Earth to the Moon, representing the great
success of the Apollo programme, is about 240,000 miles from the
earth, which happens to be roughly the entire distance the eight-
eenth-century Anglican priest and open-air preacher John Wesley
travelled on horseback during his ministry.

That may seem a long way, but *The Hitch Hiker's Guide to the*

[110] Michael Frye © 1999 Vineyard Songs (UK/Eire) CopyCare <www.copycare.
com>. Used by permission.

[111] C. F. Burney, 'Christ as the *Archē* of Creation', *Journal of Theological Studies*
27 (1925–26), pp. 160–177.

[112] Bruce, *Epistles*, p. 54.

*Galaxy* would call it only 'peanuts to space'.[113] Indeed, on a peanut scale we begin to see something of the size of the Universe. If we imagine the Sun to be the size of a peanut located in London, then the Earth would be a speck of dust about half a metre away. It takes light 8 minutes to travel to the Earth from the Sun. Nine planets with over sixty moons orbit the Sun, with a great number of asteroids and comets. However, even getting to the edge of our Solar System is only the beginning of any cosmic journey some 20 metres from our peanut. If we were to ask on our peanut scale where we would place the nearest star to our Sun if the latter were placed in London, the answer would be, another peanut some 200 miles away.

Yet that is only the nearest star. Our Milky Way galaxy of 100 billion stars is 100,000 light years across, and the Universe is at least 10 billion light years across. One light year is 9.5 trillion kilometres and if we multiply 9.5 trillion by 10 billion we can work out how long it would have taken Mr Wesley to ride across the Universe! 'Do you have the big picture of Jesus as Lord of the Universe?' says Paul.

In addition, just as Jesus is Lord of the galaxies he is also the one who holds all things together. That phrase is very important to scientists. Jesus is the one by whom the Universe coheres. To explore the Universe through science, its consistencies and laws, is to explore the one who sustains it. Science is a Christian ministry. A medical scientist once wrote, 'Jesus is Lord. It is he by whom all things exist, it is he who spiraled the DNA helix, who choreographed the genetic quadrille in cell division, who scored the hormonal symphony and who heals the wounds we bind up. And by looking to this Lord, the doctor of Galilee and sustainer of every Galaxy, we can day by day calibrate our behaviour.'[114]

Christ is the foundation of creation, sustaining its order and unity. He makes it cosmos rather than confusion. As Bruce comments, 'he is the unifying principle of its life'.[115] The Son is not solely responsible for creation, but it is the activity of the Father working in the Son. Just as the head and hands of a sculptor are together in creating something beautiful, so God the Father and God the Son are together in the work of creation.

Nor is the Son just responsible for the physical creation. The powers and rulers of verse 16 have been variously understood as spiritual beings such as angels and demons, or earthly rulers and structures such as governments. In one sense it does not matter which interpretation we take, for Paul's point is that everything finds its origin in Christ.

---

[113] D. Adams, *The Hitch Hiker's Guide to the Galaxy* (Pan, 1979), p. 1.

[114] R. F. R. Gardner, quoted in D. English, *An Evangelical Theology of Preaching* (Abingdon, 1995), p. 56.

[115] Bruce, *Epistles*, p. 66.

This would have had an immediate application to the Colossian Christians. The ancient world was often obsessed with intermediaries between heaven and earth such as principalities, authorities, demons and angels. Paul is saying that even if these things existed they were all created by Jesus. Therefore, if we have faith in him there is no need to be either obsessed or fearful about these things.

In our own time this understanding of Jesus has a great deal to say to those looking for purpose in the Universe. Science explores a Universe ordered by the laws of physics. However, science can never explain where these laws come from; it simply assumes that they are there. Paul says that the Universe 'holds together' or 'coheres' not because of an impersonal physical theory but because of the creative work of Jesus. Science is only possible because of the work of Jesus. The allusion back to Genesis 1:1 is clear. If we want to understand the origin of the Universe, then science may help in understanding how it arose; but to understand its meaning, purpose and value we have to understand that Jesus is the beginning (v. 18).

### c. Don't limit his supremacy!

Most of all, it is a challenge to get a bigger picture of Jesus Christ. The problem for Christians is often that we reduce Jesus down, seeing him in our own image. The biblical understanding critiques all such tendencies. I am a man. At times in the past and still today, men through power structures and oppression have limited the opportunities for women. But Jesus is bigger than that. I am a white Anglo-Saxon and value my history and heritage. Although whites often limit opportunities and justice for those of different ethnic origin, Jesus is bigger than that. I am a British Methodist, sometimes thinking that as Methodism started in Britain, our theology and practice is closer to the kingdom of God than anywhere else! A friend of mine from another culture once playfully said to me, 'You British doubt everything in theology, apart from your God-given right to tell the rest of us what to believe.' But Jesus is bigger than that.

I am an evangelical Christian and rejoice in the authority of Scripture, the centrality of the cross and the importance of evangelism. At times I have looked down on other Christians. I am a Protestant, thankful for the Reformation and an emphasis on justification by faith, but have at times doubted the work of God in churches outside my tradition. I am an ordained person, often part of a structure that does not free but stifles others in their ministry. I am growing older, and those who are older have often denied opportunities to young people for ministry and leadership. In all these things Jesus is bigger than that!

For all those whose ministries have been limited and devalued by my participation in unjust structures, I ask forgiveness. I am slowly learning to have a bigger picture of Jesus.

We need to ask the question 'Is the Jesus I follow and speak about big enough to communicate not only in my culture but in a different way in another culture?' Is he big enough to relate to both men and women, black and white, the elderly and children? Is this Jesus big enough to be both Lord of personal religious experience and science, my local church and the worldwide church, my life, our nation, our world? He is the source of all things and therefore there is not one part of the Universe to which Jesus is not both relevant and important.

Paul wants us to get a bigger picture of Jesus. For the one who is supreme in the Universe is the one who promises to be with us when we walk through the fire, when the water is up to our neck, and even when we despair of the church. The Colossian Christians need not fear the heavenly powers and dominions because Jesus is supreme. Yet not only is he supreme in all things; his work in the Universe involves all things and this leads us to the second point.

## 2. How far-reaching is the salvation he brings?

If you have a big enough picture of Jesus, then do you have a big enough picture of his work? Paul goes on to show the full extent of this. It is a picture that the church needs to recapture because often in the past we have reduced it again into an image of our prejudices and likes.

Some of us have so focused on the world that we have forgotten the importance of the conversion of the individual. But as David Watson once wrote, 'Revolution can change everything except the human heart.'[116] Paul says, 'Make the picture bigger.' In verse 13 of Colossians 1 he has spoken of how Jesus has delivered 'us'. At the heart of the gospel is the wonderful message that my life can be saved, forgiven, born again, empowered and renewed in personal and intimate relationship with the Lord Jesus. Jesus is the beginning (v. 18b), the first-born from the dead, causing others to be renewed in the 'image' of God (Col. 3:10–11).

Some of us have so focused on individual spiritual experience that we have forgotten the importance of the church. We have lost faith in the structures of the church. Paul says, 'Make the picture bigger.' Christ is the head of the body, the church (v. 18). As F. F. Bruce once wrote, 'one thinks of it as vitalized by his abiding presence with it and

[116] D. Watson, *Discipleship* (Hodder & Stoughton, 1981), p. 17.

his risen life in it; one thinks of it as energized by his power; one may even (without transgressing legitimate bounds) think of it as the instrument through which he carries on his work on earth'.[117] The church must be understood in relation to Jesus, and indeed it is not the church unless he is its head. He is the source of the church's life (cf. 1 Cor. 12:12–27; Rom. 12:4–5), and unless he is supreme the church dies. As Dick Lucas comments, 'When the church takes its mind and heart away from Christ and his words, human authority and tradition fills the vacuum. The ultimate consequences of this could be sterility.'[118]

And some of us have become so focused on the individual or the problems, growth and status of the church that we have forgotten God's world. Christ is not only the source of the unity of cosmos but also its reunification. Too often the image of how Christ has delivered 'us' has led to an escapist sort of theology that ignores what God says about his purposes for the world. Here Paul views salvation not as an escape but as a restoration and healing of the world. We have reduced 'Saviour of the World' to 'the Saviour of me' or 'the Saviour of my church' or even 'the Saviour of the things that are important to me'. Paul says, 'Make the picture bigger.'

From verse 18 onwards he paints a much bigger canvas. God's way of salvation is not just for the individual or the church. Here is God's purpose to bring in a new creation, the beginning of which is Jesus. Just as he is supreme in creation, here he will have the supremacy in new creation. Once again, Paul keeps stressing Christ in relationship to *all things* both in creation and new creation (vv. 16b and 20c). In fact, the word *all* appears eight times, at least once in every verse. It therefore must be of some importance!

### a. Supreme in reconciliation

Paul uses the image of reconciliation (v. 20). We are well used to the term 'reconciliation'. It presupposes some kind of separation or division that needs to be overcome. Imagine two people having a conversation as they approach a division in the road. If one decides to go to the right and the other decides to go to the left, immediately a separation forms and their communication comes to an end. In the same way, the biblical message is that men and women were created by God to be in intimate relationship with him. However, we have decided to go our own way without him, thus forming a separation between God and ourselves. Yet this is true not just of individuals.

[117] Bruce, *Epistles*, p. 70.
[118] R. C. Lucas, *The Message of Colossians and Philemon*, The Bible Speaks Today (IVP, 1980), p. 53.

The result of our separation is mysteriously and intricately linked to a separation of all things.

The good news is that the death of Jesus bridges that separation, making peace through his self-sacrifice. While the actual mechanics of what is going on here may be beyond us, we know from our own experience that reconciliation costs. In our case that cost may be pride or some things we hold dear, which must be sacrificed for reconciliation to happen. In God's case, Jesus willingly gives his own life on the cross in order to take the cost of our rebellion and restore us to a right relationship with God. For those who are Christians it is easy to pass over the full significance of this. The sacrifice that achieves reconciliation involves the shedding of his blood on the cross. Here the Lord of the billions of stars in billions of galaxies offers his blood on a small planet in an obscure part of the Roman Empire in the shame and agony of being nailed to a cross. Is your picture of Jesus big enough for this?

Partly based on the above verses, Karl Barth argued for universal salvation in terms that every individual will eventually be saved.[119] These verses however do not support such a claim. Human beings still need to acknowledge or reject his supremacy. Yet Christ's work is universal in its relevance for all things. As Hay comments, 'what God revealed and accomplished through Jesus concerns everyone and every aspect of life'.[120] Or as Wright notes:

> Redemption is not thought of dualistically, as though the created world were totally evil and salvation meant being rescued from it. Creation is God's work – Christ's work: though spoilt by sin, it still belongs to God and God still has plans for it. Redemption is not an invasion from a different or hostile realm. The Lord of this world has come to claim his rightful possession.[121]

The extent of this reconciliation knows no bounds. Paul uses a parallel in verses 19 and 20. As nothing of the fullness of God was left out of Jesus, so nothing is beyond his reconciling work. No one person, no one situation, no one community, no one nation, no one issue is beyond the reconciling work of the cross.

I spent a weekend at a church preaching some evangelistic sermons and met a woman who had been in the church for many years. Yet she had done things earlier in her life, which she felt were

---

[119] K. Barth, *Church Dogmatics* IV/1: *The Doctrine of Reconciliation*, ed. G. W. Bromiley and T. F. Torrance, 4 vols. (T. & T. Clark, 1936–75).
[120] Hay, *Colossians*, p. 66.
[121] Wright, *Colossians and Philemon*, p. 68.

beyond the forgiveness of God. This was a heavy load on her. At the end of the weekend, after talking to her nothing had seemed to change. Some time later I met her again and she was a different woman. I asked her what had happened. She said that as she read her Bible, and said her prayers (she said nothing of remembering my sermons!) she had come to see that the reconciling work of Jesus included her – 'Even me!' she squealed.

### b. Supreme in all things!

This bigger picture of God's way of salvation is a tremendous challenge to us. God's purposes in Christ are about the restoration of a world out of joint. The reference to *things on earth or things in heaven* (v. 20) no doubt refers back to the principalities and powers of verse 16. It may refer to the angels but has a broader application in expressing God's concern for the whole created order.[122] In this, God's way of salvation is not simply a return to the beginning but a new creation. As Bauckham comments, 'Salvation is both restorative (repairing the damage done by sin) and progressive (moving the work on to its completion).'[123]

Are we prepared to follow his way? His way of salvation includes reaching individuals who have never heard the name of Jesus or, as is often the case in Western culture, reject him or see no relevance in him. It will involve vibrant evangelism and imaginative apologetics. God wants to reconcile all people to himself, and in Christ there is both the mechanism and the foundation for this. As no-one is beyond Christ's reconciling work we can approach evangelism with confidence. Christ is the foundation of all things, so we can build apologetic bridges for the Christian faith from any point in contemporary culture. There is always a natural link to Jesus.

His way of salvation includes standing against racist violence, whether it be British fascists provoking violence in British cities, ethnic cleansing in the Balkans, persecution of Christians in nations where they are a minority, or in countries where the police beat people up simply because of the colour of their skin. It will involve rooting out racism in the church and in your community. God wants to reconcile all communities to himself.

His way of salvation includes helping those individuals and nations battling against AIDS. It will involve cheap health care

[122] D. Tidball, *The Reality is Christ* (Christian Focus, 1999), pp. 53–55.
[123] R. Bauckham, 'First Steps to a Theology of Nature', *Evangelical Quarterly* 58.3 (1986), p. 239.

being made available and compassionate support of the dying. God wants to reconcile all those who are sick to himself. His way of salvation includes reducing the crushing influence of unpayable debt on developing nations and moving to justice in the world economic system. It will involve campaigning for political change and changes in our own lifestyle. God wants to reconcile all nations to himself.

His way of salvation involves reducing the levels of pollutants and greenhouse gases that mess his world up and impact most those who are weak and poor. The recent report by the Intergovernmental Panel on Climate Change predicts the average temperature to rise by nearly 6 degrees centigrade by the end of the century, unless we cut back greenhouse gases. The rich nations must limit emissions. God wants to reconcile all things to himself. Step back and get a bigger picture of the saving work of Jesus.

If this is a challenge, we are also given confidence. Paul says that the life, death and resurrection of Jesus is the beginning of an inevitable process, for one day in all things he will have the supremacy. The values Jesus embodies – forgiveness for the sinner, justice for the oppressed, self-worth for the devalued, freedom for the chained, healing for the suffering, love for the isolated, hope for the despairing, extravagant generosity for the needy – values often ignored or mocked by the world, will triumph one day when Jesus reigns supreme. The way of the cross is the way of triumph, and as we take up our cross and follow him the end is assured.

Paul's answer to the Colossian heresy is to ask us to stand back and get a bigger picture of the supremacy of Jesus in revelation, in creation and in reconciliation.

In the English seaside town of Blackpool stands one of the favourite places I share with my wife. This is the world's biggest roller coaster called The Big One. We love roller coasters and when we ministered in nearby Liverpool would often drive up to Blackpool. One day we arrived and the town was humming with activity. There was so much traffic that we could not find a parking space. We drove around for ages, and I have to say the atmosphere in the car became more and more frustrated, with accusations such as 'Whose idea was this?' and 'You just missed a parking space back there!' Eventually we found a parking space and walked the four miles back. Not talking to each other by that stage we got on the roller coaster. First you go up a steep hill and at the top most people look forward down the big drop. However, if you look over your shoulder as you get to the top you see thousands of parking spaces. The problems that seem so great at one level, when seen from a different perspective seem to be much less serious!

Once we have 'full knowledge and understanding about who he is and what he has achieved, everything else will fall in place'.[124] That's Paul's response to the questions raised in the church in Colosse. It is a perspective we need to recapture in today's church.

Here also is the answer to some of today's questions asked by the world. How can we make the world a better place? What is God like? He is the image of the invisible God and through his death on the cross can reconcile all things to himself. In a world of increasing pluralism, Christians need to be at the forefront of dialogue with those who are not Christians, witnessing to the supremacy of Christ.

Charles Simeon was an Anglican minister in Cambridge. One of his final sermons in 1835 was preached on this passage from Colossians. As he came to Colossians 1:18 it is said that Simeon's old frame visibly straightened in the pulpit and he said, 'That in all things He might have the pre-eminence. And He must have it; and He will have it; and He shall have it.'[125] Many in the congregation suddenly saw in this old man of God a challenge. They looked forward to a day when every knee shall bow and every tongue confess that Jesus is Lord – but the question was 'If he is supreme in all things, is he supreme in all things in my individual life – my use of money, time, my relationships, my ambitions and dreams?'

Jesus Christ, God's way of salvation. Step back and get a bigger picture. But more than that, acknowledge his supremacy. In whatever language and in whatever culture. With that we go into all the world, to share him.

[124] Wright, *Colossians and Philemon*, p. 21.
[125] Quoted in H. C. G. Moule, *Colossian Studies* (Hodder & Stoughton, 1898), p. 84.

156

# 12. Hebrews 1:1–14
# Heir of all things

## How do I know it is true?

Truth is difficult to identify. Indeed, the news media are full of those who are found out for not telling the truth. The British Conservative politician Jeffrey Archer was jailed for getting a friend to lie for him in order to cover up that he was having dinner with a female friend. In a short space of time Archer went from being candidate for Mayor of London to having many of those in the Conservative Party saying that he should never have been trusted. Others too have fallen on 'the sword of truth' when the media have investigated, uncovering criminal activities and adulterous relationships.

Yet at the same time, can we trust the media who seem so concerned with the truth? The average person in the UK is bombarded with about 1,000 consumer messages or adverts a week. These give an impression that life can be fulfilled, yet the new washing powder will not get rid of my stains. Newspapers are full of amazing headlines such as 'Comedian ate my hamster', or the subtle spin of political stories.

Western culture is cynical of finding reliable truth. Postmodernism doubts whether there is one overarching truth to be found, and our experience of a consumer- and media-manipulated culture breeds in us doubt and questioning. In such a climate trust is not at a premium. The peace process in Northern Ireland, or reconciliation in the Middle East, has been a painfully slow process because of mistrust on both sides.

Is there any way then of judging truth? In a questioning society, we ask various questions in order to see if something that someone says to us is true. First, we ask whether they have any authority in the area. A lecture on the safety of a nuclear power plant by a textile designer may raise fears in our mind. Second, we also want to ask about a person's character. Do they appear to be manipulative, or do they seem to be honest and open? Third, do their actions fit with their words – are they consistent people? A car salesperson whom we see driving a make of car different to the one they are trying to get us to buy may not be too convincing. Fourth, we make some comparison with others who have made contributions in the area. Can we trust this person more than the others?

When we come to questions of the existence and nature of the Creator God, we have a right to ask such questions. How do we know that the Christian view is true? Is it possible to know the truth at all? In a recent sixth-form conference on the relationship of science and Christianity a very bright science student said that she did not think we could ever know the truth of whether the Universe was created, so there was no point talking about it.

In this first chapter of the letter to the Hebrews, the unknown writer gives the answers to these questions. More strictly, he presents us with the answer, the superiority of Jesus Christ:

> [1]*In the past God spoke to our ancestors through the prophets at many times and in various ways,* [2]*but in these last days he has spoken to us by his Son, whom he appointed heir of all things, and through whom he made the universe.* [3]*The Son is the radiance of God's glory and the exact representation of his being, sustaining all things by his powerful word. After he had provided purification for sins, he sat down at the right hand of the Majesty in heaven.* [4]*So he became as much superior to the angels as the name he has inherited is superior to theirs.*
>
> [5]*For to which of the angels did God ever say,*
>
> *'You are my Son;*
> *today I have become your Father'?*
>
> *Or again,*
>
> *'I will be his Father,*
> *and he will be my Son'?*
>
> [6]*And again, when God brings his firstborn into the world, he says,*
>
> *'Let all God's angels worship him.'*
>
> [7]*In speaking of the angels he says,*

> *'He makes his angels winds,*
> *his servants flames of fire.'*

*[8]But about the Son he says,*

> *'Your throne, O God, will last for ever and ever,*
> *and righteousness will be the sceptre of your kingdom.*
> *[9]You have loved righteousness and hated wickedness;*
> *therefore God, your God, has set you above your companions*
> *by anointing you with the oil of joy.'*

*[10]He also says,*

> *'In the beginning, O Lord, you laid the foundations of the earth,*
> *and the heavens are the work of your hands.*
> *[11]They will perish, but you remain;*
> *they will all wear out like a garment.*
> *[12]You will roll them up like a robe;*
> *like a garment they will be changed.*
> *But you remain the same,*
> *and your years will never end.'*

*[13]To which of the angels did God ever say,*

> *'Sit at my right hand*
> *until I make your enemies*
> *a footstool for your feet'?*

*[14]Are not all angels ministering spirits sent to serve those who will inherit salvation?*

(Heb. 1:1–14)

We know very little about this letter. As Lane sums up, 'Undefined are the identity of the writer, his conceptual background, the character and location of the community addressed, the circumstances and date of composition, the setting in life, the nature of the crisis to which the document is a response, the literary genre and the purpose and plan of the work.'[126] While commentators attempt to make progress on such issues there is still a wide divergence between them.

[126] W. L. Lane, *Hebrews 1–8*, Word Biblical Commentary (Word, 1991), p. xlvii. For further background reading to Hebrews and questions of setting, author and message see also D. A. Hagner, *Hebrews*, New International Biblical Commentary on the New Testament (Paternoster, 1995); D. Guthrie, *Hebrews*, Tyndale New Testament Commentaries (IVP, 1986); R. Brown, *The Message of Hebrews*, The Bible Speaks Today (IVP, 1982); P. Ellingworth, *The Epistle to the Hebrews* (Eerdmans, 1993).

However, a number of things are accepted by most commentators. This letter was written to a group of Christians who were affected by circumstances beyond their control, in an attempt to encourage them to stand firm in the faith. It seems that the writer was educated in both Jewish and Greek traditions, for Hebrews shows some of the best Greek in terms of vocabulary and construction of the New Testament. The encouragement offered is rooted in a fresh understanding of the significance of Jesus and his sacrifice. In particular, this is presented as the superiority of Jesus to all other modes of revelation, whether they be through the prophets or the angels (vv. 1, 4). The key to this is Jesus' unique relationship to the Creator God, and therefore he is uniquely qualified to be trusted on matters of truth.

The writer shows this in four images of Jesus.

## 1. Jesus is the royal Son of the Creator God

As Jesus is the Son and heir he speaks with the authority of God. Here he is contrasted with what went before. The writer stresses the continuity of how God spoke through the prophets (v. 1) and how he speaks through his Son (v. 2). The revelation in Christ is consistent with the revelation of the Old Testament Scriptures. They indeed point to him, as the writer will stress later in the passage (vv. 5–14).

However, even though God spoke in many and various ways, this revelation was still incomplete. Contrasting 'these last days' with 'the past' in order to signify a new era in God's unfolding work, God speaks through his Son. In this God speaks decisively and fully about himself. We can visualize this in terms of the following diagram:

**The nature of God's revelation**

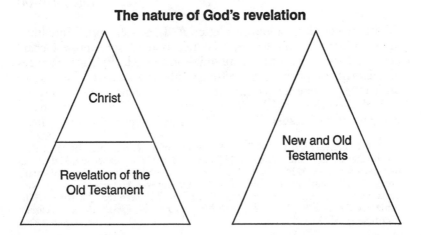

Christ

Revelation of the
Old Testament

New and Old
Testaments

The revelation of God through creation, the prophets and the law was consistent with what was to come in Christ, but pointed forward itself to that which was to come. Christ thus completes the revelation and indeed gives it a new shape. However, why should the revelation in Christ be trusted? He is the Son who has the authority of the appointed heir of all things (v. 2). This is a reference to Psalm 2:8, which is a coronation psalm celebrating the enthronement of a royal ruler. This is no mere Galilean preacher or just a good man, but the one who will inherit the whole Universe.

Ina was an unremarkable woman to look at. Small and frail she lived in a Methodist Home for the Aged and attended a Methodist church in Liverpool. Each week she would come to the church luncheon club where she would eat a two-course hot dinner for a little over £1. She was gentle and gracious. From the humble exterior few would have guessed the authority she possessed. As the sole heir of her father's business fortune, she kept little for herself but gave away hundreds of thousands of pounds to Christian and charitable causes. She had the money but as heir she also had the sole authority.

God gives his ultimate and decisive word in his Son. He therefore has the qualifications to be trusted. When Jesus speaks about God, the Universe, the end and the beginning he is to be believed!

## 2. Jesus is the divine Wisdom of the Creator God

Jesus however is not just a spokesperson for God; he has the character of God. Now the writer describes the Son in terms of the categories of divine Wisdom (cf. Prov. 8:22–30; Wisdom of Solomon 7:21–27). The wisdom tradition reflects how God related to his creation through wisdom, in creating, sustaining, revelation, and the making of friends for God. This is applied to Jesus. Further, vocabulary and formulations are used that occur elsewhere only in praise of divine wisdom. The writer has reflected on the wisdom tradition and found descriptions for Jesus as the *radiance of God's glory* and the *exact representation of his being* (v. 3). However, these categories have been refashioned to reflect the distinctly Christian tradition of the divinity of Christ.

Christ is the radiance of God's glory. This glory of God is the visible and outward expression of the presence of God. As William Barclay commented, the Son is the radiance of the glory just as the ray is the light of the Sun. He is also the exact representation of his being, just as a stamp is the exact representation of a seal. His divinity is also stressed as the agent and sustainer of the Universe (vv. 2, 3). Such a person is of the very character of God.

It is interesting to ask why the writer used these categories of divine Wisdom. Some have suggested that the context of the letter was to Christians nurtured in Hellenistic synagogues, where the wisdom tradition was greatly valued. However, it may be that the writer simply wanted to reflect the character and power of Christ as being one with God.

Certainly this is clear from the phrase *sustaining all things by his powerful word* (v. 3). This is the role of the Creator himself. Here again as we have seen in the previous two chapters, Jesus is seen as the revealer and embodiment of the Creator God, at one with the Father in the work of creation.

This character and power, in the midst of crisis, confusion and suffering, is to be trusted. He is not a deistic creator but is the one who is constantly sustaining all things, including the Christian believer.

### 3. Jesus is Royal Priest of the Creator God

Along with his sonship and character, his actions demonstrate God, both in the work of creation and in the work of salvation. The wisdom tradition would see the work of reconciling people to God as being through education. Here however the writer introduces the major themes of the letter, which are priesthood and sacrifice as the way of reconciliation (see Heb. 9, 10).

The sin that separates us from God is seen as defilement. We need to be cleansed from sin in order to enjoy the presence of God. Jesus is presented as our great High Priest who provided purification for sin (v. 3b). In fact, he made purification for sins in himself, that is, through his own sacrifice on the cross.

In addition, another major feature of the letter appears at this point. Using Psalm 110:1 the writer speaks of the power and glory of the exaltation of Jesus to the right hand of the Father. Although Christ has had such power and glory from the beginning, we need to note the importance the New Testament places on the movement through death on a cross and resurrection to exaltation. The recognition of his exalted status occurs as a result of his giving himself to death on a cross (cf. Phil. 2:5–11).

Jesus is the one who has given himself for us, so that we can see truth not just in words but also in action.

### 4. Jesus is superior to all created things

Verse 4 acts as a title that points forward to the next point the writer will make. This Jesus is superior to the whole created order and in particular the angels. Why are angels singled out in this? Some have suggested that it is to combat the false worship of angels.[127] Certainly, this is an important corrective to any society which becomes obsessed with worshipping spiritual powers, rather than the one who is Lord of all.

However, if we remember that the angels were messengers who delivered God's word, then the contrast is in terms of Jesus being superior in revelation. He is superior not just to the prophets but also to the angels.

Many commentators have pointed out the developed use of rhetoric in this letter. Here we move from the main assertions of verses 1–3 to an exposition or demonstration of their truth. This involves, for the people who will receive the letter, showing by the Scriptures in Lane's words 'the transcendental dignity of the Son'.[128] Seven quotations are used for this purpose, picking up four points in verses 2b-3. We may set them out as below:

| | Assertion | Exposition | Quotations |
|---|---|---|---|
| Son, appointed heir | v. 2b | vv. 5–9 | Ps. 2:7; 2 Sam. 7:14; Deut. 32:43;[129] Pss. 104:4; 45:6–7 |
| Agent of creation | v. 2c | v. 10 | Ps. 102:25–27 |
| Sustainer of creation | v. 3b | vv. 11–12 | |
| Exaltation to God's right hand | v. 3c | v. 13 | Ps. 110:1 |

These are the words of God to the Son, recorded in the Scriptures, whose significance we are now able to recognize. Here is God's own witness to his son.

Therefore, in asking the question of who we can trust, Jesus is superior to all others and has God's own recommendation.

## What does this mean?

The world of priesthood, angels and wisdom might seem very strange to us. Is this simply an intellectual exercise of relating Jesus to various Old Testament images? Indeed, one of the problems of truth is those who kill truth within impersonal intellectualism.

---

[127] P. E. Hughes, *A Commentary on the Epistle to the Hebrews* (Eerdmans, 1977), p. 52.

[128] Lane, *Hebrews 1–8*, p. 16.

[129] See Masoretic Text: Dead Sea Scrolls (see also Septuagint) 'and let all the people worship him'.

Marcus Barth however comments, 'Scripture exposition is . . . not an end in itself. It is a . . . service to a congregation that is in actual temptation.'[130] All exposition of Scripture should be directed to mission and ministry, for it is not just a theological text but the written Word of God.

The writer of the letter wanted to help a Christian community in crisis. From the letter itself we gain certain clues as to the main concerns. People were

- ignoring the message of salvation (2:1–4)
- losing hope (3:6; 6:18–20)
- no longer responding to the word of God in Scripture and preaching (3:7b – 4:13)
- not growing spiritually (5:11–14)
- lazy in working out their salvation (6:12)
- leaving the fellowship or, at the very least, not meeting together (10:25)
- weary, disheartened and frightened (12:3–4, 12–13)
- in danger of false teaching (13:7–9)

This is not far removed from the state of many Western churches. There is also a suggestion that because they had endured public abuse, imprisonment and loss of property (10:32–34) the church had lost its confidence. While the Western church has not suffered such persecution, it is fair to say that there is a crisis in confidence. The secularization of the West has meant that the church is increasingly marginalized. The combination of faith being seen as a private internalized matter, and the reality of living in a pluralist society means that it is easy for Christians to shrink back. The decline of the traditional churches in Britain at the scale of 100,000 members each year means that those who are left are often disheartened and weary.

The writer of the letter sees this crisis in the church directly related to their thinking about Jesus. They had lost their sense of the superiority and significance of Jesus. The pastoral response to the crisis is to point them back to Jesus. Following that comes the warning of 2:1–4, that of ignoring the word delivered by the Son, leading eventually to the climax of the letter 'See to it that you do not refuse him who speaks' (12:25). Here we have a doctrine of creation being applied to the church in crisis. What does that mean for us today?

---

[130] M. Barth, 'The Old Testament in Hebrews', in *Current Issues in New Testament Interpretation*, ed. W. Klassen and G. F. Snyder (Harper & Row, 1962), p. 57.

## 1. A challenge to those who are searching

Jesus as the Son through whom God speaks is important for those who are looking for truth in a confusing and complex society. Those who are asking what life is all about, or what the origin of the Universe is, need to be helped to see Jesus, for he has the authority, character and actions for a generation cynical about truth.

We need to recapture the confidence that Jesus embodies truth. Further, the writer's use of the wisdom tradition is a challenge for us in our own generation to find the vocabulary and images to communicate Jesus afresh. For example, the concept of the One who sustains the Universe (v. 3) is an important insight as it relates to contemporary science. Science may provide a model of how the Universe came into being, but there are many unanswered questions. Why is there a Universe at all? Where do the laws come from that science simply assumes? What makes the Universe cosmos rather than confusion?

## 2. A challenge to those who are confused

Society is full of different voices, and that is often also true of the church. Different movements say different things or at least put emphasis on different aspects. How do we stand against such a confusing climate? Jesus provides a true map through all the disagreements and vested interests.

The superiority of the revelation of God through his Son does not deny that God reveals himself in other ways, but any other knowledge of God that is true knowledge must be in line with the witness of Jesus. In any assessment of spiritual experience, or any new religious movement or theology, the test is whether this is in line with what we see in Jesus.

## 3. A challenge to those who are frightened

Many of us have lost confidence as Christians and we know at times how difficult it is to be a Christian. We have endured bad experiences or periods of doubt and it is easy to drift into anonymous church-going from time to time. Some of us will question whether God is really there at different times in our lives.

Jesus is the one we follow. He is the Son, the agent and sustainer of creation, the heir of all things and the purifier of our sins. He is Lord of the past, the present and the future. So the question naturally arises, 'Is he big enough to sustain my life or my church?'

## 4. A challenge to those who are half-hearted

If something is true we need to act on it. The truth we see in Jesus always calls us forwards. It is not an intellectual curiosity, nor simply a source of comfort, but a challenge that asks us to follow this Man day by day as Lord.

The writer puts before us a revelation of the truth that is superior and trustworthy. The truth of Jesus sustains us and challenges us to live it.

# The lessons of creation

The Bible never discusses creation as purely an intellectual interest. We have seen how the understanding of creation has been used to see the world as it really is, to call people to worship and praise and to reflect on the significance and place of Jesus in our lives.

We now turn to four passages that use creation for particular purposes within Christian discipleship – to provide comfort, to challenge our pride, to give encouragement and to undergird evangelism.

The range of different types of literature from Genesis through the wisdom literature of Job and the prophetic literature of Isaiah to Luke's record of Paul in Athens is a reminder of how fundamental the theme of creation is to the Bible as a whole.

# 13. Genesis 9:1–17
# A new trust

## How can you let that happen?

Praying with children is always refreshing because they have an honesty that most church prayer meetings will never have:

'Dear God, I am English, what are you?'
'Dear God, in Bible times did they really talk that fancy?'
'Dear God, How did you know you were God?'
'Dear God, did you mean for giraffes to look like that or was it an accident?'
'Dear God, instead of letting people die and having to make new ones, why don't you just keep the ones you got now?'[131]

We find questions like these amusing and at the same time secretly wish we could address God in that kind of way. Especially to ask the question 'God, how can you let that happen?' Indeed, if God allows liars to keep their job while your honesty is rewarded with redundancy or the sack, then this is a reasonable question to ask. Or if a woman just about to begin a new role in church leadership is diagnosed with breast cancer, it is also a natural question to ask. We may go on and say, 'Lord, if you let that happen, then can we really trust you for the future?'

If praying with children can be refreshing, then listening to the Bible stories traditionally told to children can at times be puzzling and quite disturbing. One of the favourites is the story of Noah with its associated songs, such as the classic 'God told Noah to build him an arky, arky', and accompanying merchandise of pairs of giraffes.

---

[131] S. Hample and E. Marshall, *Children's Letters to God, The New Collection* (Workman, 1992).

Most of us know the story well from such children's stories. God punishes the wickedness of the world through a flood. Noah is instructed to build an ark and he, his family and two of each animal survives. As the waters recede he sends out birds to check whether there is dry land.

It is a universal story in more ways than one, something we shall return to in a moment. However, if one looks at it seriously, then it raises some serious questions. Why did God choose to punish sin in such a way? And if he did, will he do it again? This is where Genesis 9 becomes important, but before we look at it we need to ask other serious questions.[132]

## Why, Lord?

The flood story is universal not just in its appeal across the ages but in the way it seems to be told in broadly similar forms in the different cultures of the ancient Near East. Parallels such as the salvation of one man and his family through the building of a boat and birds being sent out to test for dry land exist in a number of stories, for example in the Epic of Gilgamesh, which comes from about 1600 BC.[133]

Biblical scholars and archaeologists react to this in different ways. Some will use these parallels to suggest that they refer to a common historical event that was witnessed by different cultures in the ancient world. Others suggest that they might not refer to a historical event, but have a common source story. Other scholars will argue that the Genesis story is dependent on one of the other stories and has built on it or reacted to it by imposing Hebrew theology into the account.

Such a discussion should not be oversimplified. While there are

---

[132] For a fuller discussion of the whole of the flood story and its setting in Genesis see E. Lucas, *Can we Believe in Genesis Today?* (IVP, 2001); D. Atkinson, *The Message of Genesis 1–11*, The Bible Speaks Today (IVP, 1990); J. E. Hartley, *Genesis*, New International Biblical Commentary on the Old Testament (Paternoster, 2000); W. Brueggemann, *Genesis*, Interpretation (John Knox, 1982); D. Kidner, *Genesis*, Tyndale Old Testament Commentaries (IVP, 1967); G. von Rad, *Genesis: A Commentary*, tr. J. Marks (Westminster, 1972); G. J. Wenham, *Genesis 1–15*, Word Biblical Commentary (Word, 1987); C. Westermann, *Genesis 1–11*, tr. J. J. Scullion (SPCK, 1984); U. Cassuto, *A Commentary on the Book of Genesis*, 2 vols. (Magnes, 1961, 1964).

[133] For parallels see A. Heidel, *The Gilgamesh Epic and Old Testament Parallels* (University of Chicago Press, 1949); A. Heidel, *The Babylonian Genesis* (University of Chicago Press, 1963); W. G. Lambert and A. R. Millard, *Atrahasis* (Clarendon, 1969).

significant parallels there are also significant differences between the Genesis account and other flood stories. For example, the obvious difference with the Babylonian stories is that in them there is a multitude of deities who are fearful, ignorant and jealous. In the Genesis account, as we have seen, there is one God who is sovereign over all. Many other differences suggest that the relationship between the various accounts needs to be thought about cautiously. In addition, the classic division of the Genesis account of the flood, which has traditionally been separated into the J and P sources reflecting different names from God, has been questioned in recent years for being too simplistic.[134] The Genesis account is skilfully written, drawing on a number of sources and images, but we need a certain humility about whether it is a simple task to reconstruct that process.

If that question were not difficult enough, we then have to ask whether this is a historical or a symbolic account. It is interesting that at this point in the Genesis narrative we see a movement from 'protohistorical' to more historical account. For example, within the flood account there is an interest in dating (e.g. Gen. 7:11; 8:3–5, 13). This still does not mean that it has to be history as modern Western culture would define history, but at least the historical strand seems more important to the writer.

If we do follow the line that the account refers to a historical event that was widely known in the ancient world, the next question is about how extensive the flood actually was. Did the waters cover the whole world and was every animal therefore contained in the ark? Once again, biblical Christians have disagreed on this issue.

On the scientific side to this question, some have argued that a universal flood is important to a seven-day creationist picture. In this view the vast pressures exerted by the flood waters formed over a much shorter time than the millions of years of gradual change accepted by most geologists, the fossils and geological structures we now see. Such 'flood geology' puts forward scientific arguments for the fossils and also for questions of where the water came from and where it went.[135]

Other scientists find these arguments unconvincing. This greater majority, comprising scientists who are either non-Christians or evangelical Christians, see major problems in accepting a universal flood. Lucas helpfully summarizes these arguments and concludes that we are left with major difficulties if we take the view of a univer-

---

[134] Wenham, *Genesis 1–15*, p. 168.
[135] D. A. Young, *Creation and the Flood* (Baker, 1977); D. A. Young, *Christianity and the Age of the Earth* (Zondervan, 1982); J. C. Whitcomb and H. M. Morris, *The Genesis Flood* (Baker, 1961).

sal flood. Such a flood would not have left the geological patterns that we presently observe. In addition, the suggestions of where the water came from and where it went are not scientifically convincing. Further it is difficult to see how the animal world in its huge diversity throughout the world could have come from the animals on the ark.[136] Of course, there is always the possibility that we cannot rule out that God miraculously created the waters and then miraculously took them away without affecting the geology or atmosphere of the planet. Such a possibility is not ruled out by science, as it lies beyond it.

However, are there any indications within the text itself that the flood could have been a more local phenomenon than universal? Some commentators have suggested that the 'earth' (Gen. 7:4) refers to a particular location rather than the whole world.[137] However, we must say that the argument is not strong enough to lead us to that as an inevitable conclusion. If convinced by scientific grounds that a universal flood is not possible, then it is possible to see a local flood within the Genesis words.

If God does create the waters miraculously it heightens our final question, 'Why did he do it?' What was God doing in wiping out so many people through a flood at this time in the history of creation? The question goes beyond simply that we live in a world where such floods happen. The scale of God's destruction of what he had created, even if it were a local flood, is staggering. Going beyond the children's story, this should affect us to the depth of our being.

Some have tried to mellow the shock by suggesting that this destruction was an inevitable cause of sin. When the writer comments that God saw the corruption and violence of the world (Gen. 6:12) it is making a stark contrast with Genesis 1:31 where God saw that his creation was very good. Kidner sees in the Hebrew word 'corrupt' that what God decided to destroy had been virtually self-destroyed already.[138] This is right, and indeed we have seen in chapter 4 the clear picture that the consequences of sin affect nature as well as ourselves. We know that certain types of environmental greed can lead to floods. Global warming owing to the greed of the developed nations will raise sea levels, with the poorer nations of Bangladesh being the most vulnerable to floods. Yet at the same time, for the Genesis writer there is a clear element of God's judgment in all of this.

These four questions – the relationship to other flood accounts, the amount of historical detail in the account, the extent of the flood, and the reasons for the flood – are important. Yet they are

---

[136] Lucas, *Can we Believe?* p. 154.
[137] A. C. Custance, *The Flood: Local or Global?* (Zondervan, 1979).
[138] Kidner, *Genesis*, p. 87; See also Atkinson, *Genesis 1–11*, p. 136.

also questions of contemporary Western culture. However, the writer does not give us enough detail to solve all of them satisfactorily. Some will want to take the flood story as primarily a story, while others will want to see it as a description of the inevitability of sin. Others will want to see God at work specifically causing this to happen. All have their strengths and weaknesses and need to be continued to be examined.

Yet it seems to me that the writer interweaves these different strands of story, history and theology for a purpose. First, to say that sin cannot be separated from its consequences. Second, to say that the mercy of God cannot be separated from his judgment. But third, to say that the past cannot be separated from the future. As God speaks to Noah about building the ark he says, 'I am going to bring floodwaters on the earth to destroy all life under the heavens, every creature that has the breath of life in it. Everything on earth will perish. But I will establish my covenant with you' (Gen. 6:17–18).

In the midst of this cataclysmic event of the past, God points us to the future with the promise of a covenant that will be made in Genesis 9. It is a covenant based on both creation and the saving of Noah to new life. It asserts the seriousness of both the consequences of sin and God's opposition to sin, but also promises redemption. One of the important contrasts between the Genesis account and the Babylonian flood stories is important here. Other flood stories represent the deities as bringing the flood because human beings are making too much noise and disturbing the gods. Such triviality is a long way from Genesis, where it is the seriousness of sin that is being so strongly opposed.

We may be frustrated at not getting the answer to our questions, but God gives us in this covenant an image of his commitment to and trust of us as sinful human beings, and at the same time an invitation to trust in him. The shock of this story is meant to move us with its scale and questions. But it wants to move us to questions of trust. Now in Genesis 9:1–17 we hear God speak after the deliverance of Noah and his family:

*¹Then God blessed Noah and his sons, saying to them, 'Be fruitful and increase in number and fill the earth. ²The fear and dread of you will fall upon all the beasts of the earth and all the birds of the air, upon every creature that moves along the ground, and upon all the fish of the sea; they are given into your hands. ³Everything that lives and moves will be food for you. Just as I gave you the green plants, I now give you everything.*

*⁴'But you must not eat meat that has its lifeblood still in it. ⁵And for your lifeblood I will surely demand an accounting. I will demand an accounting from every animal. And from each human being, too, I will demand an accounting for the life of another human being.*

> *⁶'Whoever sheds human blood,*
> *by human beings shall their blood be shed;*
> *for in the image of God*
> *has God made all people.*

*⁷As for you, be fruitful and increase in number; multiply on the earth and increase upon it.'*

*⁸Then God said to Noah and to his sons with him: ⁹'I now establish my covenant with you and with your descendants after you ¹⁰and with every living creature that was with you – the birds, the livestock and all the wild animals, all those that came out of the ark with you – every living creature on earth. ¹¹I establish my covenant with you: Never again will all life be cut off by the waters of a flood; never again will there be a flood to destroy the earth.'*

*¹²And God said, 'This is the sign of the covenant I am making between me and you and every living creature with you, a covenant for all generations to come: ¹³I have set my rainbow in the clouds, and it will be the sign of the covenant between me and the earth. ¹⁴Whenever I bring clouds over the earth and the rainbow appears in the clouds, ¹⁵I will remember my covenant between me and you and all living creatures of every kind. Never again will the waters become a flood to destroy all life. ¹⁶Whenever the rainbow appears in the clouds, I will see it and remember the everlasting covenant between God and all living creatures of every kind on the earth.'*

*¹⁷So God said to Noah, 'This is the sign of the covenant I have established between me and all life on the earth.'*

## 1. A God who trusts us

After a story of God destroying human life apart from a preacher of righteousness and then for the preacher of righteousness to make a drunken fool of himself after 600 years of godly living (Gen. 9:18–29), this passage seems extraordinary. In the midst of all this human sinfulness, God repeats the sense of the Genesis 1 promises in terms of dominion and then makes his covenant with Noah and his descendents. Ancient readers of Genesis would probably not be asking about the historicity because they would be so startled by the story. What is going on? At one level should not God have known better? He has wiped out sinful humanity, started again and found his 'righteous man' who walked with him (Gen. 6:9) as bad as the rest of them.

Yet in a sense that is the whole point of the story. Here in the midst of human sinfulness and God's total opposition to that sin, he still believes in human beings. Verses 1 and 7 take us back to Genesis 1 before the sin of Adam and Eve. There human beings created in the image of God were told to be 'fruitful', 'increase in number' and 'fill the earth' (Gen. 1:28). There God delighted in his creation and human beings were given intimacy and responsibility before God. However, human beings have broken that by rejecting God. Does that mean the end of the story? The consequences of that rejection are serious but they are not the end. Here now in a world where sin and its consequences are part of human experience, God is still committed to us.

The world of broken relationships is very different from Eden, as the goodness of creation now exists side by side with suffering. The consequences of sin affect both the wicked and the righteous. Although Noah was saved, the flood had an impact on him. The investment in the building of an ark and the destruction of his home were not trivial matters, not to say anything of the smell of the animals in the ark! In our own lives we may despair of the scale of sin in the world and how it affects us. Many of the people of Afghanistan had nothing to do with the actions of Osama bin Laden or the Taliban regime yet found themselves caught up in the war that followed. Sin touches every part of our lives. The images and values of television, the person who is jealous towards us, or the material expectations of our society mean that even if we were living totally righteous lives, sin would still affect us. In such a world is there any hope?

This passage says 'yes'. However harsh the consequences of sin are, they can never remove hope, as our hope is based on God. The beginning of the flood account expresses the depths of God's concern for his human creation. His heart is grieved and filled with pain at the state of the world (Gen. 6:6). But the turning point of the account is Genesis 8:1, 'But God remembered Noah and all the wild animals and the livestock'. The account has moved from sin to the rising of the waters. Now they begin to recede and we see hope.

To be remembered is a very important thing. I was once part of a committee interviewing a person for a job. After 40 minutes he was asked to describe any events in his university that had been popular with students. He replied that the most popular was a lecture on cosmology and creation. He went on to say that it was 'an appalling lecture given by a nobody'. I suddenly realized that he was speaking about me! I had been sitting in front of him for 40 minutes and he did not remember me. When he left I had to admit to the committee that I was the nobody who had given the appalling lecture! I excused myself from the discussion but the rest of the committee did not feel that such a man could be trusted and he did not get the job.

However, to be remembered (for the right reasons) is an expression of interest, care and love. Here in the midst of the consequences of sin, God remembers not just Noah but all the animals. In Old Testament usage, to 'remember' combines the ideas of faithful love and timely intervention. Indeed, the idea of action is important. The rest of Genesis 8:1 goes on to say, 'and he sent a wind over the earth, and the waters receded'. As Childs comments, 'God's remembering always implies his movement towards the object of his memory.'[139] When God remembers he acts, with the consequences that the waters recede.

This is a lovely image for those who feel forgotten in society. They may be characterized by others as 'nobodies' in a far more serious way than as a result of a lecture. It may be the single parent isolated from family, the abused child with no-one to turn to, the person who has messed up his life, or the teenager nobody ever talks to at church. God remembers in the midst of a sinful world and acts. So should we.

The result of his remembering is that he gives a new start. God renews his blessing (9:1–7) but what is significant here is that it is a command given to sinful men and women. The blessing is given in the midst of the reality of a sinful world. He gives the gift of responsibility again to men and women, whom he knows are sinful, have let him down and will let him down again. The Lord recognizes the sacrifice of Noah (8:20–22), promises to ensure the stability of nature 'even though every inclination of his heart is evil from childhood' (8:21).

Here is recognition of the reality of fallen human beings and yet, at the same time, God gives responsibility and hope. God is about remembering, delivering and blessing his people in the midst of a sinful world. This is reflected in the modifications to the earlier blessing from Genesis 1. The command to stewardship (Gen. 1:28b) now has a different context and a different edge to it. This is the command to stewardship in a world where the relationship between human beings and the natural world has been affected (v. 2). The *fear and dread of you* reflects the reality of a sinful broken world. The gift of food is expanded to include animals, but within it God reminds his people of the importance of respecting life (vv. 3–4). Indeed, this

---

[139] Quoted in Kidner, *Genesis*, p. 92.

is strongly stated in respect of human life with severe punishment for those who take human life (vv. 5–6).

There are three important applications of this. First, God demonstrates his trust in us by asking us to be stewards within a sinful world. Adam and Eve messed the first opportunity up. However God does not give up on us. For those who have messed up, God offers salvation, a new start and the opportunity for new service. While the church needs to be careful and wise in reinstating those who have got it wrong, there needs always to be an offer of a new start. All of us are sinful people but God loves, cares and wants to use us. Of course, this does not mean that those who have committed certain actions should be allowed back to their former ministries. God takes into account the power of sin and the church needs to do that too. Restoration for the person who has abused children will not be back to children's ministry. We need to recognize that we live in a sinful world and any future ministry will be in another area of church life and will be closely supervised.

Second, in a sinful world structures of justice that limit the sinfulness of human beings are essential. We may not think that the death penalty is applicable today as it was in ancient society, but punishment is an important part of any judicial system that keeps society together.

Third, as Atkinson helpfully notes, 'We cannot simply read off God's creation intention from the way things happen to be in this world . . . Nor can we identify every expression of God's law with his perfect will . . . We are "after the Deluge" not "back in Eden".'[140] Atkinson wants us to take into account the difference between God's creation intention and his providential will in our thinking about ethics; that is, Genesis 1 needs to be held together with Genesis 9, and they both need to be held with the New Testament ethics that set out the pattern for those who are empowered by the Holy Spirit. Thus for example in terms of the environment, Christians will want to respond to God's intention for us to be good stewards of the planet. They will also want to recognize the difficulties of how that can be worked out in a world of greed and injustice. Legislation involving incentives and punishments through economics will be involved for both individuals and nations. At the same time, Christians will want both to affirm and to demonstrate the power of the Holy Spirit in helping us to live more simply and to overcome greed.

The trust that God has in us gives us a new beginning, and the covenant made on this basis is a promise of this commitment for the

---

[140] Atkinson, *Genesis 1–11*, p. 158.

future, not just to Noah but to all people and indeed all creation (vv. 8–11). As a research student in physics I remember preparing for my first public lecture to the staff of the department. As I walked along to the lecture room, a colleague said not very helpfully, 'Good luck. Remember, if you mess this up, it will be the end of your career.' Fortunately God is more encouraging. We mess up his creation, his church and our lives. But the message of Genesis 9 is that God remembers us, forgives us and is prepared to trust us again.

## 2. A God we can trust

This all sounds very encouraging but is it really true? Broken trust needs to be restored on both sides. We shall only receive his trust if we are prepared to trust him.

In this God takes the initiative. All through this story God is always taking the lead. He is the one who establishes the covenant on the basis of his earlier promise to Noah. We have already seen a glimpse into the mind of God where he says that 'As long as the earth endures, seedtime and harvest . . . will never cease' (Gen. 8:22). Now God states this promise publicly to Noah (vv. 8–11). The covenant is a public commitment, a solemn pledge of God's intimate care and future commitment to human beings. It is an encouragement to trust.

In its immediate context it is about a commitment in the midst of God's opposition to sin. The writer is using the story of the flood to affirm that God opposes sin but gives mercy to the sinner who trusts in him. The obvious question is whether God can accept someone who is part of such a fallen creation and fallen humanity. But he is the God who comes to us and invites us to entrust ourselves to him.

The wider application is the promise of the security and stability of this creation in the midst of the consequences of sin. As Westermann comments, 'Underlying the history of nature and . . . of mankind is an unconditional divine Yes, a divine Yes to all life, that cannot be shattered either by any catastrophes in the course of history . . . or by the mistakes, corruption or rebellion of man.'[141]

The consequences of sin are real but they will be limited, in that they will not overcome God's ultimate purposes for good. In the movie *The Last of the Mohicans* there is a moment when the character played by Daniel Day Lewis has to leave his girlfriend to be captured by his enemies. At the moment when the music builds and half the audience in the cinema clutch tightly to their partners and get ready to cry (and some of the women do this as well) he says,

[141] Westermann, *Genesis 1–11*, pp. 633–634.

'Whatever happens, stay alive, I will find you.' He fulfils this promise, and after many difficulties they walk away in the sunset to give birth to a few more Mohicans. God's covenant is that whatever happens, he is committed to us and to this creation. As we shall see in later chapters, his purpose, to transform this creation and us, will be fulfilled.

Not only does God give a public promise, but he also gives a public sign of that promise. Verses 12–17 repeat with variation the covenant and its sign. Perhaps this is to emphasize in the midst of the shock of the story that God is committed to us. This covenant is far-reaching and is between God and

- you and every living creature (v. 12)
- the earth (v. 13)
- you and all living creatures (v. 15)
- all living creatures (v. 16)
- all life on the earth (v. 17)

The sign of this covenant is the rainbow, a sign ordained by God to be a reminder of his activity and purpose in creation. But is it there simply as a kind of reminder note for God in case he forgets? 'I will remember my covenant' (v. 15) picks up the crux of the story in Genesis 8:1. God's remembering involves his saving action. The sign is for human beings to know that God is a God of saving action.

The covenant sign was there to give reassurance. Some commentators have suggested that the Hebrew term for rainbow normally means the 'bow of a warrior'. Thus Atkinson suggests that the sign means 'The hostility is over: God hangs up his bow.'[142] While this may be true the rainbow itself may be just a reminder of the diversity and order of creation that God sustains. There is no need to believe that up until this point there has been no rainbow. God gives natural phenomena significance through his word to us.

God is to be trusted both on the basis of his covenant and the sign of that covenant. The story of the flood was known widely and therefore there was the question of whether God could be trusted for the future. At the same time, one of the features of the flood stories of other cultures is that there are a number of gods who are capricious and fighting with one another. Some are frightened by the flood waters and ignorant of what has happened. Such a view of the divine does not lead to confidence for the future. The Lord God however is different. He is the one Lord of creation who opposes sin but does so offering hope and commitment to those who trust in

[142] Atkinson, *Genesis 1–11*, p. 164.

him. The Genesis account stands over the other flood stories, comparing the Lord God with the gods of other cultures.

Thus today the Lord God is the one to be trusted compared to those things in the world we are tempted to put our trust in but that ultimately let us down. We put our faith in someone at work and they let us down. We put our faith in someone we love and they let us down. We put our faith in politicians and they let us down. We put our faith in the leaders of the church and even they let us down. In a world dominated by the consequences of sin this will always be the case. The question however is, do we trust in the Creator God who makes an everlasting covenant?

A man once fell over a cliff and was fortunate to grasp a branch protruding from the cliff wall. It stopped his fall. He looked down to certain death on the rocks far below. Feeling his hand beginning to slip he called out, 'Is there anyone there to help me?' A voice replied, 'This is God. I am here to help you. Don't worry. All you need to do is to trust me. Let go of the branch and I will keep you safe.' The man thought for a moment and then called out, 'Is there anyone else there?'

How often do we look for our security in other things? In the New Testament, the new covenant is represented in the visible signs of baptism, bread and wine and the cross. The waters of baptism remind us of the new start. The bread and wine use this creation to remind us of God's commitment to us and point us to the heavenly banquet. The cross is a testimony to the fact that God remembers us and acts. 'While we were still sinners, Christ died for us,' writes Paul in Romans 5:8. The promise is that all who trust in him, whatever the circumstances and whatever our unanswered questions, will be saved by his grace. There are many crosses in this world and there were many crosses in the time of Jesus. But God has given two pieces of wood on a hill outside Jerusalem eternal significance by being in Christ and reconciling the world to himself. At the cross God opposed sin by taking the full cost of its consequences himself, while offering us hope.

# 14. Job 38:1 – 42:17
# A new understanding

## 'God has taken him because he wanted another star in heaven'

David Watson used to tell the story of two men meeting in the street not having seen one another for some time. One man said, 'And how is your wife?' His friend replied, 'She's in heaven.' 'Oh, I am sorry,' the first man immediately responded, then worried whether that was the best response. Quickly he tried again, 'Oh, I am sad.' Once again that did not seem to be the right thing to say! So in increasing panic, he blurted out finally, 'Oh I am surprised!'

All of us know how difficult it is to say something to a person who is bereaved, sad, depressed or ill. Yet in order to express our concern we want to say something. Unfortunately, we often go beyond a reassurance of love and prayers, to feeling that we have to give some explanation or interpretation of the situation. I remember when an elderly relative had died after a long life and long illness, saying to someone who enquired, 'He died last week, but it's not serious'!

Perhaps it is our inability to communicate love and sympathy honestly (especially those of us who are male) that we are led to say the most inappropriate things. We feel that the person will be helped if we give an explanation of why something dreadful has happened. A woman was interested in the Christian faith but found it difficult to make a Christian commitment. She talked to the pastor at the church and eventually told the story of how as a child she had been playing with her younger brother. The boy had stumbled on to the road where he was killed by a motorist who was drunk and driving over the speed limit. A well-meaning Christian friend of the family had said to the young girl, 'God has taken him because he wanted another star in heaven.' For years the woman had struggled with that, trying to make sense of her own sense of guilt at not protecting her brother, the sin of the motorist and the kind of God who needed to create stars in that kind of way. Although rationally she could understand the inadequacies of the explanation, the emotions and the awful image of God took a long time to heal. How could she trust herself to a God who did this type of thing?

Western culture does not cope well with innocent suffering. The dominant model that every effect has some easily identifiable cause means that we feel we must give some kind of explanation. Our belief that our rationality can understand everything in the world means that the explanation should be logical and simple. And underneath we feel undermined by innocent suffering because after all we feel we should be able to cope with and control life. Our comfortable and controlled culture, which provides warmed car seats on a cold morning, is shocked when death, depression or illness hits us.

## Why me, Lord?

It is a long way from our culture to the culture of the book of Job, but there are similarities in terms of the difficulty of coming to terms with innocent suffering. There is a vast amount of literature on the book of Job with no general agreement as to when the book was put together in its final form or in what context.[143] It may have developed over a number of years within a number of historical situations including the Babylonian exile. It consists in its present form of a mixture of narrative (Job 1 – 2; 42:7–17), lament (Job 3; 29 – 31) and dialogues (Job 4 – 27; 38:1 – 42:6).

Job is presented as a moderately wealthy man in terms of herds and flocks with a large family. More importantly he is presented as someone who was 'blameless and upright' (Job 1:1). He 'feared God and shunned evil'. Here was a man who embodied piety and virtue. More than that 'the fear of the LORD is the beginning of knowledge' (Prov. 1:7). So Job is described as someone reflecting the wisdom tradition. As we saw in chapter 5 in our snapshot into the wisdom

[143] For detailed questions concerning the date, background and commentary on the book of Job as a whole see R. L. Alden, *Job*, New American Commentary (Broadman & Holman, 1993); J. A. Wharton, *Job* (Westminster, John Knox, 1999); L. G. Perdue, *Wisdom and Creation* (Abingdon, 1994); D. Kidner, *Wisdom to Live by* (IVP, 1985); J. E. Hartley, *The Book of Job* (Eerdmans, 1988); D. Atkinson, *The Message of Job* (IVP, 1991); R. Fyall, *How Does God Treat His Friends?* (Christian Focus, 1995); N. C. Habel, *The Book of Job: A Commentary* (SCM, 1985); F. I. Andersen, *Job*, Tyndale Old Testament Commentary (IVP, 1976). For introductory issues see D. J. A. Clines, *Job 1–20*, Word Biblical Commentaries (Word, 1989), and R. Fyall, *Now my Eyes Have Seen you: Images of Creation and Evil in the Book of Job* (IVP, 2002).

tradition in Proverbs 8, wisdom was fundamental to the Universe and living by it is the right way to live.

What then happens to Job means that following such a way does not lead to an easy life. In a series of disasters affecting his livestock, family and eventually himself he loses everything. The reason for these disasters is not due to Job's faults, but to God allowing Satan to test Job. His initial reaction of chapters 1 – 2 is to accept and go with God's will, but the continued physical and mental suffering begins to take its toll. He wishes he had never been born, and longs to die. His suffering is so great that he wishes he had died at birth (Job 3:11). He curses creation and demands God to tell him why this has happened.

Into the midst of this situation come a series of friends who try to help, but make things worse. They give rational explanations of why this is happening based on retribution and justice. They assume that Job has sinned and call on him to repent. Within their many words of advice Eliphaz advises that 'human beings are born to trouble as surely as sparks fly upwards' (Job 5:7), Bildad comments that 'God does not reject the blameless, or strengthen the hands of evildoers' (Job 8:20) while Zophar comforts that 'God will vent his burning anger against him, and rain down his blows upon him' (Job 20:23). Here are the explanations that ' life is like this', 'this is why it is happening' and 'let me tell you what God is doing'. Finally, Elihu gives a list of excellent reasons why Job cannot get an answer to his plea for help, echoing themes of Job's sin and the need to repent. However, in chapter 37 he acts as a bridge from the far-away God of the three friends to a return to the value of wisdom.[144]

It is at this point, just as Elihu has finished his excellent reasons why God will not speak to Job, and things seem to have come to a halt that the Lord speaks out of the storm. We cannot reproduce the whole of God's speech here but these two excerpts from Job 38 and 40 are crucial in terms of the doctrine of creation:

> *¹Then the LORD answered Job out of the storm. He said:*
>
> *²'Who is this that darkens my counsel*
> *with words without knowledge?*
> *³Get ready to defend yourself;*
> *I will question you,*
> *and you shall answer me.*
>
> *⁴'Where were you when I laid the earth's foundation?*
> *Tell me, if you understand.*

---

[144] Atkinson, *Message of Job*, p. 135.

*⁵Who marked off its dimensions? Surely you know!*
*Who stretched a measuring line across it?*
*⁶On what were its footings set,*
*or who laid its cornerstone –*
*⁷while the morning stars sang together*
*and all the angels shouted for joy?*

*⁸'Who shut up the sea behind doors*
*when it burst forth from the womb,*
*⁹when I made the clouds its garment*
*and wrapped it in thick darkness,*
*¹⁰when I fixed limits for it*
*and set its doors and bars in place,*
*¹¹when I said, "This far you may come and no farther;*
*here is where your proud waves halt"'?*

*⁴⁰:¹The LORD said to Job:*

*²'Will the one who contends with the Almighty correct him?*
*Let him who accuses God answer him!'*

*³Then Job answered the LORD:*

*⁴'I am unworthy – how can I reply to you?*
*I put my hand over my mouth.*
*⁵I spoke once, but I have no answer –*
*twice, but I will say no more.'*

*⁶Then the LORD spoke to Job out of the storm:*

*⁷'Get ready to defend yourself;*
*I will question you,*
*and you shall answer me.*

*⁸'Would you discredit my justice?*
*Would you condemn me to justify yourself?*
*⁹Do you have an arm like God's,*
*and can your voice thunder like his?*
*¹⁰Then adorn yourself with glory and splendour,*
*and clothe yourself in honour and majesty.*
*¹¹Unleash the fury of your wrath,*
*look at all who are proud and bring them low,*
*¹²look at all who are proud and humble them,*
*crush the wicked where they stand.*

> <sup>13</sup>*Bury them all in the dust together;*
>   *shroud their faces in the grave.*
> <sup>14</sup>*Then I myself will admit to you*
>   *that your own right hand can save you.*
>
>                              (Job 38:1–11; 40:1–14)

Throughout the book Job has been in torment not only at what has happened but also at the silence of God. He has asserted his innocence and integrity, struggled with the views of his friends and vented his anger and despair. When the Lord speaks he *answered Job* (38:1). The reference to the storm reminds us that this is often the context for God's revelation of himself (cf. Exod. 19:16–19).

The nature of God's answer is not immediately easy to see, but a number of clues are given. We notice that he speaks as 'Yahweh' the covenant Lord. This name is used primarily in the narrative at the beginning of the book, but is not used in the discussions of chapters 3 – 37 where God the 'Almighty' signifies a less personal God. Whatever the Lord's answer to Job is going to be, it is the Lord who is the Redeemer who will speak.

While some commentators have pointed out that God could have been a little more sympathetic and comforting to Job, Wharton makes an interesting suggestion. He argues that in Psalms where people cry out for an answer from God as innocent people in need of vindication (e.g. Pss. 4:1; 13:3; 22:2), 'answer' could be translated rescue, vindicate or deliver. Thus when God *answered* Job it means 'God's unqualified yes' to Job.[145] This is supported in the use of Yahweh and the reminder of the theophany of the exodus. God is Job's deliverer and vindicator. Therefore, this is not about the Lord humiliating Job or criticizing his anger and attitudes. The questions that the Lord will pose to Job and indeed Job's response are on the basis of Job having already received unqualified approval.

A number of other commentators agree that the tone of God's speech is not about condemnation. Hartley comments that in these opening verses the Lord 'addresses Job like a teacher instructing a student who fails to understand an important matter, for he wishes to open up for him new ways of understanding the created order and his wise care of that order'.[146] Of course there is an open and honest engagement between the Lord and Job. The image of get *ready to defend yourself* (v. 3) is an image reminiscent of tucking the robe into the belt in order to get ready for wrestling. There is at times a brutal

---

[145] Wharton, *Job*, p. 166.
[146] Hartley, *Book of Job*, p. 487.

wrestling: as Job has questioned the Lord so the Lord now questions Job.

Yet this is wrestling on the basis of intimate relationship. Atkinson suggests a sense of irony in the Lord's questioning, as a good teacher may help a child by asking questions.[147] Other commentators have suggested the playfulness and honesty of parent and child.[148]

Job has attacked God in his speeches, yet God sees this as a demonstration of integrity (Job 42:7-8). We should never be afraid of honesty before God. The nature of his gift of relationship with us allows a questioning and a wrestling with him. Part of prayer is that honest openness which asks God the difficult questions while being open to his posing of questions to us. We might also note in passing the importance of encouraging an atmosphere in the church where people can ask the questions and where the people of God wrestle with the answers. It is in the wrestling that relationship is deepened.

Taking the image of parent or teacher and child, the Lord takes Job on a walk through creation and points things out along the way. Here is some of the greatest poetry of the Old Testament in terms of a description of creation. It is interesting that the friends had used creation to speak to Job earlier in the book. Here God points out the inadequacies of their answers by reflecting on creation himself. He uses creation to remind Job of three things about himself.

**1. The Lord is greater than our intellects**

The tour of the creation is not simply an educational science tour but is meant to give Job a new perspective. As Wharton comments, 'the reader is left in a state of wide-eyed, open-mouthed, slack-jawed wonder at the unapproachable splendour and majesty of God as reflected in nature and in God's mastery of chaotic powers'.[149] Job's horizon is broadened and in particular his focus is taken away from his present concerns. Job has been concentrating on what has happened and the attempt to understand the will of God in this. The purpose stays as part mystery, but the Lord cautions against those who would try to explain everything.

The Lord's sovereignty in creation in the earth (38:4-7), the sea (38:8-11), the heavens (38:12-15) and the underworld (38:16-18) is presented in the traditional wisdom metaphors of artistry, birth and word. Job has questioned whether God is in control and here is the unequivocal answer. The earth's foundation (vv. 4-7) is a major

---

[147] Atkinson, *Message of Job*, p. 137.
[148] J. W. Whedbee, 'The Comedy of Job', *Semeia* 7 (1977), p. 24.
[149] Wharton, *Job*, p. 167.

building project, planned, built and sustained by the Lord. The chaos represented by the sea is under his control; in fact the Lord is the midwife who brought forth the sea (vv. 8–11). His word has created light that confines the work of the wicked (vv. 12–15).

The Lord questions Job's understanding in terms of time and space. As Job was not there when the earth's foundations were laid, does he understand everything (v. 4)? In addition, Job's ignorance of the extremities of the creation, whether the depths of the sea (vv. 16–18), the distant horizon (vv. 19–21) or the heights of the heavens (vv. 22–24), means that his understanding is limited. Here is a reminder of the limits of the creature, however pious or wise.

The images continue to be stacked up to emphasize that human wisdom cannot comprehend everything (vv. 36–38). From 38:39 onwards the Lord turns to the animal world to illustrate the point. The diversity of the animals is under the control of the Lord but beyond human understanding in terms of its purpose. Some of this diversity is for efficiency, but in the Lord's playfulness some of it seems just for fun! Even the silliness of the ostrich is part of God's plan (39:13–18).

Here creation is used to encourage epistemological humility, or the limits of our own understanding. Images from creation had been used by Job's friends to tell Job what the Lord was doing. Now the Lord uses images from his creation to remind Job that there are certain things that are simply beyond his understanding. While Job has rejected the explanations of his friends he has been tempted to construct his own explanations, which suggest an image of God as cruel sadist. God is reminding Job of the fallacy and folly of this.

This is an important reminder. It is not saying that reason in either science or theology is unimportant. As we saw in chapters 1 and 11, the Bible encourages us to use our minds to discern the nature of the Universe and how that reflects the nature of God. Science is given as a gift, as God is the source of the order and intelligibility of the Universe. Yet science can be pushed too far. Reductionism is based on the order of the Universe but says that everything should be reduced to its constituents, which is the only level of explanation. Thus the human person is nothing but a collection of atoms and molecules, and physics will one day give us an explanation of everything from mind to religion.[150] But there is more to this than just atoms. Complex systems cannot be reduced simply to their constituents. A level of understanding is thus needed that is not dependent on the atoms and molecules. In a similar way, science itself will never

---

[150] See R. Dawkins, *River out of Eden* (Weidenfeld & Nicolson, 1995); P. Atkins, *Creation Revisited* (Freeman, 1992).

give us all of the 'mind of God'. A God who created the Universe is always bigger than our minds can comprehend. Science may give us useful, and indeed beautiful, insights but never the answer to every question.[151]

Theology too needs to be mindful of its limits. God has given us minds to think about him, and in his revelation of himself in many ways, but supremely in Jesus, has given the basis on which such thinking should be built and tested. However, it is always easy to get carried away. The perceived triumphs of human wisdom in the scientific revolution led to the attempt, and indeed pride, of achievement of proving God through design, cosmological and ontological arguments. However, the logically consistent God who came out of these arguments was a long way from the Lord of the Bible.

While the proofs of the existence of God may not be popular today, there are dangers in systematic theology of the same kind. Systematic theology attempts to define the doctrines of Christian faith and looks for the patterns that relate them together. Such an attempt is important in guarding against heresy, enabling dialogue between different groups of Christians and defining the Christian message in mission and ministry. Yet such a programme of systematization can become an end in itself.

For example some theologians concerned to free God of any responsibility for innocent suffering in the world, rule out miracles, or indeed any intimate involvement of God in the world. God brings creation to birth and then has nothing more to do with it. This might be a logical answer to the problem of holding a good God and the existence of innocent suffering together, but it does little to reflect the complexity of God's action in the world reflected in the Scriptures. Another example is the way that some parts of Calvinism promoted predestination to be the leading doctrine of all systematic theology. This doctrine became the controlling principle in understanding the Christian gospel, with a subsequent loss of much of the biblical witness to the both/and of God's sovereignty and human free will.

We have a tendency in theology to present the nature of God in a way that makes sense to us. Yet we must remember that God is personal and always beyond our intellects. The former Bishop of Durham, David Jenkins, said, 'God is no object of critical investigation. He is the subject of faith and hope, of obedience, of love, of

---

[151] Robust defences against reductionism are given in A. R. Peacocke, *Creation and the World of Science* (OUP, 1979); D. M. MacKay, *The Open Mind* (IVP, 1988); J. C. Polkinghorne, *Science and Christian Belief* (SPCK, 1994); I. Barbour, *When Science Meets Religion: Enemies, Strangers or Partners?* (SPCK, 2000).

longing.' This means that systematic theology must always stand under the Bible and be judged by God's self-revelation, even if this revelation is more complex than we would want it to be.

We also have a tendency in pastoral ministry to oversimplify the truth. Job's friends, out of the need to provide comfort, tried to give logical explanations, but in that attempt faith became sterile and God was far away. Their arguments at times were 'sound' in reflecting God as Creator and the wisdom tradition, but they were applying these things inappropriately.

The Lord's answer to Job is a condemnation of that approach. As Kidner comments, 'It attacks the arrogance of pontificating about the application of these truths, and of thereby misrepresenting God.'[152] We need to be careful in the pastoral situation when ministering to someone who is suffering. We may want to apply general principles that may have some truth to them, but in the specific situation may end up misrepresenting what God is doing.

## 2. The Lord is greater than our circumstances

If the Lord uses his guided tour of creation to question Job's ability to understand everything, he also uses it to help Job 'recover a place of security and belonging within the rich panorama of God's creation'.[153]

The world may seem dangerous and chaotic but it is ultimately under the Lord's control. Whether it be the sea (38:8), the weather (38:25–30) or the movement of the constellations (38:31–33), God is sovereign. It is interesting that the Lord uses the same constellations – the Pleiades, Orion and the Bear – that Job used earlier in both recognizing God's power and justice but also in expressing despair (Job 9:9 in the context of 9:1–35). Here is a recognition that the Lord has heard Job and indeed affirms part of what Job was saying. However, rather than a source of despair, creation is a reminder of the sovereignty of the Lord.

Even the animal kingdom is used to convey this (38:39 – 39:30). From the lion to the raven and from the huge and dangerous wild ox to the silly ostrich, the Lord is in control. The Lord looks after the wild animals and provides food for the lions.

The implication is that even in Job's inexplicable suffering, the Lord is still sovereign. In addition, if the Lord gives wild animals both freedom and care, does he not care for Job even more? The calamities Job has suffered do not demonstrate that the Lord is not

---

[152] Kidner, *Wisdom*, p. 61.
[153] Atkinson, *Message of Job*, p. 147.

in control. Having said this, we need to be careful of interpreting the Lord's will in the way Job's friends have done. Hartley comments, 'Just like the wild ass which has to go hungry in exchange for its freedom, so Job has had to endure suffering in exchange for the integrity of his relationship with Yahweh.'[154] Bob Fyall helpfully reminds us, 'The God of the Friends has certainly been too small, trapped in a universe of laws of cause and effect of which he is apparently the slave.'[155] But Job's relationship with the Lord is beyond these circumstances. He is not the slave to circumstances but is presented with a challenge to trust the Lord who is ultimately in control.

Charles Simeon said while enduring pain and illness before his death, 'What do you think especially gives me comfort at this time? The creation! The view of God in his work of creation! Did Jehovah create the world or did I? I think he did! Now if he made the world, he can sufficiently take care of me!'

This is not to trivialize innocent suffering in any way. It is not to say to a person who is in horrific pain, 'Well just look at a hippopotamus and that will sort you out,' a caricature attributed to a number of people including George Bernard Shaw and the novelist Charles Williams. Job is being challenged on the basis of creation to re-examine the nature of his relationship with God, to see whether that deserves trust which looks beyond the present circumstances. The nature of that re-examination is not something that can be forced upon people in a series of shallow soundbites. It is something that people themselves have to come to, and the wise pastor will give space, time, understanding and acceptance for this to happen.

Richard E. Byrd was a polar explorer, born in Virginia in 1888. His amazing life included travelling alone to the Philippines at the age of eleven and flying during the First World War. He made the first flight across the South Pole but nearly died trying to winter alone in a tiny cabin on the ice. Out of the experience he said, 'Near the axis of the world, I knew that a beneficent intelligence pervaded the whole. It was a feeling that transcended reason; that went to the heart of man's despair, and found it groundless.'[156]

Before we leave this point it is worth noting that there is a sense here in the intimate playfulness of the Lord's answer to Job that uses humour and points to the enjoyment of creation. The word pictures and plays suggest that creation is a place of joy and laughter (e.g. 39:7, 13, 18, 22). Humour too points us beyond our circumstances. An enduring theme of humanity in the midst of suffering and

[154] Hartley, *Book of Job*, p. 516.
[155] Fyall, *How Does God?* p. 107.
[156] D. Chater, 'Arctic Adventures', *The Times* 2, 3 December 2001.

oppression has been the use of humour. Humour subverts the oppressor and the circumstances, and often points to a deeper reality. Laughter is good for the body and the soul and can allow a person to open up to a new perspective. The Lord seems to use that to help Job see a new perspective. I am convinced that laughter and common enjoyment of creation is essential in both preaching and pastoral ministry. In addition to opening up new perspectives it also deepens relationships.

### 3. The Lord is greater than our expectations of him

Throughout the Lord's answer, Job is being reminded that it is not nature that he needs to encounter but the Creator himself. The climax of this occurs in 40:1–5. The Lord asks Job whether he wants to *correct*, or *accuse* God (40:2)? The question is whether Job is judging God and his purposes by his own standards.

The Lord then turns the tables on Job asking him on what basis Job would judge him (40:6ff.). Job has objected to the way God governs the world (Job 21) but the Lord says could you do it better? Do you have my power and my perspective? Am I controlled by your expectations of me? Job's views are too anthropocentric, putting himself at the centre of everything. Thus Job believes in God's justice but has linked that with his own vindication. He needs to be reminded that God alone has power to vindicate him. Andersen points out that the thrust of this section is to convince Job 'that he may and must hand the whole matter over completely to God more trustingly, less fretfully. And to do it without insisting that God should first answer all his questions.'[157]

The Lord then speaks about the Behemoth and Leviathan at some surprising length (Job 40:15 – 41:34). We may ask why the hippopotamus and crocodile are of such importance. It is not clear whether they refer to the animals themselves or supernatural monsters. However, the Lord has chosen two animals that are greatly feared. They are beyond the human ability to control or indeed to understand. The detailed descriptions, using a great deal of irony, emphasize that again and again. Yet the Lord created and controls them, as 'Everything under heaven belongs to me' (41:11). The implication is clear. Job's attempt to judge or even control God by his own expectations of what God should be like is simply silly.

Some commentators see in these animals a picture of supernatural forces, reflecting the cosmic dimensions of Job's plight. They point us back to the Satan of the prologue and raise the issue of understanding

---

[157] Andersen, *Job*, p. 287.

God's ultimate control. Why does the Lord allow Satan to do these things to Job, and why does he permit such animals to exist in creation? A full answer to this is never given. Kidner sees in the book of Job the pointer that 'Where we might wish to argue that omnipotence ought to have stamped out evil at its first appearance, God's chosen way was not to crush it out of hand but to wrestle with it; and to do so in weakness rather than in strength, through men more often than through miracles, and through costly permissions rather than through flat refusals.'[158] That may be pushing the message of the book a little too far. However, it is certainly reflected in the overarching narrative of the Bible, culminating in an innocent man who is tortured and put to death on a cross in weakness, but in that way achieves victory over sin, death and evil.

For those who want to find an easy answer to innocent suffering, the book of Job will be a major disappointment. In fact it warns us of the danger of the very attempt. Creation reminds us that we are creatures, not God. God is always beyond our human-centred expectations of him. We need to remember this in prayer and indeed in the way we think about the circumstances that affect us in life.

Through his wander through creation Job has encountered the Lord afresh. It is in that that he can rest with his questions unanswered (Job 40:3–5; 42:1–6). He has not been humiliated but responds in humility. He has not been condemned but, overwhelmed by God's presence, he sees himself afresh. The final part of the book concerns the rebuke of the friends (42:7–14) and he receives God's restoration (42:10–17).

At the end we are left not sure why Job has suffered or God's purposes in it. That is true of many Christians who have suffered. Yet in meeting with God he is aware of God in a new way and a new perspective has been given to his life. He has struggled with unanswered questions and they are still there, but a new relationship undergirds the future. The key is that God has spoken, not revealing everything but revealing enough.

Creation can point us to the limits of our own intellect, our own circumstances and our own expectations of the Creator. Yet it too is limited. Only in the Lord who speaks can we find the reassurance we need. The Word becoming flesh does not answer all of our questions but does point us to a God of power and authority, who loves us, shares our human suffering and dies our death upon the cross. A God who is with us, but also a God who points us away from the past to the hope of the future where sin, suffering and death will be no more. The resurrection of Jesus points us beyond the limits of our

---

[158] Kidner, *Wisdom*, p. 59.

own intellects, our own circumstances and our human expectations. The German theologian Jürgen Moltmann states, 'Faith in the resurrection is the faith in the God of lovers and the dying, the suffering and the grieving. It is the great hope that consoles us and gives us new courage.'[159]

[159] J. Moltmann, 'The Resurrection of Christ: Hope for the World', in *Resurrection Reconsidered*, ed. G. D'Costa (Oneworld, 1996), p. 73.

# 15. Isaiah 40:9–31
# A new strength

## Can I ever trust again?

From the outside he seemed to be a person who could be trusted with a great deal of confidence. Trained in medicine, he had been in general practice for decades, looking after patients in his surgery and in their homes. He appeared to be a kindly older doctor who understood especially the elderly women who called him for help.

Yet under this exterior lay a terrifying reality. The doctor was a serial killer who administered overdoses to vulnerable patients, seemingly rejoicing in having the power of life and death. He was christened Dr Death by the media and was jailed for life for the murder of fifteen patients.

The case of Dr Harold Shipman is shocking for a number of reasons. The large number of victims and the fact that there did not seem to be any obvious motive is shocking enough. However, what intensified the shock and public outrage was that the murders had been carried out by a doctor, someone we should be able to trust. Doctors are people in whom we put our trust, confident that they will make us better, not that they will kill us.

For the vast majority of us, the health of our body and mind involves concepts we do not understand. It is an area where we have to trust. We cannot stay awake during a heart operation and check that the surgeon is doing her job properly. That is why we feel so betrayed if things go wrong.

Harold Shipman may be an extreme example, but it is easy to feel betrayed in other more everyday ways. We entrust ourselves to the covenant of marriage and then find that our partner is cheating. We find ourselves cheated out of money that is rightfully ours, or let down by a friend.

When we have experienced a betrayal of trust the hurt is so intense that we do not want it to happen again. In order to protect ourselves the temptation is to do everything in our power to control things so that such betrayal never happens again. In the public sphere a betrayal of trust leads to more and more legislation, as society tries to protect itself against every possibility. In our private lives, some of us retreat from real relationships, hiding behind superficiality and not wanting to risk ourselves into honesty and openness.

Have you felt such an experience in your relationship with God? You may not want to admit it publicly for fear of other Christians questioning your lack of faith, or for harming your witness to those who are not Christians, but deep down many Christians feel as if God has let them down. It may be that life has been really difficult and you have gone through a time of suffering. Or maybe you have seen family or friends endure illness, injustice or failure. You say, 'God, we trusted you. We have lived faithful Christian lives, yet you have not looked after us.' You may feel you have made sacrifices, tried hard in the Christian life, but everything has gone wrong. Maybe you have prayed for something but God seems to have been silent.

This passage is written to a group of people who felt betrayed, let down by God and worried about the future. The Jewish people had a strong sense of a God who could be trusted. They looked back to the exodus when God had delivered them from Egypt, but now found themselves in a very different situation.

The high point of their national life had come during the reign of David and his son Solomon, which brought unparalleled political and economic success. However, following Solomon's death the kingdom fell apart. It split into Israel in the north and Judah in the south. During the first half of the eighth century both Israel and Judah enjoyed rich economic rewards and military success. Yet disaster was not far off.

Tiglath-Pileser III came to power in Assyria in 745 BC, and became a strong threat to other nations. Then the death of king Uzziah, who ruled Judah from 791 BC to 740 BC, marked the decline of the kingdom. Economic division was rife in society. In addition, religious practices were continued but their ethical implications were disregarded.

The first part of the book of Isaiah deals with this period of time, Isaiah giving prophecies in 740 BC, 'the year that King Uzziah died' (Is. 6:1). Ahaz, against Isaiah's advice, formed an alliance with Tiglath-Pileser but it was a bad decision leading to economic decline and an acknowledgment of imperial gods. Meanwhile, the northern

195

kingdom, which had formed an alliance with Damascus, fell in 722 BC. This meant that the Assyrian Empire was on Judah's doorstep.

The next ruler, Hezekiah, brought reforms, and sided with Babylon and Egypt against Assyria. However, Assyria razed the Judaean countryside in 701 BC, but Jerusalem was miraculously saved. This salvation was again short-lived. In 587 BC the southern kingdom fell to the Babylonians.

What were the people to make of all of this? Was their God really a God who could be trusted? Why save them from the Assyrians and not from the Babylonians?

The second part of Isaiah (chapters 40 – 66) deals with these questions.[160] Was God still to be trusted? Did he have power over the nations and was he in control? But not only was he able to look after them – did he want to look after them? Did a sinful nation still have a place in his plan? These are questions about the character of God.

Isaiah's response forms some of the most glorious poetry in the Old Testament.[161] Chapter 40 is about a renewal of trust. Verses 1–11 describe the Lord as a comforter. The answer to the question of whether God wants to restore the nation is a resounding 'yes'.

If God wants to restore them, the question remains of whether he can restore them? The answer is once again a resounding 'yes' and the prophet points to creation to back up his bold assertion.

> *⁹You who bring good tidings to Zion,*
>    *go up on a high mountain.*

[160] Many contemporary scholars accept that Isaiah is a collection of writing from different periods of time and indeed from different authors. Thus Isaiah 40 – 66 is written at the time of the exile rather than at the same time of the first part of the book. The evidence for this revolves around differences in vocabularly and style and a debate over whether Isaiah could have prophesied with such detail about events to come. A full account of this position and objections to it can be found in J. D. W. Watts, *Isaiah 1–33*, Word Biblical Commentary (Word, 1987); A. Motyer, *The Prophecy of Isaiah* (IVP, 1993); and J. N. Oswalt, *The Book of Isaiah, Chapters 1–39*, New International Commentary on the Old Testament (Eerdmans, 1986). Oswalt makes the important point that whatever their origin, they have been skilfully put together into a whole that has a development of themes throughout the whole book.

[161] For further background and detailed comments on this section of Isaiah see J. N. Oswalt, *The Book of Isaiah, Chapters 40–66*, New International Commentary on the Old Testament (Eerdmans, 1986); J. D. W. Watts, *Isaiah 34–66*, Word Biblical Commentary (Word, 1987); C. Westermann, *Isaiah 40–66* (SCM, 1966); B. S. Childs, *Isaiah* (Westminster, John Knox, 2001); W. Brueggemann, *Isaiah 40–66* (Westminster, John Knox, 1998).

*You who bring good tidings to Jerusalem,*
*lift up your voice with a shout,*
*lift it up, do not be afraid;*
*say to the towns of Judah,*
*'Here is your God!'*
[10]*See, the Sovereign LORD comes with power,*
*and his arm rules for him.*
*See, his reward is with him,*
*and his recompense accompanies him.*
[11]*He tends his flock like a shepherd:*
*He gathers the lambs in his arms*
*and carries them close to his heart;*
*he gently leads those that have young.*

[12]*Who has measured the waters in the hollow of his hand,*
*or with the breadth of his hand marked off the heavens?*
*Who has held the dust of the earth in a basket,*
*or weighed the mountains on the scales*
*and the hills in a balance?*
[13]*Who has understood the mind of the LORD,*
*or instructed him as his counsellor?*
[14]*Whom did the LORD consult to enlighten him,*
*and who taught him the right way?*
*Who was it that taught him knowledge*
*or showed him the path of understanding?*

[15]*Surely the nations are like a drop in a bucket;*
*they are regarded as dust on the scales;*
*he weighs the islands as though they were fine dust*
[16]*Lebanon is not sufficient for altar fires,*
*nor its animals enough for burnt offerings.*
[17]*Before him all the nations are as nothing;*
*they are regarded by him as worthless*
*and less than nothing.*

[18]*To whom, then, will you compare God?*
*What image will you compare him to?*
[19]*As for an idol, a metal worker casts it,*
*and a goldsmith overlays it with gold*
*and fashions silver chains for it.*
[20]*People too poor to present such an offering*
*select wood that will not rot.*
*They look for a skilled worker*
*to set up an idol that will not topple.*

*²¹Do you not know?*
  *Have you not heard?*
*Has it not been told you from the beginning?*
  *Have you not understood since the earth was founded?*
*²²He sits enthroned above the circle of the earth,*
  *and its people are like grasshoppers.*
*He stretches out the heavens like a canopy,*
  *and spreads them out like a tent to live in.*
*²³He brings princes to naught*
  *and reduces the rulers of this world to nothing.*
*²⁴No sooner are they planted,*
  *no sooner are they sown,*
  *no sooner do they take root in the ground,*
*than he blows on them and they wither,*
  *and a whirlwind sweeps them away like chaff.*

*²⁵'To whom will you compare me?*
  *Or who is my equal?' says the Holy One.*
*²⁶Lift your eyes and look to the heavens:*
  *Who created all these?*
*He who brings out the starry host one by one,*
  *and calls them each by name.*
*Because of his great power and mighty strength,*
  *not one of them is missing.*

*²⁷Why do you say, O Jacob,*
  *and complain, O Israel,*
*'My way is hidden from the LORD;*
  *my cause is disregarded by my God'?*
*²⁸Do you not know?*
  *Have you not heard?*
*The LORD is the everlasting God,*
  *the Creator of the ends of the earth.*
*He will not grow tired or weary,*
  *and his understanding no-one can fathom.*
*²⁹He gives strength to the weary*
  *and increases the power of the weak.*
*³⁰Even youths grow tired and weary,*
  *and young men stumble and fall;*
*³¹but those who hope in the LORD*
  *will renew their strength.*
*They will soar on wings like eagles;*
  *they will run and not grow weary,*
  *they will walk and not be faint.*

(Is. 40:9–31)

## 1. He's got the power!

Has God still got power to work in history? Isaiah points to creation to show that the Lord is incomparable as both Lord of creation (vv. 12–20) and Lord over creation (vv. 21–26).

Maybe some in exile felt that if Babylon had conquered Jerusalem, then this surely meant that God is not all-powerful, that nations of the world must be as powerful as he is. Furthermore, the Babylonians had gods, and did not the defeat of Judah mean that these gods were more powerful than God himself? The prophet responds with a forceful reminder that there is no-one like God, whether in the cosmos (vv. 12–14, 22, 25–26) or in the realm of world history (vv. 15–17, 23–24). The Lord is without compare and can do whatever he wants to.

Some scholars have suggested that there is no progression of the argument in the passage and therefore it must have been constructed from separate segments. Yet there is a continuity of theme, where the author is using reinforcement rather than progression. Just as people who want to communicate that they had a good holiday will show you their holiday pictures in no particular order, this passage piles one picture on top of another. They all add up to say that the Lord is unique and there is no-one like him.

Look at some of the pictures.

### a. More powerful than the cosmos

He holds the oceans in the hollow of his hand (v. 12). As I write this I am flying at 35,000 feet across the Atlantic Ocean. Even at 575 mph the journey will take some 7 hours, which the cramped conditions make tedious and uncomfortable. Yet he holds the vastness of this ocean in the hollow of his hand. The heavens are like the breadth of his hand. When the Hubble Space Telescope takes pictures of galaxies ten billion light years away, that unimaginable distance is nothing to the greatness of God. God is so much greater than the created world's awe-inspiring oceans, heavens, earth, mountains and hills. Indeed, who can fully understand God and tell him what to do (vv. 13–14)? Stephen Hawking may use the image that a new quantum theory of gravity may show us the 'mind of God', but it will only be a very small part of it.

### b. More powerful than the nations

Then the images move from the cosmos to the nations. However powerful they seem to be they are no match for God (vv. 15–17).

No doubt the exiles had been impressed by Babylonian culture and military might. They would also be impressed by those able to overthrow this might. Yet this power is but a drop in the bucket or a speck of dust. Another image is placed on these images. Even Lebanon with its vast cedar forests and abundant animals could not provide enough for the altar fires that God deserves. Compared to God, the nations are not on the same plane of existence. They are as nothing before him (v. 17).

These are images that speak to a people in exile, conquered by the mighty power of Babylon. God was not defeated by the power of armies or the Babylonian gods. Whatever happened, he allowed this situation in his sovereign purpose. Today the power of nations may seem overwhelming. Communism seemed so powerful, persecuting the church and denying religious freedom. Yet Soviet communism fell, and the church in China continues to grow at an amazing rate. Weapons of mass destruction, economic strength and intellectual development need to be seen from the perspective of the power of God.

This cautions those who look for security purely in military or economic might. Perhaps Israel herself had to learn that the pride, military power and success of the days of David and Solomon were not something to trust in or aspire to in the future as an imperialist dream. While the defence of a nation state and the health of its economy are important, they are not the things to trust in. Nationalism can be as much an idol as anything else that we worship or trust in. Ultimately, compared to the power, justice and love of God, they are nothing. Those who exercise power in our world need to remember that. Conversely, here is encouragement for those who are weak and oppressed in the world. The power of God is so much greater than human structures.

### c. More powerful than our imagination

Verse 18 returns to the main theme, that there is no-one like God. The author uses the word *'ēl* for God, not the more usual *'elōhîm*. The former is identical to that of the high God in the Canaanite pantheon, and seems another way to stress the superiority of God.

The implication of this is that you cannot make an image of such a God. The danger of idolatry is in making something trivial into a god, wanting something at our level and something that we can control. Here the prophet uses sarcasm to show how silly this is (vv. 19–20). Such 'gods' are simply made by human hands. They are created from the stuff of creation, whether they are metal or wood. So useless are they that the worshipper has to be careful that they do not fall over! But the Lord is the everlasting God, creator of the entire world.

Of course, we do use analogies to think of God, and the Bible gives us pictures to think about God. In fact, this passage itself is full of them; for example 'shepherd' (v. 11). However, it is very easy to reduce God to these pictures. The danger is that we then think we fully understand him and place ourselves as his counsellors. It is said that Field Marshall Montgomery paused while reading the Scriptures during a service to say, 'And the Lord said, quite rightly in my opinion . . .' God is always greater than our pictures of him.

Verses 21–26 now develop the theme of God being the Lord over creation. Again God's transcendence over the cosmos (vv. 21–22) and world history (vv. 23–24) are stressed.

The question of verse 21 assumes that the hearers have known the answers. Some commentators suggest that the prophet is saying that creation in its origin points to a Creator, so Delitzsch translates, 'Has no understanding of the foundations of the earth dawned on you yet?'

This may be pushing too far. The prophet assumes the key to the answer is that God has declared or revealed himself. The Babylonians were accomplished astronomers and had looked at the same sky and saw the greatness of the heavens. Yet they had not understood the nature of the Creator. Some commentators suggest that the prophet is stressing the importance of God's self-revelation in history. It may be that 'the foundations of the earth' refer to the occupation of Canaan, as the earth may be a reference to the land of Canaan as well as to the whole earth.

The prophet again returns to God's otherness (v. 22). Perhaps the *circle of the earth* is the circular horizon or perhaps the movement of the sun and stars. Whatever it specifically refers to, the image is clear. From God's perspective, the things of this world that seem so powerful are insignificant compared to his power. Just as seeing the earth from an aircraft gives an entirely different view of things, so those who trust in the Lord should not be overawed by the power of Babylon.

The people are encouraged to see things from this new perspective. *Lift your eyes* (v. 26) and see God's power in creation. The text uses the word 'create' found in Genesis 1 – 2, and this term is also used extensively in Isaiah 40 – 66. The extravagance and incomparability of creation is used here, reflecting the Genesis 1 themes (see chapter 1). The sense of God's power stated by 'He also made the stars' (Gen. 1:16) is given here in an image of God bringing out each star and calling it by name. It is an image of power but also an image of intimate sustaining care of the created order.

It is worth noting in passing how important this sense of God's transcendence is to Christian theology. Christians do want to assert God's immanence in his creation but we need to maintain that he is distinct from nature. Models of God's action in the world that see the Universe as God's body or see the relationship of God and creation as that of a mother and child in the womb may be attractive in some ways but do not do justice to this text's view of the greatness of God compared to all creation.

## 2. Power to the people!

A BBC sitcom of the 1970s entitled *Citizen Smith* told the story of a Marxist revolutionary called Wolfie Smith attempting to start a revolution in Tooting! One of the catchphrases was 'Power to the people'. The irony was that he was powerless to do anything and so the people of Tooting were never liberated!

However, the Lord has the power. He is the dependable one even during their exile (vv. 27–31). It would be natural to ask and even complain that the Lord had forgotten them. But the people's complaint is strong; it stresses *my way* and *my cause*. These do not feature strongly enough in God's plans.

It is natural to question God during times of national or personal crisis. Does God understand what I am going through? Does God really care about me? Yet often we want to go further and tell God what he should do. Intercessory prayer can quickly move from a relationship of cooperating with God to a lecture of what God has to do for me!

While the book of Isaiah says that their behaviour had an inevitable consequence, it also pictures God as the one who is intimately involved both in judgment and restoration. The circumstances we go through are not because God forgets us or because we are too small for him to have no more than a passing interest in us.

First, God has a wider perspective than just us. He is Lord of all history and all places (v. 28b). His plans and his answers to prayers are not just concentrated on our moment and our problem but on the whole creation. He does not grow tired or weary in working out his plans with patience and care (v. 28c), and we cannot control him. Religion has often been used as an attempt to control God, but his ways are greater than that.

Second, we might not be able to understand all of his ways, but we should be assured that he is committed to us (v. 28c). Earlier in the chapter in verse 11 there is the beautiful description of God's care:

> *He tends his flock like a shepherd:*
> *He gathers the lambs in his arms*
> *and carries them close to his heart;*
> *he gently leads those that have young.*

Later we read about the suffering servant who gives himself for us. This is the same Lord who is the everlasting God, the Creator of the ends of the earth (v. 28a). Webb comments, 'The glory of God is not just, or even essentially, his power, but his servanthood; the fact is that no-one and nothing is too small to be important to him or worthy of his attention and care.'[162]

This Creator God is so committed to us that he is into sharing his power (v. 29). In verses 6 and 7 of the chapter, human beings are seen as fragile plants. This is often our human experience. We are fragile creatures in a difficult world. We often feel weary. We feel failures under life's pressures, constrained by not enough time, pressurized in work or family by those around us. We often also feel weak, lack innate strength to stand up for that which we know is right or to battle against evil. To such people God promises to give strength and increase their power. All of us need his help (v. 30). In a classic picture of renewed strength the Lord is shown to give power and endurance (v. 31).

How then do I get this power? The way of the world is to get power by manipulating others. Tolstoy once wrote, 'In order to obtain and hold power a man must love it. Thus the effort to get it is not likely to be coupled with goodness, but with the opposite qualities of pride, craft and cruelties.' In contrast, strength from the Lord comes from hoping in him or waiting on him (v. 31). The key is not our own strength but his strength. To receive this power involves understanding who God is and then trusting in him. William Booth, founder of the Salvation Army, said, 'The greatness of a man's power is the measure of his surrender.'

Yet the images suggest that this is not simply a 'sit back and let God'. The power comes as you take the risk and give of yourself. It is while walking and running that you do not grow weary. Even to soar like eagles involves that committing of yourself by jumping into the air and trusting that the power will be there.

The model of God giving his power to the weak is an important model for our own use of power. Power can be used to oppress or to liberate. Often the power structures of our culture preserve power for those who already have it. Men cling on to power through sexism, and whites maintain their status through racism. Even within

---

[162] B. G. Webb, *The Message of Isaiah* (IVP, 1996), p. 165.

the church such power structures exist. In addition to sexism and racism, those in leadership are often threatened by those younger in leadership. But God gives power for growth and liberation. Secure in his own identity he gives freedom and encouragement. The holding on to power is often because of basic insecurity. If our security or hope is in the Lord, rather than in our status, rank or fame, then we shall share power. In the church we dare not resist the power of the Holy Spirit at work in the young, women, or different ethnic and cultural groups. The godly leader will be committed to God's greater purpose, and committed to individuals. He or she will encourage the weak and weary and help rather than hinder them in their development as leaders.

At the end of the day Israel cannot be what God intends them to be because they do not trust him. They look to their own history or the nations around them to find their source of hope. Do we do that? Nationalism is on the rise all around the world, whether it be in devotion to a national soccer team or the struggle for independent nation states. While the life of a just and caring nation can be a helpful way to structure human society, patriotism can soon become an idol. We can trust in our military or economic power. But such trust is fragile and the idol can easily topple over into destruction or oppression. The real power of a nation comes from godly trust.

The same is true for our individual lives. Are we in a place and attitude in our own life where the power of the Spirit, the lordship of Christ and the love of the Father are the motivating and empowering aspects? If not, why are we trusting other things?

# 16. Acts 17:16–34
# A new life

### 'When I said keep the faith, I didn't mean from other people!'

How do you motivate people for evangelism? Any pastor will probably acknowledge this is one of the hardest tasks of Christian leadership. How does a church switch from a survival mentality to a mission agenda? How can we encourage people to bring along their friends to a seeker service or be confident enough to share the good news in their place of work? In addition, I wonder whether most of us would also admit that we find it hard to motivate ourselves. The busy life of church leadership makes it hard to make the time to make non-Christian friends and most of us are far more nervous in personal conversation than we are when behind a pulpit with a well-thought-out set of notes in front of us!

Within the Western church guilt plays a great part in the motivation for evangelism. Many sermons and exhortations on the need for evangelism can get us to such a state of shame that we occasionally feel compelled to rush out of the safety of our churches for a brief 'guerilla' raid, to snatch a non-believer and then make it quickly back to the sanctuary. The trouble is that guilt is self-defeating. It is short term and limited and does not exactly express the joy of the gospel.

Another contemporary motive for evangelism is given in the numerous new methods that help Christians and churches to share their faith. In the last few decades we have had Evangelism Explosion, Power Evangelism, the Decade of Evangelism, Two Ways to Live and Alpha, to name but a few. All of them are useful and have been blessed by God. They have helped the sharing of good news by equipping Christians and giving them opportunities.

However, the strongest motivation for evangelism is also the most enduring. In the end evangelism needs to be motivated by theological conviction. The person who has just been converted is often the most powerful witness because she believes that this wonderful new relationship with Jesus that she has received is available for all, whoever they are. Donald English, the Methodist preacher and theologian, was once asked where he got his confidence from in doing a weekly 'Thought for the Day' on BBC Radio 4. This high-profile opportunity for the gospel depended on the invited person being able to speak about one of the day's news stories and connecting it with Christian faith. Donald's answer was 'My confidence comes from John 1, Colossians 1 and Hebrews 1.' He went on to explain how those passages speak of the cosmic significance of Jesus as the one in whom all things are created and in whom all things hold together. His point was that because he had a big enough understanding of Jesus, there was not one thing in creation that did not have a natural path to Jesus. Therefore any news story should have such a path to Jesus. You may not see immediately where the path is, but you start with the confidence that it is there.

The apostle Paul had such a theological conviction, which motivated his missionary work and also determined his strategy. Here in Athens we see this theological conviction being worked out. Of course the sermons in Acts have been selected by Luke not only to give an account of how the church preached the gospel, but also to give us an understanding of why they preached the gospel. The content of the sermons both explains the gospel to the unbeliever and is an account of the emerging missiology, that is, the theology of mission, that was developing as God led them by his Holy Spirit.

In this account of Paul's work in Athens we learn a great deal of his understanding of creation and how this informs his motivation for evangelism:[163]

*16While Paul was waiting for them in Athens, he was greatly distressed to see that the city was full of idols. 17So he reasoned in the synagogue with the Jews and the God-fearing Greeks, as well as in the market-place day by day with those who happened to be there. 18A group of Epicurean and Stoic philosophers began to*

---

[163] For a fuller discussion of the context and background of this passage see J. R. W. Stott, *The Message of Acts*, The Bible Speaks Today (IVP, 1990); I. H. Marshall, *The Acts of the Apostles*, Tyndale New Testament Commentaries (IVP, 1980); C. K. Barrett, *A Critical and Exegetical Commentary on the Acts of the Apostles*, vol. 2 (T. & T. Clark, 1998); D. J. Williams, *Acts*, New International Biblical Commentary on the New Testament (Paternoster, 1995); J. A. Fitzmyer, *The Acts of the Apostles*, Anchor Bible (Doubleday, 1998); J. D. G. Dunn, *The Acts of the Apostles* (Epworth, 1996).

*dispute with him. Some of them asked, 'What is this babbler trying to say?' Others remarked, 'He seems to be advocating foreign gods.' They said this because Paul was preaching the good news about Jesus and the resurrection.* <sup>19</sup>*Then they took him and brought him to a meeting of the Areopagus, where they said to him, 'May we know what this new teaching is that you are presenting?* <sup>20</sup>*You are bringing some strange ideas to our ears, and we want to know what they mean.'* <sup>21</sup>*(All the Athenians and the foreigners who lived there spent their time doing nothing but talking about and listening to the latest ideas.)*

<sup>22</sup>*Paul then stood up in the meeting of the Areopagus and said: 'People of Athens! I see that in every way you are very religious.* <sup>23</sup>*For as I walked around and looked carefully at your objects of worship, I even found an altar with this inscription: TO AN UNKNOWN GOD. Now what you worship as something unknown I am going to proclaim to you.*

<sup>24</sup>*'The God who made the world and everything in it is the Lord of heaven and earth and does not live in temples built by hands.* <sup>25</sup>*And he is not served by human hands, as if he needed anything, because he himself gives all life and breath and everything else.* <sup>26</sup>*From one man he made all the nations, that they should inhabit the whole earth; and he determined the times set for them and the exact places where they should live.* <sup>27</sup>*God did this so that they would seek him and perhaps reach out for him and find him, though he is not far from each one of us.* <sup>28</sup>*"For in him we live and move and have our being." As some of your own poets have said, "We are his offspring."*

<sup>29</sup>*'Therefore since we are God's offspring, we should not think that the divine being is like gold or silver or stone – an image made by human design and skill.* <sup>30</sup>*In the past God overlooked such ignorance, but now he commands all people everywhere to repent.* <sup>31</sup>*For he has set a day when he will judge the world with justice by the man he has appointed. He has given proof of this to everyone by raising him from the dead.'*

<sup>32</sup>*When they heard about the resurrection of the dead, some of them sneered, but others said, 'We want to hear you again on this subject.'* <sup>33</sup>*At that, Paul left the Council.* <sup>34</sup>*Some of the people became followers of Paul and believed. Among them was Dionysius, a member of the Areopagus, also a woman named Damaris, and a number of others.*

(Acts 17:16–34)

Athens was in decline when Paul arrived there but it was still the region's intellectual metropolis. Paul finds himself waiting for Silas and Timothy after a difficult time of divisions, imprisonment and mob violence (Acts 15:36 – 17:15). He may have been tired, hurt or dispirited. However, alone in this powerful city Paul still had the central theological conviction that the God and Father of Jesus Christ was Lord of all.

## He does not live in temples built by hands!

Perhaps Paul was enjoying his break in Athens and the chance to be a tourist. However, he sees the city *full of idols* and this has an emotional effect on him (v. 16). Why does it provoke such a reaction? The answer is surely that the worship of idols denies all that Paul holds dear about who God is. As he explains in his subsequent sermon, *The God who made the world and everything in it is the Lord of heaven and earth and does not live in temples built by hands* (v. 24). There is no-one like God and he alone is to be worshipped.

Indeed, in the sermon we see Paul clearly stating that the UNKNOWN GOD has made himself known and is nothing like their objects of worship (vv. 23, 29). In fact, look at the way Paul describes the God whom he proclaims. Notice the 'alls' and 'everythings' in the sermon, repeated in order to emphasize the point of the greatness and universality of the Lord:

- created everything (v. 24)
- gives life to all people and everything else (v. 25)
- made every nation inhabiting the whole earth (v. 26)
- not far from each one of us (v. 27)
- commands all people everywhere to repent (v. 30)
- given proof to all (v. 31)

First, Paul clearly sees God as the creator of all things, *the world and everything in it* (v. 24). He is not a minor deity whom Christians follow but the Lord of heaven and earth. The implication is clearly that there is no-one like him and it would be simply stupid to compare idols to such a God. Why bother with such idols when you can know this God?

Second, he is the source of all human life. There is an allusion back to Genesis 2 in the creation of human beings. God is the creator (v. 25) and sustainer of all life (v. 28), which means that we are his offspring. It is therefore folly to think that God needed us to serve him. He is the source of all that is good and gives us life itself.

Third, he made and controls the nations. Again in the phrase *from*

*one man* Paul is referring back to the Genesis 1 command to be fruitful and multiply and fill the earth. The Lord is sovereign over the
power of the nations. He determines their rise and fall and the extent
of their empires (v. 26).

Fourth, while being so powerful he is also personal. As he is the
source and sustainer of our lives, he is not aloof, but wants to be in
relationship with every person (vv. 27–28).

Fifth, his call to repentance is universal, for he is the judge of all.
An idol can be controlled. Here God is the one who is in control and
the one to whom each of us will answer (v. 30). Finally, his action in
the space-time history of the Universe in the resurrection of Jesus
stands as a universal statement of his nature and purposes (v. 31). It
is important to note Paul's holding together of creation, redemption
and judgment in this sermon. As we shall see later he may use creation for a particular purpose but he never uses it in isolation from
the rest of the gospel. At the same time it is interesting to see how in
this context he does major on creation, where in other contexts he
does not.

Here is a huge picture of God that builds on the Genesis account
but presents it in the context of Jesus and the resurrection (v. 18b). It
is this picture of God that gives Paul his confidence. It is a picture of
God that sustained the growth of the church into the Gentile world
and beyond. It is a picture that Luke asks us in our day to recapture.

How then does this confidence translate into evangelistic strategy? If the Lord does not live in temples built by human hands, then
the implication is, neither should we!

## We should not live within temples built by hands!

Athens was a tough place for the gospel. The region was a centre of
ethnic, cultural and religious pluralism, and was one of the leading
cosmopolitan cities in the world. Paul began with a twofold strategy
of reasoning in the synagogue, but also in the market place (v. 17). It
is this latter ministry that attracts Luke's attention. It has already
been recorded in chapter 17 how Paul preached to Jews in
Thessalonica (Acts 17:1–9) and Berea (Acts 17:10–15). Here we see
another form of evangelism.

The synagogue would have been Paul's home ground. He would
have understood the context, the rules of speaking, and been at home
with the Scriptures, stories and illustrations. In one sense he was
ideally suited to preaching in the synagogues and could have been
tremendously successful. Why then did he venture out in the market
place with people who were largely ignorant of the Scriptures?

## 1. There is no place in which Jesus is not relevant

Paul's understanding of the Christian good news meant that there was no place where Jesus is not relevant. That is not to say that every place is an easy context in which to preach the gospel. Athens seems to have been a very difficult place. The market place would have highlighted that. Paul would not have been able to start with the Scriptures in a context where most people would have been largely ignorant of them. In addition, it was a culture of pluralism, that is, with many options concerning religious choices. The many different statues and temples of Athena, Apollo, Jupiter and Diana jostled with new teachings, foreign gods and the latest ideas (vv. 16–21) in this forest of idols.

It also seems to have been a culture where there were few converts (vv. 32–34). Older commentaries suggested Paul got it wrong in Athens and so had to change his message when he went on to Corinth where he simply preached Christ crucified (Acts 18:1–17; cf. 1 Cor. 2:1–5).[164] While most commentaries show how shallow this interpretation is,[165] we need to recognize that Paul had relatively little response in Athens. The claim that among the *few* who became followers were significant people in the early church is partly made to cover over the fact that a *few* really means a *few*!

Yet Paul was not going to let the number of converts he could mark up determine his evangelistic strategy. Of course in his ministry he would make strategic choices based on gifts and resources, which in part is why he always began in synagogues. But as he encountered the idolatry it affected him deeply. The NIV English translation *greatly distressed* does not convey the seriousness of this. In fact, it sounds as if Paul was disappointed in the way that we might be disappointed to see that there are no second helpings of our favourite dessert left! The verb however is much stronger. It is a verb that can be used to speak of a seizure or epileptic fit, and is the same word used in the Old Testament to refer to God's reaction to idols (Deut. 9:7).

Whatever the place, Paul could not live with Jesus so dishonoured. The Lord of heaven and earth had been sidelined to one of many in this place and Paul was not going to let that situation continue. His venture into the market place was due to a confidence that not even this place of idolatry was beyond Jesus. It was a place where he

---

[164] This view was popularized by W. M. Ramsay, *St Paul the Traveller and the Roman Citizen* (Hodder & Stoughton, 1895), p. 252.

[165] E.g. N. B. Stonehouse, *Paul Before the Areopagus: And Other New Testament Studies* (Tyndale, 1957), pp. 33–34.

would be mocked and misunderstood (vv. 18, 32), but that did not ultimately matter.

There are some significant parallels here to those of us who live within Western secular society, which is now largely post-Christian and often aggressive towards Christian truth claims. This is sometimes represented in a bias against Christians within the media. It is a society largely ignorant of the Bible and, in terms of its ethnic diversity and postmodern understanding of truth, is pluralistic in its view of God and truth. In addition, it is a society where large numbers of people are not presently being converted to the gospel. In other countries around the world, the church is growing at an astonishing rate. Part of the reason is no doubt that the church in those nations is more Bible based and dependent on the power of the Holy Spirit than churches in Britain. However, another important reason is the nature of the culture itself. Some societies, owing to a complex mix of historical, sociological and spiritual factors, seem more open to the gospel than others. We need to be real about that and not always blame our lack of substantial growth on the sin of the church.

However, whatever the openness of the culture, Paul challenges us to take seriously the work of evangelism in all places. His understanding of the Lord in creation and redemption means that there is no culture in which Jesus should not be shared or to which he is irrelevant. In a society or nation where Christians are barred by law or discouraged by the prevalent culture from preaching the good news of Jesus we must stand firm. To speak of the Lord of heaven and earth is not optional for Christians; it follows from God's revelation of himself.

Therefore we might pose the question 'Where is our Athens?' To an extent Western culture can be viewed as an Athens where it has been easy for the church to build the barricades and retreat into a Christian subculture, afraid of those who sneer. Yet Jesus is relevant in both the football club and the university debating society, in the media and in our consumer culture. Do we have the confidence to be there? The inner cities of Britain are difficult places for the gospel but will only be changed if Christians are prepared to live and witness there. Do we have the confidence for that? At the same time there are countries in the world that are hostile to the Christian faith. Do we have the confidence to work there?

## 2. There is no philosophy to which Jesus is not relevant

In the market place Paul meets a group of philosophers and begins today what would be termed a 'dialogue'! The Epicureans were into

211

detachment. They believed that the gods were remote from this world, having no part in creation and that the world resulted from a chance collision of atoms. For them there was no afterlife and thus no judgment, as one's atoms were simply dispersed. The gods were detached, so that was the ideal for human life as well. Life was ideally to be lived free from pain, and happiness was to be sought.

The Stoics believed in God but were mostly pantheists, seeing God and the world as one. They taught that human beings were 'a spark of the divine' whose souls at death would be reabsorbed into God. The gods of popular mythology were all expressions of God. Believing the Universe was governed by unchanging laws the Stoics taught that human beings must submit to fate. Indeed, training would allow the person to rise above all the circumstances of life and become self-sufficient or 'a god'.

Paul could have preached condemnation of these views from afar. After all, some Christians would argue that it was dangerous to get too involved. The danger would come in trivializing the gospel, they would say. The gospel should not be reduced to the level of people who do no more than debating the latest ideas. Another danger could be a pollution of the gospel by these strange philosophies. Or perhaps these philosophers might find holes in the gospel for which there are no ready answers.

Paul has no such fears! His confidence in the gospel demands that he dispute day by day (vv. 17–18). Then, when the invitation to the Areopagus comes, he goes. This makes Paul vulnerable. He is used to working in teams, but here he goes to the Areopagus alone. The Areopagus itself was not just a debating hall but also had a sense of trial about it. Paul also knows that he will continue to encounter those who characterized him as a *babbler* (v. 18).

He goes, and it is clear from the address he gives that he has done considerable homework. He has observed their worship (v. 23), studied their poets (v. 28) and from the theological points of his talk seems to understand well both Epicurean and Stoic philosophy. Quoting from such sources as Epimenides of Knossos and the Stoic poet, Aratus, Paul presents God as both immanent and transcendent. He both connects with and critiques the philosophers' own views.

The Epicureans attacked the superstitious belief in the gods and attacked idolatry. They would have agreed with Paul as he argued that God does not live in temples (v. 24). The Stoics would have nodded when Paul said that God is not far from us (v. 27). However, in so doing he was challenging the Epicureans' belief that God was remote. He further challenged their views that it was unnecessary to seek after God, and there would be no judgment. Meanwhile, the Stoics would have been challenged by God's transcendence. On the basis of this Paul presents God as the one who can be known, and therefore idolatry just does not make sense. It follows that life in this world is not to be pursued only for pleasure, or viewed as if nothing will change.

It is interesting to see how Paul does this. C. K. Barrett has suggested that Paul identifies and uses resonances between the Old Testament view of creation and Greek philosophy.[166] Paul does this first to side with the philosophers, and then demonstrate that they did not go far enough. To support this argument he is unafraid to use statements of a pagan origin. He takes over these Greek poems, expressive of Stoic philosophy, and applies them to God. This strategy is based on the belief that God does not leave himself without witness even within pagan culture. In Howard Marshall's words, Paul is able to identify the 'glimmerings of truth'.[167] God is not confined to churches built by human hands. He is at work in his world, preparing the way for the reception of the gospel. Luke's account challenges those of us who are preachers, theologians or evangelists to take apologetics seriously in terms of building bridges between Christian faith and contemporary culture. It will involve looking for those glimmerings of truth and allowing them to resonate with the Scriptures.[168]

Those resonances of God's transcendence and immanence in creation are then presented as proclamation (v. 23) whose focus is on the man raised from the dead (vv. 18, 31). Jesus is the integrating point. This identification and then integration of the resonances is not an easy thing to do. It would seem that Paul has adopted this message as a result of his daily discussions with the philosophers in the market place. Not only does his activity in the market place lead to the opportunity of speaking in the Areopagus but also the market place crystallizes the message. He begins in the market place only because he is confident about Jesus.

This account asks us whether we in our time are prepared to engage with the philosophies of today, whether postmodernism,

---

[166] Barrett, *Acts of the Apostles*, vol. 2, p. 839.

[167] Marshall, *Acts of the Apostles*, p. 289.

[168] Recent examples of this approach can be found in books such as W. D. Romanowski, *Eyes Wide Open: Looking for God in Popular Culture* (Brazos, 2001); R. Bauckham and T. Hart, *Hope Against Hope: Christian Eschatology in Contemporary Context* (DLT, 1999); J. C. Polkinghorne, *Belief in God in an Age of Science* (Yale University Press, 1998); A. Peacocke, *Paths from Science Towards God: The End of All our Exploring* (Oneworld, 2001); P. Plyming, *Harry Potter and the Meaning of Life: Engaging with Spirituality in Christian Mission* (Grove, 2001); C. Rees, *The Divine Embrace: Discovering the Reality of God's Love* (Fount, 2001); R. Frost, *A Close Look at New Age Spirituality* (Kingsway, 2001); D. Wilkinson, *The Power of the Force: The Spirituality of the Star Wars Films* (Lion, 2000).

reductionism, Marxism, consumerism or the folk religion of the pub. In order to do this we need to do our homework. We need to understand the philosophies and we need to speak to the 'philosophers'. Many Christians are often afraid of witnessing to their friends because they are worried that their friends might respond with arguments that destroy their Christian faith. But if the Christian faith is true about the Lord of heaven and earth we should not be worried or defensive about discussing truth.

If Paul was confident that Jesus could stand up in the Areopagus, he also believed strongly that this gospel claimed universal and public truth. This was not a privatized belief that had an intellectual attraction to it. It was more than just one of the latest ideas. When Paul makes his case that this gospel is for all and that the truth of this is written into the space-time history of the Universe in the resurrection of Jesus, he divides his audience (vv. 32–34).

There will be those in our culture who will be quite happy for Christians to believe their 'thing', as long as that thing is a kind of private hobby. However, when Christians make claims for a truth that everyone needs to respond to, then some will sneer. Yet Christians can do no other.

### 3. There is no person to whom Jesus is not relevant

At the heart of Paul's concern is that men and women come to the Lord. His confidence in Jesus may allow him to engage in any place and with any philosophy, but he is also convinced that his faith is relevant to any person. Luke records that Paul reasoned in the market place with *those who happened to be there* (v. 17). As we are all God's offspring (v. 28) and he is not far from each of us (v. 27) Paul was confident that individuals could come to the Lord. In fact, there is a sense that Paul argued that pointers towards God are written into creation (v. 27).

Evangelism is difficult work. We are often misunderstood and made fun of, if not to our face, then behind our back. We make ourself vulnerable by talking about the things that are most important to us, and if these are rejected we can often feel rejected as a person.

Paul experienced those emotions. Some accused him of being foolish. The question of *what is this babbler trying to say* (v. 18) has a great deal of cynicism to it. It has the sense of calling Paul a parrot or a bird picking up scraps from the gutter. The implication is that he does not know what he is talking about and in terms of ideas is poor and pathetic. Then some misunderstood him, thinking that he was advocating foreign gods (v. 18). Even at the finish of his

Areopagus address his reception was mixed. As preachers throughout the world know, we are at our most vulnerable at the end of an address. Some people will avoid eye contact and simply say, 'Nice hymns vicar'! Others will take us to task on a point they disagree with. However, most difficult to cope with are those who sneer and seem to judge us as not being good enough.

It is remarkable that in that environment Paul remains so confident. Indeed, he begins his address at the Areopagus with genuine respect for his hearers. He says that he sees that they are *in every way ... very religious* (v. 22). I do not take the view of some commentators that this is said with irony or sarcasm. I think it is genuine respect that leads on to the sharing of common ground by referring to the inscription he has seen, TO AN UNKNOWN GOD (v. 23). Yet at the same time Paul is clear about the way the gospel critiques their religious beliefs. These Athenians were ignorant of the truth.

It is partly this respect that steers him to the Areopagus. At the same time it is undergirded by the conviction that there is no-one beyond the saving work of Jesus. God creates every person and every person has the capacity to know him. Further, the resurrection is a public event in history and therefore the need for repentance is essential for every person. It is not enough for the Athenians to be religious – every person needs to know about Jesus.

The question posed for us is clear. Who is the person that God is asking us to connect with? It might not always be the person we assume or the person who seems to be the most open to the gospel. What about those who mock or sneer? Of course, God will often use us with people with whom we easily relate. I often wonder what the Epicurean and Stoic philosophers would have made of Peter rather than Paul! I suspect Peter would not have been invited to the Areopagus, and if he had been it would have been interesting to see what he would have spoken about! Paul was the right person at the right time. God had used the circumstances of Thessalonica and Berea to bring Paul to Athens, but Paul still had to have both the courage and the conviction to be vulnerable in the market place and at the Areopagus.

However, having said that, this does not mean that as individuals or as a church we neglect everyone else. Are there people whom we consider are beyond the gospel? Perhaps no-one would have suspected that a member of the Areopagus such as Dionysius would have become a Christian.

This big theological vision of God in Christ also poses questions about the nature of the church. The church needs to reflect this. God does not live in just one kind of church. The diversity of the church reflects the diversity of creation that God rejoices in. Here in his new community, which points forward to his new creation, the church's ministry and mission needs to reflect that no person is unimportant to Jesus.

The growth of ethnic, age or cultural network churches that reach out to people of their own subculture is an effective means of growth and evangelism. Often churches do not realize that this is what they are doing, but effectively by the subtle messages they give they limit who can be part of the church. However, such work always needs to be critiqued by the bigger vision. The alienated need to be seen as part of the church's mission and we always need to ask the question of what kind of churches can relate to those who feel estranged by much of the culture of today's churches. It is interesting that in this context John Stott uses Paul's theology of this passage to address the issues of racial justice both inside and outside the church.[169]

If the church of today were to attempt to evangelize the Athens of Paul's time I wonder how we would do it? Perhaps the first thing we would do would be to buy a building, and then send a group of Christians from a strong church as a large church plant into the building. The church would need finance and be covered by a bishop or an apostle (delete as appropriate!). Some money would be invested in publicity in order to get people to come into our building, where they would be handed at least four pieces of paper and it would be assumed that they would be able to follow both the choruses and the liturgy.

Forgive me for the caricature. Each of these elements may be proper in any evangelistic strategy. However, our confidence is often in the methods, leaders, finance or buildings rather than in the Lord of heaven and earth. Paul goes alone into power structures where he is not in control, indeed where he is very weak. But his confidence is in the Lord who does not live in temples made by human hands.

John Drane comments that two things characterized the early church.[170] One was confidence in the power of the Spirit, and the other was vulnerability in the face of the world. What characterizes the church of today?

[169] J. R. W. Stott, *Issues Facing Christians Today* (Marshall Pickering, 1990), pp. 221–226.
[170] J. Drane, *Faith in a Changing Culture* (HarperCollins, 1997), p. 73.

# The fulfilment of creation

You can never understand the beginning or middle of a story without the ending. The story of God's work as creator and sustainer of the Universe needs to be held together with his future work of new creation.

The following four passages give us different pictures of that movement from creation to new creation: the poetry of Isaiah, the closely argued theology of Romans, the pastoral concern of 2 Peter and the apocalyptic vision of Revelation. Each engages us in a different way, but the message is the same – the Lord who is sovereign and caring in creation is sovereign and caring in new creation. New creation is the work of the Lord and we are invited to join him in it.

# 17. Isaiah 65:17–25
# The Creator of a new heaven and earth

## What can happen when an apple falls

The young man who arrived at the University of Cambridge was shy, small and not physically strong. He was prone to stammer and did not show any great signs of brilliance. However, the plague changed all of that. Sent away from Cambridge because of the plague, he took home with him his fascination for mathematics. Years later, the world would marvel at how Isaac Newton produced the mathematics of mechanics, gravitation and calculus, although it must be said that not all generations of teenage students have thanked him for differential equations!

The achievement of Newton was monumental. Not only did he affect science and mathematics forever; his discoveries had a profound effect on how we view the world, with serious consequences for biblical theology. Newton's equations of planetary motion suggested that the Universe was rather like a clock, a precise mechanism created by God and running smoothly. Models of the solar system would adorn museums and private houses, suggesting that the world was predictable and reliable.

In all of this Newton saw God. The perfection of the mechanism was a reflection of the faithfulness of the Creator. In fact, Newton needed God occasionally to intervene in the solar system to push the planets back into their orbits gently, but when Laplace reworked the theory he proclaimed to Napoleon that he did not need Newton's hypothesis of God. The solar system may have been created by God but he was not needed to stick his finger into the mechanism. Science could predict what the world would be like in the future and indeed what it was like in the past.

This was a major problem for biblical theology. If God had made such a perfect mechanism, then why should he interfere with it? Indeed, any unusual interference by God would indicate that the world was not perfect, just as a watch that needs constant repair is a bad buy. But this removed God from the proceedings of the Universe. He could wind up the clock to start it off but then his work was done. He could step back and have nothing more to do with the Universe. God became in many people's minds, a distant divine mathematician, able to design the Universe but not a personal reality. The personal God of the Bible became the logical theory beloved by philosophers.

The problem that inevitably followed was what then to make of the miracles of the Bible. Philosophically, God could not work by miracles. Therefore, what are these accounts of Jesus breaking the laws of gravity and walking on water? There was a ready solution to this. Perhaps the biblical miracles did not actually occur but were made up by the early church in order to convey truth about Jesus. The German scholar D. F. Strauss saw them as myths. The resurrection for example did not lead to the Christian church; the Christian church produced the story of the resurrection to convey their faith in Jesus. The Bible had to be demythologized to make it acceptable in the modern scientific world, bequeathed to us by Newton.

Yet there was one further thing that stemmed from the work of Newton that caused difficulty for biblical faith. The success of the scientific method of prediction and explanation suggested that this was the way to certain knowledge. Things about the world could be proved by the application of the scientific method, which seemed quite a contrast to the Christians, who talked about the need of faith. Quickly a view became widespread that science was the area of facts and certainty, while Christian belief was just a matter of faith, in the sense of the definition of faith once given by a child, 'Faith is believing things you know aren't true'! Such an attitude is around today. The biologist Richard Dawkins comments, 'faith is the great cop-out, the great excuse to evade the need to think and evaluate evidence'.

So we have been left in Western culture with the model of the Universe as a predictable machine. It is a model we have applied widely, not only to God's relationship to the Universe. We have applied it to ourselves, seeing ourselves embedded in a causal network of relationships and circumstances. Our genes determine us, the pressures of life confine us and ultimately we live with the consequences of our actions.

We are at the mercy of the predictable world, yet our human spirit cries out for something more. We dream of a land 'somewhere over the rainbow' where things are different, and a time when we wish upon a star and our 'dreams come true'. Such talk can be dismissed as childish fantasy, but the entertainment industry is full of escapism. The growth of astrology and New Age shows a spiritual hunger that wants to look beyond the mere mechanistic view of the world and human nature. Even in the search for that special relationship we desire a new start that will clear away all that has gone before and that will bring us happiness.

The British pop singer Geri Halliwell, formerly of the Spice Girls, in her song 'Lift me up' asks whether there is a world where life naturally lifts us up. Rather than life dragging us down, is there any possibility of new life?

## What happens when a nation falls

As we saw in chapter 15, the Jewish people felt these emotions keenly during their time in exile in Babylon. They were suffering the consequences of their own disobedience and sin. They were now at the mercy of a powerful empire that had destroyed their temple in Jerusalem. Was there any future for them? If there was a future, was it going to be here in Babylon and was their faith simply now dead in the ruins of Jerusalem?

Into this situation, this passage from Isaiah speaks:[171]

> *17'Behold, I will create*
> *new heavens and a new earth.*
> *The former things will not be remembered,*
> *nor will they come to mind.*
> *18But be glad and rejoice forever*
> *in what I will create,*
> *for I will create Jerusalem to be a delight*
> *and its people a joy.*
> *19I will rejoice over Jerusalem*
> *and take delight in my people;*
> *the sound of weeping and of crying*
> *will be heard in it no more.*

[171] For a more detailed consideration of the issues of authorship and context of this passage see J. D. W. Watts, *Isaiah 34–66*, Word Biblical Commentary (Word, 1987); C. Westermann, *Isaiah 40–66*, tr. D. M. G. Stalker (Westminster, 1966); B. S. Childs, *Isaiah* (Westminster, John Knox, 2001); J. N. Oswalt, *The Book of Isaiah, Chapters 40–66*, New International Commentary on the Old Testament (Eerdmans, 1986); W. Brueggemann, *Isaiah 40–66* (Westminster, John Knox, 1998).

> <sup>20</sup>'Never again will there be in it
> an infant who lives but a few days,
> or older people who do not live out their years;
> those who die at a hundred
> will be thought mere youths;
> those who fail to reach a hundred
> will be considered accursed.
> <sup>21</sup>They will build houses and dwell in them;
> they will plant vineyards and eat their fruit.
> <sup>22</sup>No longer will they build houses and others live in them,
> or plant and others eat.
> For as the days of a tree,
> so will be the days of my people;
> my chosen ones will long enjoy
> the works of their hands.
> <sup>23</sup>They will not toil in vain
> or bear children doomed to misfortune;
> for they will be a people blessed by the LORD,
> they and their descendants with them.
> <sup>24</sup>Before they call I will answer;
> while they are still speaking I will hear.
> <sup>25</sup>The wolf and the lamb will feed together,
> and the lion will eat straw like the ox,
> but dust will be the serpent's food.
> They will neither harm nor destroy
> on all my holy mountain,'
> says the LORD.

(Is. 65:17–25)

## 1. A God of new possibilities

One suggestion is that this is part of a prophecy into the fifth century BC, portraying the time of Ezra and Nehemiah and the rebuilding of Jerusalem after the exile. The bright hope portrayed in Isaiah 60 had not yet been fulfilled in terms of stable economy or government. Here Isaiah 65:17–25 describes the fulfilment of that hope, alongside Yahweh dealing with his opponents (Is. 65:1–16) and Yahweh confirming his servant in his new city (Is. 65:17–25).

The reason for this setting is the two issues of the nature of worship and plans for building the new temple. The passage attacks the exclusivity of temple worship (Is. 66:1, 3), that is, the claims that God is only present in the temple, that only certain priests can sacrifice and that worship primarily is a matter of sacrifice. This may reflect the conflict that Nehemiah experienced in wanting to build the city of Jerusalem rather than just the temple.

However, the opening exclamation of 'Look at me' or 'Behold' (65:17) sets the central message. Whatever the circumstances, God says, 'See what I can do!' This is given in an image of God's new creation for his new city.

The key verse is of course verse 17:

> *Behold, I will create*
> *new heavens and a new earth.*
> *The former things will not be remembered,*
> *nor will they come to mind.*

The verb *create* is a rare word in the Old Testament, found primarily in Genesis 1 – 2, a few psalms and Isaiah 40 – 66. Here in verses 17–18 it is used three times. A personal pronoun places the emphasis on the Lord who calls attention to himself in the process of creating. The link with Genesis is important. The Lord who created the Universe is also the Lord of new possibilities. His intention is clear and there is no-one like him.

The word *new* may mean several different things. It may mean a temporal newness in the sense of something that has never existed before and therefore is unknown in this time. Alternatively it can be used to distinguish what is different from what has already existed. Or it may mean something that is 'fresh, pure, young . . . or sharp, polished, bright'.[172] The word is contrasted here with *the former*, something that is done in a number of places (Is. 42:9; 43:9, 18; 46:9; 48:3; 61:4; 65:7, 16, 17).

God is the Lord of all these possibilities. He can create something new or renew something already in existence. He is the source of novelty in the Universe, and therefore this Universe is not a closed predictable system.

Watts comments on the 'Vision' of the passage: 'Emphasis on these words supports the Vision's view that the creator of the world is creating a brand new situation for his restored temple-city and its worshippers. That God does a new creative thing is not simply a feature of the time which the Vision pictures, but is a characteristic of Yahweh God as the Vision understands and presents him.'[173] The

---

[172] J. Fürst, *Hebrew and Chaldee Lexicon*, 3rd ed., tr. S. Davison (Williams & Norgate, 1867), p. 1404; G. J. Botterwick and H. Ringgren (eds.), *Theological Dictionary of the Old Testament*, tr. D. E. Green, vol. 4 (Eerdmans, 1974– ), pp. 225–244.

[173] Watts, *Isaiah 34–66*, p. 120.

prophet sees hope for a new era for Jerusalem and the people based on the sovereign work of the Creator. An understanding of God as Creator also helps us to dismiss the confines of Newton's mechanistic Universe. The laws of physics that science discloses in a worldview without God become prescriptive laws; that is, they determine what can and what cannot happen. However, in a worldview that sees the world as creation, these laws are seen as descriptive of the Creator's constant sustaining work. They describe God's usual ways of working rather than setting limits for what he might or might not do.

In the twentieth century both quantum theory and chaos theory fatally undermined the Newtonian worldview. Both say that the Universe is subtler than a predictable clock. At this level the Universe itself seems to recognize the importance of the novelty, mystery and spontaneity that reflect the character of a God of new possibilities. Newton was thus right to detail, understand and use the regularities, but the philosophy built upon it was wrong to rule out that God was a God of new possibilities.

At an individual level this understanding of God is much more personal than the divine logician. The prophet says that with this God a new start is possible (v. 17b). The consequences of sin are real but there is always hope. Here the time of suffering and mourning is changed into joy and delight (vv. 18–19).

For those who are aware of their own sin this is a message of good news. Through the work of Jesus on the cross we are freed from both the guilt and power of sin. We are given a new start. That does not mean that we are separated from what our sin has done. A marriage that goes wrong owing to one person's sin leaves a broken family. The guilt may be dealt with, but the emotional scars for all involved can take a long time to heal. Yet with God new possibilities are always before us. He wants to bring healing and joy, renewal and restoration. Sometimes that is possible within the same family. Sometimes the partners need to move on and, in my view, churches are right to struggle in holding together the seriousness of the commitment of marriage vows with the possibilities of a new relationship in marriage.

The joy of such new possibilities is shared by God himself (v. 19).

## 2. A God of surprising possibilities

The prophet continues with this picture, contrasting the new heavens and new earth with the *former things*. Here are imaginative pictures that say to the people that they should not limit the new possibilities that God can give. It is a place of contrast to the *former things* (vv. 19b–25):

224

| The former things | The new creation |
|---|---|
| Crying, distress | Rejoicing |
| An infant dying a few days old | A child living to be a hundred |
| An elderly person dying prematurely | One hundred deemed an early age to die |
| Build and another live there | Build houses and live in them |
| Plant for another to eat | Plant vineyards and eat their fruit |
| Animals in opposition | Animals in harmony |

The new creation promises security and longevity in contrast to the history of some three centuries past. In that way it is somewhat surprising! The political situation of the return to Israel would not have been thought about in this kind of way. The political and economic situation was not secure. The walls of Jerusalem were in ruins and life was hard.

Is this a promise of an idyllic existence in the near future? Certainly the image of the wolf and the lamb feeding together questions that. It parallels Isaiah 11:1–9, on which Brueggemann helpfully comments that

> it is clear that aggression and domination belong to the animal world, and it was ever thus. Therefore this poetic scenario is unreal. However, this poem is about the impossible possibility of the new creation! The coming king will not only do what the world takes to be possible, but will also do what the world has long since declared to be impossible. If there is a coming time when 'death will be no more' (Rev 21:4), then it is entertainable that devouring competition and the old practice of the big ones eating the little ones is not the way of the future.[174]

These images are meant to give confidence that with God nothing is impossible. God is, in the words of Gerard Hughes, 'A God of surprises'.[175]

This means that we must not be tempted to box God into our expectations. In terms of the natural world this has an impact on how we think about miracles. The laws of physics are a description of God's faithful relationship with the Universe. This faithful relationship maintains a world of order, and thereby provides us with an environment where exploration and responsibility are possible.

Yet at the same time, if we have a big enough view of God as Creator, then we cannot rule out his prerogative to go beyond his normal ways of working for specific purposes. Such miracles may be

---

[174] W. Brueggemann, *Isaiah 1–39* (Westminster, John Knox, 1998), p. 103.
[175] G. Hughes, *God of Surprises* (DLT, 1996).

surprising to us both in their nature and in their rate of occurrences, but we cannot limit God. That such miracles were especially associated with the King who was also the suffering servant and who inaugurated the new era of new creation therefore makes sense.

Once again, in our personal lives, this is good news. God is able to do in us the most surprising or even impossible work. He may give to us surprising gifts or new ministries. He may also do that with other people and we need to be careful not to limit God. A fourteen-year-old who feels he is called to preach may be told by the pastor that he first needs time to mature. While this is sensible advice, in this unusual case the pastor would have been wrong. A woman in her late fifties, still struggling with post-viral syndrome has to resign her secular job but feels an overwhelming call to leadership and pastoral ministry. The church tells her initially that she is too old and not well enough. Wise advice again but in this unusual case the church was wrong. Both the young preacher and the older minister now have powerful ministries because sometimes God does surprising things. And I as the pastor had to learn that!

This is not a justification for understanding God as capricious. It is simply to say, 'How large is your vision for what God can do in your life?' Brueggemann concludes his comments on Isaiah 11:1–9 in this way: 'This poem is about deep, radical, limitless transformation in which we – like lion, wolf and leopard – will have no hunger for injury, no need to devour, no yearning for brutal control, no passion for domination.'[176]

## 3. A God of real possibilities

Some suggest that this vision is God restoring the Garden of Eden. Yet here is a vision of peace set in the real world of rulers, questions about worship, the return to Palestine after the exile and the building of the temple (66:1–5).

This picture of new creation is based on his faithfulness as Creator, and pictured in ways that emphasize his amazing power, but is earthed in the context of political and social reality.

For example, the Hebrew root of the word *heavens* refers to height and brilliance. Within the Old Testament it often refers to the sky or God's dwelling place, but when used with the earth is usually a description of the whole created order. However, Watts argues here in Isaiah 65:17 that it may represent a new, divinely instituted order in which the Persian Empire has the Lord's sanction and Israel is called to be a worshipping, pilgrim people with Jerusalem as its focus.[177]

[176] Brueggemann, *Isaiah 1–39*, p. 103.
[177] Watts, *Isaiah 34–66*, p. 354.

Throughout his commentary Watts has translated 'the earth' as 'the land' suggesting that it is primarily referring to Palestine. The 'new creation' may therefore refer to agricultural fertility or a new political or social reality for Palestine.

This is contentious but he has rightly indicated that this vision is earthed in reality. The view of God as creator of new and surprising possibilities is now applied to the plans for the temple (Is. 66:1), the nature of worship (Is. 66:3–5) and community relationships (Is. 66:5).

The temple needs to be seen from God's perspective (vv. 1–2). Worship should not be idolatry, but the personal God is interested in personal response (v. 2b). God is not to be controlled by sacrifice for he is beyond any attempt for us to control him. His sovereignty is a sovereignty of care, joy and delight in his people. And if his people are rejected, then the God of the whole creation is on the side of his people.

We need to apply these things into our own situation. In terms of situations in the world that seem so desperate or locked into cycles of hate, Christians believe that God always offers possibilities. Further, we Christians are called to go into those situations trusting in the sovereignty of God.

The church also needs to earth these understandings. The debate about temples is always with us! Arguments about architecture, worship, liturgy or music often reduce God to what we like and prefer. Will the way we worship God reflect his extravagant diversity? In addition, will we come before God with a humble and contrite spirit?

Further, our mechanistic Universe has sometimes encouraged us to misrepresent the practice of prayer. Some say that prayer just changes us rather than having an influence at all on God. While it is true that we are changed through the experience of prayer as our wills are aligned with God's will, there are indications from the Bible that prayer is more than that. From the story of Abraham interceding for the people of Sodom (Gen. 18:16–33) to Jesus' own teaching about prayer (Matt. 7:7–11), God seems be to able and willing to weave our prayer requests into the working out of his will. Prayer is the gift of the mutual realization of possibilities through relationship.

Others view God as a 'divine slot machine' where you put enough prayer into the top and get the answer you want out of the bottom. It is a view that leads to the condemnation of the believer for not having enough faith if the answer is not delivered as expected.

More importantly this view does not take the personal aspect of God seriously. We need to acknowledge God's sovereignty over

prayer. We can pray with confidence, as he is the God of new possibilities who wants both to cooperate with and delight in his people.
At the same time we need to be ready for the answers of 'yes', 'no'
and a few surprises. The nature of the Universe and the God who
created it are not, thankfully, bound by our laws or expectations!

# 18. Romans 8:18–30
# The Creator liberates

## 'Death concentrates the mind wonderfully'

'Death concentrates the mind wonderfully,' said my friend whose son's goldfish had just died. She talked about how her son needed to be helped at such a time and then somewhat spoilt it by adding that she had planned to have fish for lunch!

In the face of death we say some funny and profound things. The movie star Brooke Shields once said, 'Smoking kills. If you're killed, you've lost a very important part of your life.'[178] Often as we face the 'ultimate statistic of human existence' our minds can focus on ourselves. As Woody Allen once said, 'I don't want to achieve immortality through my work. I want to achieve immortality by not dying.' Alternatively we can focus on the cause. The gravestone of a Mr Donald Robertson in a Sheffield cemetery reads:

> He was a peaceable, quiet man, and to all appearance a sincere Christian.
>
> His death was very much regretted – which was caused by the stupidity of LAWRENCE TULLOCH of Clotherton who sold him *nitre* instead of *Epsom salts* by which he was killed in the space of three hours after taking a dose of it.[179]

We smile at such comments partly as a way of avoiding the pain of it all. Many of us will have experienced the death of someone close to us. The grief of loss affects people in different ways, but few can remain unmoved by the tragedy of it all. The journalist Ruth Picardie died of breast cancer early in her life. In the book written by her

---

[178] Quoted in the *Observer*, 5 April 1998.
[179] F. Spiegl (ed.), *A Small Book of Grave Humour* (Pan, 1971)

before her death, articles and letters are reproduced showing the depth of human emotion and the love of her family and friends in the face of death. However, her husband concludes with an essay in which he writes, 'Ruth's poor, hunched silhouette, half-lit by a shaft of light from the door . . . was the saddest thing I ever hope to see. I knew then that, like Eurydice, she was lost to the Underworld, and that the true meaning of dying is its absolute loneliness.'[180]

A distinguishing feature of the Christian faith is the way that it has helped women and men face the pain and grief of death. A philosopher was once giving a talk about the meaning of life. At the end of an excellent lecture, a female student asked him, 'But what happens at death?' His reply was 'I don't know; I've never died.' The audience laughed at the witty response, but the woman persevered and asked the question again. This time the philosopher replied, 'I don't know and never will know. The only way we would know is if someone came back from the dead and told us.'

The Christian hope of life beyond death is based on such a conviction. It is based on a God who raises Jesus from the dead, who then both tells and shows us what resurrection life is all about. Yet Christian thought about the future has often been concentrated on the individual. We have seen the Christian faith in terms of deliverance from this world to a new existence in heaven. Personal immortality has been seen in terms of leaving physical existence and this sinful creation behind. Yet this is not true to the Bible, or in particular to the bodily resurrection of Jesus. Richard Bauckham and Trevor Hart comment:

> Whereas a hope for purely spiritual immortality envisages human destiny as apart from this world and tends to envisage it in individualistic terms, the hope of bodily resurrection cannot stop at either the human individual, without human sociality, or at humans without the rest of God's creation, in which as bodily creatures we are so deeply embedded. Modern scientific insight into the depth and extent of our continuity with the rest of the animal creation merely reinforces what the Christian hope of bodily resurrection already implies, as Paul recognized in Romans 8:19-23. Our destiny is bound up with that of the world, and our resurrection will be our participation in God's new creation of all reality.[181]

[180] R. Picardie, *Before I Say Good-bye* (Penguin, 1998), p. 102.

[181] R. Bauckham and T. Hart, *Hope Against Hope: Christian Eschatology in Contemporary Context* (DLT, 1999), p. 127.

The New Testament in general and this passage from Romans 8 in particular question the individualistic view. Before we look at the passage, it may be helpful to summarize some New Testament themes that provide the background to Paul's view of the future.

## What's the end of the story?

One of the important things about any narrative such as a detective story or a joke is that the beginning only makes sense from the perspective of the end, and indeed the end only makes sense from the perspective of the beginning. There is a tendency in Christian theology to separate the beginning of the story from the end. That is, we talk about a doctrine of creation purely in terms of the beginning. Likewise, we often talk about eschatology, that is, the end, without reference to the doctrine of creation. In contrast, the New Testament holds the two together.

So, to understand a passage like Romans 8 we need to see it in its context, not only of its place in Romans but also in its general context of Pauline eschatology, which in turn is set in its own context of Jewish and Christian eschatology.[182]

The first thing about such a context is that creation and consummation are held together.[183] Paul reflects the Jewish sense of the linear nature of history that is dependent on the purposes of God being worked out between creation and consummation. Second, the link between creation and consummation is Christological,[184] that is, it is Christ who is both Creator and Consummator (Col. 1:15–17). In commenting on the Colossians passage, Wright states, 'The true humanity of Jesus is the climax of the history of creation and at the same time the starting point of the new creation.'[185] Third, there exists the strong sense of the idea of transformation of this creation into new creation. Here Dahl rightly comments, 'The fundamental idea here is not the conformity of the eschatological salvation with the original creation but that creation as described in Genesis prefigures the whole history of the world, including its eschatological fulfillment.'[186]

---

[182] B. W. Witherington, *Jesus, Paul and the End of the World: A Comparative Study in New Testament Eschatology* (IVP, 1992).

[183] F. Bridger, 'Ecology and Eschatology: A Neglected Dimension', *Tyndale Bulletin* 41.2 (1990), p. 297; N. A. Dahl, 'Christ, Creation and the Church', in *The Background of the New Testament and its Eschatology*, ed. W. D. Davies and D. Daube (CUP, 1964), pp. 422–443.

[184] C. Gunton, *Christ and Creation* (Eerdmans, 1992).

[185] N. T. Wright, *Colossians and Philemon* (Eerdmans, 1986), p. 70.

[186] Dahl, 'Christ, Creation', p. 429.

The new creation is not a return to Eden. The new creation is better than the old since it is freed from the corruption of sin. This is highlighted in the Adam/Christ contrast in Romans 5 where the curse of Genesis 3:17–18 is lifted by the obedience of the second Adam. This sense of discontinuity between the old and new creation is also present in thinking about the physical Universe both in Paul and in Messianic Judaism. The resurrection is to incorruptibility (1 Cor. 15) and even the light of the heavenly bodies in new creation exceeds that of the old (Is. 30:26).

Although there may be differences of detail and image along the way, in terms of the purposes of God, the significance of Christ and the idea of transformation, New Testament thought holds together the beginning and end of the story. This is important for how we do theology, or use creation and eschatology in evangelism, ethics and apologetics.

## What's the meaning of it all?

We now turn to Romans 8:18–30. I do so with a great deal of hesitation, reflecting the large amount of literature and disagreement that has been generated by these few verses. Of course, there is a wealth of literature on Romans, not least three substantial commentaries by professors of my own university.[187] Within that there is a great deal of work on Romans 8 in particular. However, this passage is often quoted but rarely understood or explained in detail. At the same time it is a crucial passage both to Paul's argument in Romans and to our doctrine of creation. We shall need to tread quite carefully as we ask what the passage gives to our understanding of creation. Indeed, as the reader might have picked up already, the visit to this particular village will need a lot of referring back to certain guidebooks!

Dunn points out three important strands of the relationship of this passage to the whole of the letter and argues that it plays a key role in Romans. First, it is the climax of chapter 8 picking up the earlier language of liberation, sonship, resurrection and the role of

[187] For a fuller discussion of this passage and its context within Romans see J. D. G. Dunn, *Commentary on Romans 1–8*, Word Biblical Commentary (Word, 1988); C. E. B. Cranfield, *The Epistle to the Romans*, vol. 1, International Critical Commentary (T. & T. Clark, 1975); C. K. Barrett, *A Commentary on the Epistle to the Romans* (A. & C. Black, 1957); L. Morris, *The Epistle to the Romans* (Eerdmans, 1988); J. R. W. Stott, *The Message of Romans*, The Bible Speaks Today (IVP, 1994); D. Moo, *The Epistle to the Romans*, New International Commentary on the New Testament (Eerdmans, 1996).

the Spirit. Second, it is the climax of the argument presented by Paul up to chapter 8, that is, the answer to the problem of sin. Third, it is the preparation for chapters 9 – 11 where 'God's salvation completes both his purpose in creation and his purpose in calling Israel.'[188]

Already in this we encounter some key questions. What does it mean for creation to be 'liberated'? How does sin affect the physical creation? Finally, what is God's purpose in creation? They are questions that we touch on in other chapters in this book but here are drawn together for us in quite dense theological writing:

> [18]*I consider that our present sufferings are not worth comparing with the glory that will be revealed in us.* [19]*The creation waits in eager expectation for the sons of God to be revealed.* [20]*For the creation was subjected to frustration, not by its own choice, but by the will of the one who subjected it, in hope* [21]*that the creation itself will be liberated from its bondage to decay and brought into the glorious freedom of the children of God.*
>
> [22]*We know that the whole creation has been groaning as in the pains of childbirth right up to the present time.* [23]*Not only so, but we ourselves, who have the firstfruits of the Spirit, groan inwardly as we wait eagerly for our adoption, the redemption of our bodies.* [24]*For in this hope we were saved. But hope that is seen is no hope at all. Who hopes for what he already has?* [25]*But if we hope for what we do not yet have, we wait for it patiently.*
>
> [26]*In the same way, the Spirit helps us in our weakness. We do not know what we ought to pray for, but the Spirit himself intercedes for us with groans that words cannot express.* [27]*And he who searches our hearts knows the mind of the Spirit, because the Spirit intercedes for the saints in accordance with God's will.*
>
> [28]*And we know that in all things God works for the good of those who love him, who have been called according to his purpose.* [29]*For those God foreknew he also predestined to be conformed to the likeness of his Son, that he might be the firstborn among many brothers and sisters.* [30]*And those he predestined, he also called; those he called, he also justified; those he justified, he also glorified.*

(Rom. 8:18–30)

Following Paul's lead of personifying creation in order to describe it, let us look at creation under five headings.

---

[188] Dunn, *Romans 1–8*, p. 467.

## 1. A suffering creation

Paul has been setting out that we are 'heirs of God and co-heirs with Christ' (v. 17) but now has to ask how this relates to our earthly existence? If we have been given such a privileged position, then does this mean that we will be protected from suffering, and further, is there any point to our earthly existence? However, the sufferings of this world are real and Paul interprets them as sharing in the sufferings of Christ as a necessary part of sharing in his glory. Here we have a strong link between the sufferings of this creation and the glory of the new creation.

However, Paul wants his reader to get this into perspective, pointing out that the present suffering is outweighed by the future glory (v. 18). Paul's use of *I consider* signifies strong assurance, not doubt. Cranfield speaks of 'firm conviction reached by rational thought on the basis of the gospel', while Dunn rightly qualifies this by effectively adding 'and experience of the Spirit'.

Commentators generally see the reference to the *present* as a reference to the era between the coming of Christ and his second coming. This eschatological tension between the beginning of the new creation and the end of this creation leads to some disagreement on *the glory that will be revealed in us*. Some see this revelation as being already real in some sense, a revelation of God's glory in the lives of the persons transformed by it. Others however see it as something future, belonging to the transition to heaven and new resurrection bodies. In terms of the rest of Pauline thought it is probably both/and rather than either/or. There is a future glory awaiting us in heaven (Phil. 3:21) but there is also the sense of that glory being revealed in our bodies now (2 Cor. 4:7 – 5:5).

The present sufferings Paul speaks of may be from a number of sources such as sin, the persecution of Christians, or the suffering of living in this fragile world. It is not clear what kind of sufferings Paul is specifically thinking of, but he does see them as sharing in the suffering of Christ (v. 17). Christians therefore need to come to terms with the reality of suffering in this world. An escapist view of Christian discipleship that promises a life free of suffering is not the message of the New Testament. At the same time our suffering needs to be seen in the perspective of that which is to come (Rev. 21:4; see chapter 20). It is not entirely clear why we have to live as part of a suffering creation rather than be translated immediately to God's new creation. All we can say is that the road to glory for Jesus was the way of the cross. We too are asked to walk that road.

We should be careful not to use these truths to give trite and insensitive words to those who are going through the most intense times of suffering. As we saw in chapter 14, there is always a mystery about suffering. Certainly we need to be careful not to become Job's friends in saying that God has given someone a disability so that he or she is more effective in shining for him.

Notice that Paul owns this suffering himself in terms of speaking of *our present sufferings*. As Gore put it, 'here we have, as nowhere else in the Bible – perhaps nowhere in ancient literature – a man who feels with the pain of creation'.[189] Theologians and preachers are often tempted to forget that those who are able to speak with depth on the subject of suffering are those who have had a depth of suffering. At the same time Paul wants to share his bigger perspective on suffering by seeing it in the light of the future. There is an end to it, there is a time of healing and there is a time of justice. This creation involves suffering in a way that the new creation will not, and that gives us a different view on it. Suffering often concentrates the mind totally on our illness or ourselves; it is a natural human emotional response. Yet those who are able to cope better with suffering are those who have a wider perspective.

## 2. An expectant creation

In fact the creation itself waits in eager expectation for the revelation of that glory (v. 19). The *eager expectation* is indicative of stretching the head forward or craning the neck. While some such as Fitzmyer suggest that this involves both curiosity and some uncertainty,[190] most commentators follow Denton as interpreting the image as confident expectation.[191]

More disagreement has been in what Paul means by *creation*. The most obvious meaning would be the subpersonal creation.[192] However, other contemporary commentators find the personification of creation and its need for liberation difficult and so think *creation* refers to human beings, for example 'the world in so far as it is distinct from the church'[193] or the 'non-believing human world',[194] that is, those who are not Christians. Manson finds it difficult in seeing how the material world can be liberated and therefore sees *creation* as

---

[189] C. Gore, *St Paul's Epistle to the Romans*, vol. 1 (John Murray, 1902), p. 305.

[190] J. A. Fitzmyer, *Romans* (Doubleday, 1993), p. 505.

[191] D. R. Denton, 'Apokaradokia', *Zeitschrift für die neutestamentliche Wissenschaft* 73 (1982), pp. 138–140.

[192] Morris, *Romans*, p. 320.

[193] F. J. Leenhardt, *The Epistle to the Romans* (Lutterworth, 1961), p. 123.

[194] J. G. Gager, 'Functional Diversity in Paul's Use of End Time Language', *Journal of Biblical Literature* 89 (1970), p. 329.

'mankind'.[195] Christian tradition has also given a variety of interpretations such as 'mankind both believing and unbelieving and also the angels',[196] 'all mankind',[197] 'unbelieving mankind',[198] 'angels only'[199] and 'sub human nature together with mankind in general'.[200]

None of these interpretations is convincing. Käsemann[201] and Cranfield[202] have argued strongly that it refers to 'sub-human nature only', which is also the position of Ambrosiaster, Cyril, Chrysostom, Calvin and the majority of recent commentators.[203] Believers must be excluded, since in verse 23 they are contrasted with creation. The phrase in verse 20 *not by its own choice* seems to rule out human beings as this includes Adam, and the suggestion that Paul is referring here to angels seems unlikely.

The creation therefore, both animate and inanimate objects from lions to asteroids, is waiting in eager expectation. But what is this personal language meant to convey? The personal language when referring to creation is not unusual in the context of Old Testament passages that do a similar thing. Isaiah 35:1–2 sees creation as demonstrating the glory of the Lord, while Isaiah 55:12–13 speaks of creation rejoicing and as a sign to the Lord. Other passages, such as Psalm 96:11–13, link the rejoicing of creation to the Lord's coming in judgment.

This raises an interesting parallel that has relevance to our understanding of creation. The personification of nature is used to see creation pointing towards the glory of the Creator God (e.g. Ps. 19:1). Indeed, Paul has already emphasized the way that God reveals himself through the natural world (Rom. 1:20). Such a biblical base is often used by those who speak of a revival of natural theology within the dialogue between science and religion.[204] Such a revised

---

[195] T. W. Manson, 'Romans', in *Peake's Commentary on the Bible*, ed. M. Black and H. H. Rowley (Thomas Nelson, 1962), p. 946.

[196] Origen, *Commentaria in epistolam b. Pauli ad Romanos* (Latin tr. by Rufinus), in *Patrologia Graeca*, ed. J.-P. Migne, vol. 14 (Paris, 1857–66), cols. 1109ff.

[197] Augustine, *Expositio quarumdam propositionum ex epistola ad Romanos*, in *Patrologia Latina*, ed. J.-P. Migne, vol. 35 (Paris, 1844–64), cols. 2074–2075.

[198] A. Schlatter, *Gottes Gerechtigkeit: Ein Kommentar zum Römer-brief* (Calwer, 1959), pp. 269–275.

[199] E. Fuchs, *Die Freiheit des Glaubens: Römer 5–8 ausgelegt* (Kaiser, 1949), p. 109.

[200] K. Barth, *A Shorter Commentary on Romans* (SCM, 1959), pp. 99–100.

[201] E. Käsemann, *Commentary on Romans* (Eerdmans, 1980), p. 233.

[202] Cranfield, *Romans*, p. 411.

[203] Such a view is seen in old and new commentaries such as W. Sanday and A. C. Headlam, *A Critical and Exegetical Commentary on the Epistle to the Romans*, International Critical Commentary (T. & T. Clark, 1902), p. 212; J. A. Fitzmyer, *Romans* (Doubleday, 1993), p. 505.

[204] E.g. D. Wilkinson, 'The Revival of Natural Theology in Contemporary Cosmology', *Science and Christian Belief* 2.2 (1990), pp. 95–116; J. C.

natural theology does not fall into the traps of the classical proofs for the existence of God, but identifies insights into the nature of the world revealed by science that point to something beyond the scientific description of the Universe. Thus the Universe's extraordinary balances in the laws and circumstances, which make life possible, its intelligibility and the awe it invokes can be pointers to a Creator God. They are not proofs and they fall short of any full and reliable description of the nature of such a God, but they point to transcendence.

The image of creation craning its neck forward is a helpful image in suggesting that the nature of this creation points forward to its own limitations and the coming of new creation. Just as some aspects of the Universe give pointers back to a Creator God, other aspects may point forward to a new creation achieved by the sovereign act of God. These aspects include the *present sufferings*, but also include the sense of futility concerning the future of the Universe revealed by science, which we shall look at in the next chapter. The Christian doctrine of creation would therefore expect certain pointers forward to new creation. These may be of value in evangelism and apologetics. Certainly Christians have often used the apparent futility of death as a pointer that there must be a hope that transcends death.

Barrett suggests that Paul in this particular argument 'is not concerned with creation for its own sake'.[205] Paul sees creation as a stage in God's purposes that has already within it pointers towards a better future. This is in line with the expectation in Judaism of a renewal and transformation of nature, and is an important corrective for those who would build a doctrine of creation in isolation from its future end.

Paul understands crucially that creation is important in pointing forward to new creation and the importance of redeemed human beings as key to that new creation. This passage does not say that this creation is worthless, for God is working his purposes out through this creation. Central to those purposes is the role of human beings (v. 19). The link between creation and the *sons of God* is a clear allusion to the Genesis narratives. So Dunn comments, 'as creation in the beginning had its role in relation to man, the crown and steward of creation, so creation's rediscovery of its role depends on the restoration of man to his intended glory as the image of God'.[206]

Polkinghorne, *Science and Theology* (SPCK, 1998); D. Wilkinson and R. Frost, *Thinking Clearly about God and Science* (Monarch, 2000), p. 56; J. T. Houghton, *The Search for God: Can Science Help?* (Lion, 1995).

[205] Barrett, *Romans*, p. 165.

[206] Dunn, *Romans 1–8*, p. 487.

Such an understanding challenges those who would underestimate the importance of both human beings and the material creation. At the same time it questions any eschatology that stresses too much continuity at the expense of discontinuity between creation and new creation. The very nature of this creation points forward to a qualitative difference in the new creation.

The revelation of the sons of God is likened by Dunn to a play when the final curtain is drawn back to show actors in their real characters. Such reality of sonship is only recognized by faith at this time. As Cranfield comments, 'they themselves have to believe in their sonship against the clamorous evidence of much of their circumstances and condition which seems to be altogether inconsistent with the reality of it'.[207] How then does this help creation? To understand this we need to go on to another of Paul's images.

## 3. A frustrated creation

Paul now describes in more detail why creation waits in eager expectation, linking with the word *for* (v. 20). It is because it has been subjected to *frustration*. This word is found thirty-seven times in the Septuagint translation of Ecclesiastes and has the sense of emptiness, futility, purposelessness and transitoriness. What does this mean for the physical creation? Some have suggested that it refers to the corruption to which humanity has subjected God's creation. However, this has the sense of human beings doing the subjecting. More helpful is to think of the subjection being the result of the relationship of God, human beings and nature being corrupted.

Cranfield sees the frustration as the ineffectiveness of that which does not attain its goal. Thus he states, 'the sub-human creation has been subjected to the frustration of not being able properly to fulfil the purpose of its existence, God having appointed that without man it should not be made perfect'.[208] The environmentalist and leading genetics expert R. J. Berry follows this line, arguing that Paul's point is that as long as we refuse to play the part assigned to us by God, that is, to act as his stewards, then the entire world of nature is frustrated and dislocated: 'an untended garden is one which is overrun by thorns and thistles'.[209] Cranfield helpfully uses the following picture:

[207] Cranfield, *Romans*, p. 413.
[208] Ibid., p. 414.
[209] R. J. Berry, 'Creation and Environment', *Science and Christian Belief* 7 (1995), p. 39.

What sense is there in saying that 'the subhuman creation – the Jungfrau, for example, or the Matterhorn, or the planet Venus – suffers frustration by being prevented from properly fulfilling the purpose of its existence?' The answer must surely be that the whole magnificent theatre of the universe, together with all its splendid properties and all the varied chorus of subhuman life, created for God's glory, is cheated of its true fulfilment so long as man, the chief actor in the great drama of God's praise, fails to contribute his rational part . . . just as all the other players in a concerto would be frustrated of their purpose if the soloist were to fail to play his part.[210]

Creation is thus caught up in the human fallen state, as human beings are not able to play their part. Once again allusion is made to Genesis 1 – 3. The subjecting of creation may refer to the dominion given by God to human beings (Ps. 8:6), but more likely refers to the consequences of sin (Gen. 3:17–18). Paul's use of the aorist tense looking to a single occasion seems to suggest that he was referring to the consequences of the fall, that is, the curse of Genesis 3:17–19.

The question is then 'who subjected it?' Some have suggested that Paul is referring to Adam, idols, or even celestial powers.[211] However, the vast majority sees Paul referring to God as the one who subjected the creation to futility. Yet it is an odd construction in the Greek. Dunn is helpful on this point and it is worth engaging with him in full. He states, 'The reason for the difficulty is probably Paul was attempting to convey too briefly quite a complicated point: that God subjected all things to Adam, and that included subjecting creation to fallen Adam, to share in his falleness.'[212]

Why should God do this? Dunn continues: 'God followed the logic of his purposed subjecting of creation to man by subjecting it yet further in consequence of man's fall, so that it might serve as an appropriate context for fallen man: a futile world to engage the futile mind of man . . . There is an out-of-sortedness, a disjointedness about the created order which makes it a suitable habitation for man at odds with his creator.'[213]

However, this process has a purpose: 'It is not an end of God's dealings but a stage in his purpose, the means by which the self

---

[210] C. E. B. Cranfield, 'Some Observations on Romans 8:19–21', in *Reconciliation and Hope: Essays on Atonement and Eschatology*, ed. R. Banks (Eerdmans, 1974), pp. 224–230.

[211] E.g. J. A. T. Robinson, *Wrestling with Romans* (SCM, 1979), p. 102; B. Byrne, *Reckoning with Romans* (Glazier, 1986), pp. 166–167.

[212] Dunn, *Romans 1–8*, p. 471.

[213] Ibid., p. 488.

destructiveness of sin can be drawn out and destroyed, and creation restored to its proper function as the environment for God's restored children.'[214]

Thus creation, as it now is, is both necessary to new creation and a pointer to new creation. The 'out of jointedness of creation' is testimony that it was not always intended to be like this and that it will not always be like this in the purposes of God. Christian commentators have often used the present fragility and suffering of this world to point backward to the seriousness of the fall. Here Paul also points forward to the seriousness of new creation. For it was subjected *in hope* that the judgment itself included the promise of a better future.

The hope for creation is that the effect of sin will be no more and creation will be set free to be what God wants it to be (v. 21). Creation itself, rather than just human beings, will be redeemed. Paul images it as *liberated from its bondage to decay*. He has already used this image of liberation in liberation from sin (Rom. 6:18, 22) and from the law (Rom. 7:3; 8:2). But what does this liberation mean for the physical Universe?

This has not been an easy verse to understand. In trying to interpret what *decay* means for the physical universe, some have suggested mere 'transitoriness'.[215] This of course raises serious questions concerning the nature of time. Our experience of time is that it is associated with decay, but time is also key to the growth of complexity, life, organization and creativity. There is deterioration in the Universe, but part of that deterioration as we have seen can point forward to new creation. However, in speculating too much on the physical Universe we may miss what is central here. The disjointedness of this creation will not continue forever. The creation will be brought into the same experience of freedom as the children of God through the action of God. The key feature of that environment is the freedom of the incorruptible for resurrected embodiment (1 Cor. 15:42–50), not at the mercy of sin, deterioration or death.

### 4. A groaning creation

Paul now appeals to common knowledge amongst believers that the creation is in trouble (v. 22), but again sees this groaning as a process and sign for the future. Moffatt's translation of 'the entire creation

---

[214] Ibid., p. 471.
[215] F. S. Jones, *'Freiheit' in den Briefen des Apostels Paulus* (Vandenhoek & Ruprecht, 1987), p. 132.

sighs and throbs with pain' may be a little extravagant in that it takes the emphasis away from the reason for the groaning. As Calvin pointed out this is meaningful pain in the sense not of death pangs but birth pangs. The image of childbirth was frequently used in Christianity and Judaism (e.g. Is. 26:17–18; Jer. 22:23; Hos. 13:13; Mic. 4:9–10; Mark 13:8; John 16:21; Acts 2:24; 1 Thess. 5:3; Rev. 12:2). Some have suggested that it was therefore common in contemporary apocalyptic and Rabbinic Judaism as well as in Greek thought to speak of a period of suffering until new creation.[216]

Paul's use of this image of birth pangs suggests that creation both prepares for and points to new creation. The groaning of creation is echoed in the groaning of believers (v. 23). Believers are part of this creation with its present sufferings, frustration and decay, but they have been given the *firstfruits of the Spirit*. Jewish custom was to bring the first of the harvest to the temple and offer it to God. This would consecrate the whole harvest and would also be a sign that there would be later fruits. Dunn argues that this harvest image is an allusion to the final resurrection of believers (1 Cor. 15:20, 23), with the first-fruits being the gift of the Spirit. The image further means that just as the first-fruits are of a piece with the whole harvest, then there is continuity between the gift of the Spirit, his work in the believer and the final product of resurrection.

Here we encounter again the importance of holding a tension between creation and new creation in terms of continuity and discontinuity. The believer reflects such a tension. The Spirit does not free the believer from such a tension but in fact heightens it. The experience of adoption and calling 'Abba, Father' (Rom. 8:15) is held in the frustration that the life of the Spirit cannot find full expression in this creation. The groaning is a sign of the Spirit's presence, his work within us and a sign of the new creation to come. Paul uses the same *wait eagerly* as in verse 19 to highlight both the parallel and the link between the future of the believer and the future of creation.

This passage is helpful in eschatological thinking as it constantly challenges views that see creation as meaningless compared to future glory, or new creation as meaningless compared to present experience. New creation is part of God's purpose from the beginning, but creation is necessary for that purpose to be fulfilled.

[216] J. Zeisler, *Paul's Letter to the Romans* (SCM, 1989), p. 218; D. Allison, *The End of the Ages Has Come* (Fortress, 1987); D. S. Russell, *Apocalyptic Ancient and Modern* (SCM, 1978); G. Vermes, *The Dead Sea Scrolls in English* (Penguin, 1975), p. 157. However, a different view is taken by E. P. Sanders, *Jesus and Judaism* (SCM, 1985), pp. 124, 130.

## 5. A hopeful creation

Paul then has to defend against any sense that this eschatological perspective on creation might lead to dualism, which values spiritual experience over against present reality (vv. 24–25). The hope for the future is based on the work of salvation and the present experience of the Spirit, but in the light of all that Paul has already said, it cannot ignore this creation. Indeed it is a new *creation* that is to come, not a disembodied spirit world.

Yet the Christian perspective is not determined by the frustrations of the present, but by its future hope. This means that the believer must wait in this creation patiently for the new, which means a positive endurance rather than quiet acceptance. As Grundmann comments, 'In virtue of the reception of the Spirit the Christian attitude is one of burning expectation in conformity with the divine plans.'[217]

The groaning of creation and the believer is also linked to the groaning of the Spirit (vv. 26–27). The Spirit helps believers in their weakness, when not just words fail but when they do not know fully God's will in the transition and tension between creation and new creation.

Paul then turns again to the certainty of Christian hope (vv. 28–30). Note the emphasis here on the initiative and work of God, who

- works for good (v. 28)
- calls according to his purpose (v. 28)
- foreknows (v. 29)
- predestined (v. 29)
- justified (v. 30)
- glorified (v. 30)

From creation to glorification this God is working his purposes out. We may not fully understand how he foreknows and how he predestines while at the same time giving freedom, but we do know that our hope is located in him rather than the circumstances around us. Hope for the future must be based on the action of God the Creator.

Having said that creation is not just a process towards new creation, but also has within itself pointers to the new creation; that is, creation and new creation existed together in the mind of God from the beginning. Furthermore, the very suffering, frustration and decay that results from the sin of human beings can become point-

---

[217] W. Grundmann, in *Theological Dictionary of the New Testament*, vol. 2, ed. G. Kittel and G. Friedrich (Eerdmans, 1964–76), p. 56.

ers to God's future purposes. The disjointedness and present sufferings of the natural world can point beyond themselves. By themselves they can be interpreted in different ways, not least in the problem of evil-type arguments against the existence of God. Yet if such pointers are seen from the perspective of Jesus, and in particular his resurrection, they point forward to a new creation. Paul discusses this hope as part of his overall exposition of God's work in Christ here in Romans. The cross and resurrection help us to see a suffering, expectant, frustrated and groaning creation in the context of hope.

The recognition that creation is both a process towards and pointer to new creation has implications for providence and ethics. Systematic theologians such as Maurice Wiles have a picture of God effectively creating the Universe and letting it explore its own potential, which is inadequate to do justice to the complexity of the biblical literature.[218] The biblical writers do not underestimate such complexity but they do want to emphasize the sovereign actions of God in both creation and new creation.

In terms of ethics, Becker uses Romans 8 to comment that 'Paul's apocalyptic faith in the transformation of the creation at the time of God's coming reign compels an ethic that strains and labours to move God's creation toward that future triumph of God promised in Jesus Christ and to which the presence of the Spirit propels us.'[219] Thus, this picture of hope does not mean that we opt out of the world. Our minds should not be concentrated on our own death or our own suffering – God's perspective points us beyond that. That means that churches need to be places that take seriously the suffering, frustration and groaning of this world of sin and death. They need to be places of listening, sympathy, support and bereavement counselling. At the same time, the life of the Spirit in fellowship, evangelism, social action, preaching and worship should point joyfully to the hope of new creation.

It is to the working out of this that we turn next.

[218] M. Wiles, *God's Action in the World* (SCM, 1986). See also D. Wilkinson, 'The God of the Physical Universe', in *Science, Life and Belief*, ed. R. J. Berry and M. Jeeves (Apollos, 1998), pp. 89–106.
[219] J. C. Becker, *Paul's Apocalyptic Gospel: The Coming Triumph of God* (Fortress, 1982), p. 111.

# 19. 2 Peter 3:3–16
# The Creator transforms

## Is there any point to it all?

'The more the Universe seems comprehensible, the more the Universe seems pointless.' So writes the cosmologist Steven Weinberg as he reflects on the future of the Universe.[220] Weinberg, one of the greatest scientists of his generation, had good grounds for such cosmic despair. The great triumph of understanding the origin of the Universe as the rapid expansion of space, which we call the Big Bang, brought with it a down side.

It predicted that in the future the expansion would slow down leading to two scenarios.[221] The first was that the expansion would continue forever, and in so doing the Universe would cool down to the point that life would cease to exist and the fate of the Universe would be 'heat death'. The other scenario was that gravity would eventually reverse the expansion and the Universe would end in a fireball the opposite of a Big Bang, a 'Big Crunch'. Once again all life would be extinguished. While the timescale for either of these scenarios was over 20 billion years, the future destined to futility in terms of the existence of life and a creative Universe seems to pose the question 'what is the point of it all?'

In fact, if Weinberg had made his remark in the year 2000 the situation would have been even more comprehensible and even more pointless. From 1998 onwards work by the physicist Saul Perlmutter and others on distant supernovae explosions has suggested that far from the expansion of the Universe slowing down, in fact it is speeding up. This was unexpected and seems to indi-

---

[220] S. Weinberg, *The First Three Minutes* (Andre Deutsch, 1977), p. 154.
[221] P. Davies, *The Last Three Minutes: Conjectures About the Fate of the Universe* (Weidenfeld & Nicolson, 1994).

cate that heat death awaits the Universe, a little sooner than expected.[222]

What then is the point of it all? Some physicists such as Freeman Dyson[223] and Frank Tipler[224] have tried to salvage a point by attempting to give cosmological scenarios where life, or at least intelligent machines, can go on existing for ever. While being unconvincing in a scientific sense, they are interesting examples of the need to say that the Universe and life will continue.

Such a desire to see things continue can also be seen in the way that people think about another cosmic problem for the future, that is, the end of our Sun. The Sun, our local star, will eventually use up all of its available hydrogen fuel. When that happens in about 4.5 billion years time, it will begin to swell up and its outer layers will burn the earth up, before being ejected into space. Again we see the pessimists and the optimists in this. The pessimists bemoan that the human achievements that stand as physical monuments will be destroyed, whether the Parthenon or the Eiffel Tower or the Human Genome Project.

However, many others are currently thinking of how science will deliver us by allowing us to travel away from the Earth to different planets that may support life or could be engineered to support life. Such 'terra-forming', that is, changing a planet's atmosphere to support human life, is an extension of the scientific belief that we can control our own future, whatever the Universe has to throw at us.

Others looking at all of this, simply ask what the point is of being worried about such things in the far future. After all, they say, my life will never see 4.5 billion years into the future. During my lifetime the world goes on as it normally does, they say. Indeed, even when faced with the damage we are currently doing to the environment, global warming over 100 years will not affect my life. Even if we are causing problems now, we know that science in the future will deliver us, because it always has. For such people this Universe will go on forever; time is judged simply from the perspective of our human life and the future has no effect on the present.

## God's point

The world of the letter of 2 Peter may seem a long way removed from twenty-first-century cosmology. Yet, as always,

---

[222] M. Livio and A. Sandage, *The Accelerating Universe: Infinite Expansion, the Cosmological Constant, and the Beauty of the Cosmos* (John Wiley & Sons, 2000).
[223] F. Dyson, *Infinite in All Directions* (Harper & Row, 1988).
[224] F. J. Tipler, *The Physics of Immortality* (Weidenfeld & Nicolson, 1994).

human attitudes are similar and this letter speaks both to the those who think this world is pointless and to those who think this world will simply go on for ever. Both are mistaken, and only by understanding God's perspective on the future can life be lived rightly today.

> [3]First of all, you must understand that in the last days scoffers will come, scoffing and following their own evil desires. [4]They will say, 'Where is this "coming" he promised? Ever since our ancestors died, everything goes on as it has since the beginning of creation.' [5]But they deliberately forget that long ago by God's word the heavens existed and the earth was formed out of water and by water. [6]By these waters also the world of that time was deluged and destroyed. [7]By the same word the present heavens and earth are reserved for fire, being kept for the day of judgment and destruction of the ungodly.
>
> [8]But do not forget this one thing, dear friends: With the Lord a day is like a thousand years, and a thousand years are like a day. [9]The Lord is not slow in keeping his promise, as some understand slowness. He is patient with you, not wanting anyone to perish, but everyone to come to repentance.
>
> [10]But the day of the Lord will come like a thief. The heavens will disappear with a roar; the elements will be destroyed by fire, and the earth and everything in it will be laid bare.
>
> [11]Since everything will be destroyed in this way, what kind of people ought you to be? You ought to live holy and godly lives [12]as you look forward to the day of God and speed its coming. That day will bring about the destruction of the heavens by fire, and the elements will melt in the heat. [13]But in keeping with his promise we are looking forward to a new heaven and a new earth, the home of righteousness.
>
> [14]So then, dear friends, since you are looking forward to this, make every effort to be found spotless, blameless and at peace with him. [15]Bear in mind that our Lord's patience means salvation, just as our dear brother Paul also wrote you with the wisdom that God gave him. [16]He writes the same way in all his letters, speaking in them of these matters. His letters contain some things that are hard to understand, which ignorant and unstable people distort, as they do the other Scriptures, to their own destruction.
>
> (2 Pet. 3:3–16)

This is a letter to a specific church or groups of churches (v. 15) with an apologetic content directed against specific objections to

Christian teaching.[225] Bauckham also points out that the use of language is that of a 'farewell speech' or 'testament' that contained the characteristics of ethical admonitions and predictions of the future (e.g. 2 Pet. 1:12–15).

The letter gives a response to objections raised by false teachers against Peter's teaching on ethics and eschatology, that is, what will happen in the future. It addresses the difficult question raised by some that the second coming of Jesus had been expected by the first generation of Christian believers but had not happened. These Christians were dying (vv. 4, 9a) and there was still no sign of the Lord's return in judgment and glory. From this fact some were suggesting that the expectation of the Lord's return was simply a mistake. There would be no judgment or divine intervention, but instead life would continue as it always has.

In fact a number of arguments seem to have been put forward against the Lord's return in judgment. These included that the parousia was invented by the apostles as an instrument of moral control (2 Pet. 1:16–19), that the Old Testament has been interpreted mistakenly (2 Pet. 1:20–21), and that without an expectation of the second coming and judgment life should be more enjoyable and free (2 Pet. 2:3b–10a). Here in this passage before us, Peter responds to further arguments. His counter-argument is that those who deny the Lord's return in judgment are mistaken about creation, mistaken about the Lord and mistaken about discipleship. And far from being irrelevant, these things are of utmost importance.

## 1. Mistaken about creation

Peter begins by reassuring those he is writing to that *in the last days*, that is, the period between Jesus' first and second coming, there will be those who will mock both moral and prophetic revelation from God (v. 3). They do so as a way of justifying their own lifestyle. Obviously, the implication is that they want to avoid any concept of judgment so that they can be free to define their own morality.

However, underlying their denial is both a genuine problem for the early Christian community and a subtler but very serious theological mistake. The genuine problem was the apparent delay of the

---

[225] For a fuller discussion of the background of this letter and context of this passage see R. J. Bauckham, *Jude, 2 Peter*, Word Biblical Commentary (Word, 1983); M. Green, *2 Peter and Jude*, Tyndale New Testament Commentaries (IVP, 1983); R. C. Lucas and G. Green, *The Message of 2 Peter and Jude*, The Bible Speaks Today (IVP, 1995); A. Chester and R. P. Martin, *The Theology of the Letters of James, Peter and Jude* (CUP, 1994); N. Hillyer, *1 and 2 Peter, Jude*, New International Biblical Commentary on the New Testament (Paternoster, 1992).

Lord's return. We can have genuine sympathy with those who longed for the second coming, especially in situations of persecution and difficulty. Expectations of an imminent return would have an attraction, just as they had for many others over centuries of Christian history.

So, as the first generation of Christians died, there were those who questioned whether the promise of Jesus to return could be trusted (v. 4a). Indeed, this genuine problem was then used by false teachers to support their argument.

However, in doing so they made a fundamental theological mistake. That was that this creation is all there is, and exists independently of God. Their eschatological scepticism was based on a common-sense rationalistic view of the world where the world continues on its course for ever (v. 4b). 'The Sun will come out tomorrow' as the orphan Annie would sing! The argument of the scoffers was that the world goes on in a regular pattern. It has done so since the beginning of creation. Indeed, there is the subtle suggestion that this is God's intention for this creation. He created those regular patterns and is quite happy with them. Such a God would not intervene in such a Universe. The Universe is reliable and self-contained and we can make of it what we want.

Peter will take up the genuine problem of the apparent delay later (vv. 8–10) but first he must deal with the theological mistake about creation (vv. 5–7). The Universe is not self-sufficient and independent but depends and continues to depend solely on the will of God. Far from creation denying that God can intervene in the Universe, it reinforces the view that God will intervene in the Universe. The world has not continued without intervention, and the same word of God, which created the Universe, has also decreed that judgment will come.

Bauckham suggests that the first part of verse 5 should be translated as 'For in maintaining this, they overlook the fact'. Their theological mistake was to overlook the nature of creation and God's action in the flood (vv. 5–6). The reference to creation *out of water and by water* reflects the view that the heavens and earth emerged out of God's creative activity of creating, separating, gathering and holding back the waters of chaos (Gen. 1:2, 6–7, 9; Pss. 33:7; 136:6; Prov. 8:27–29). That was not just a one-off event but a reflection of God's continuous sustaining and protecting of creation.

Not only is God intimately related to creation by his sustaining of it; he has also given evidence of special intervention. The link here may be a reference to Genesis 7:11 where, in the flood narrative, the waters of chaos that were confined at creation above the firmament poured through to the earth. This image is a reminder of God's cosmic sustaining and also his freedom to work in unusual acts in the cosmos.

By his word and water God created the Universe. He also intervened at the flood, and so by the same word and this time by fire he will intervene in judgment in the future. These images may be influenced by contemporary Jewish apocalyptic sources such as 1 Enoch, but Peter uses them to remind his readers of the nature of creation. However he goes further. This present creation although good and created and sustained by God is not the end point of God's purposes. The scoffers were making the mistake of equating the past and present with the future. God's purposes are in fact greater than this creation.

The image used to convey this is one of fire (v. 7). That the world would be engulfed by fire was not uncommon in the time of this letter. For example, the Stoics viewed the world as being periodically dissolved and renewed by fire. However, the image is not as much about periodic purification as about judgment. This reflects more Jewish apocalyptic than Stoic thought. The idea of destruction by fire is rooted in the Old Testament; for example in the story of Sodom and Gomorrah (e.g. Deut. 32:22; Ps. 97:3; Is. 30:30; 66:15–16; Ezek. 38:22; Amos 7:4; Zeph. 1:18; Mal. 3:19). The function of fire was to consume the wicked, not destroy the world. Indeed, in Jewish eschatology in the post-biblical period such judgment with fire was seen to have a parallel with the flood.

We need to be careful in interpreting this image. Even such an outstanding biblical scholar as Bauckham is a little misleading when he comments that as an 'apocalyptic image, it is an image which remains powerful today, evoking both the threat of nuclear holocaust and the eventual reabsorption of our planet into the expanding Sun'.[226] While nuclear holocaust in the popular mind may be an image of fiery judgment, it is worth noting that in fact fire is not the important factor in nuclear holocaust. More destruction would be caused by the so-called nuclear winter and longer-term radiation damage. The better image of nuclear holocaust is of a never-ending cold dark night! Nuclear holocaust is an image of the technological arrogance and violence of human beings. However, the eventual reabsorption of our planet into the Sun has no relation to judgment at all, as it is simply the way the solar system will develop, and by the time it happens human beings will have moved out. We need to very careful in linking these apocalyptic images with our contemporary physical understanding.

[226] Bauckham, *Jude, 2 Peter*, p. 302.

For example Michael Green's 1983 commentary quotes a commentator who identifies these biblical verses literally with the scientific picture of the end of the Universe: 'The solar system and the great galaxies, even space-time relationships will be abolished ... All elements which make up the physical world will be dissolved by heat and utterly melt away. It is a picture which in an astonishing degree corresponds to what might actually happen according to modern theories of the physical universe.'[227]

The problem is not only of identifying current scientific thinking and terminology of events that will happen in billions of years' time with a biblical text that does not think in such terms, but more importantly we lose the focus of the text, which is that of judgment. There are many of us who would far rather take part in eschatological speculation than respond to the coming judgment of God on lifestyle and attitudes. The letter is reminding its readers that God is in control of all of the patterns and forces of creation and judgment. This is an important reminder for today.

Though apocalyptic in its language and character, this argument has relevance to our understanding of eschatology and the future of the Universe. Scientific predictions of the future of the Universe are based on the assumption of the regularity of the Universe shown in the laws of physics. Within their own realm such predictions are valid and useful. However, it is not valid to build a philosophical or theological picture of the future simply on the scientific predictions. Such 'scientism' does not recognize that the laws themselves may be the description of God's faithful upholding of the Universe (Heb. 1:3) or that the God who in creation gives regularity to the Universe may at the same time allow himself freedom to work within the Universe in acts that go beyond those regularities.

Those who see the Universe as pointless see it as a closed system inevitably heading for futility. However, recognizing a Creator God who has purposes beyond this Universe gives a wider perspective to the discussion.

The same principle that 2 Peter uses in terms of the flood could be used more positively in terms of the resurrection. The resurrection gives evidence that God can go beyond the constraints of the normal pattern of human life and death to new creation. Indeed, this is the argument that is foundational to Paul's discussion in 1 Corinthians 15. The promise of the resurrection is that there will be a new creation, of which the resurrection body of Jesus gives us a model (see chapter 20). It is interesting to note also that Paul uses the resurrection as a pointer to the future judgment (Acts 17: 31; see chapter 16).

[227] B. Reicke quoted in Green, *2 Peter and Jude*, p. 138.

Yet 2 Peter does not help us much in relating just how the new creation will be different from this present creation. Verse 6 says that the world of that time was *destroyed*. However, destruction by the flood does not mean annihilation. The world was created out of the primeval ocean and then submerged again. It was a transforming process but it is difficult to know how that applies to the fire of judgment.

In such questions however we must not lose the twin foundations of Peter's response. They are that this creation is not the end in itself and that God is sovereign both in creation and in new creation.

## 2. Mistaken about the Lord

Peter now addresses the genuine problem used by the scoffers in attacking the understanding that Jesus would return. This is the problem of the delay (vv. 8–10).

His response is to say that it is a mistake to judge God from our own perspective. In terms of our perspective of time, *With the Lord a day is like a thousand years, and a thousand years are like a day* (v. 8). This is a reference to Psalm 90:4. Some people thought that the Day of Judgment would last a thousand years. This eschatological chronology was based on the exegetical formula 'A day of the Lord is a thousand years'. Here Peter reflects Jewish literature where Psalm 90:4 is used to contrast the short human lifespan with God's purposes.

The implication is clear. Those who find it hard to understand the delay have made the mistake of putting God into our human perspective rather than seeing human history from God's perspective. From the perspective of eternity the delay in the parousia is only a short time. Indeed, if God is not constrained by linear time in the way that we are, the very idea of a delay becomes meaningless. In such a view, Christians can hold together in tension an imminent expectation and the reality of delay, a position that has been argued to be characteristic of Jewish and Christian apocalyptic.[228]

Nevertheless Peter needs to go further in his response to the scoffers. There may be a philosophical response but there also needs to be a pastoral response. This is an important point to remember in Christian apologetics. We may be able to provide an intellectual solution to problems that people pose about the Christian faith, but we need to go further and address the pastoral issue behind the question. The pastoral issue here is the issue of the nature of God, as often

---

[228] R. Bauckham, 'The Delay of the Parousia', *Tyndale Bulletin* 31 (1980), pp. 3–36.

is the case. What is God's motive and can he be trusted? The scoffers were saying that God was not keeping his promise.

Peter may have suggested a solution at an intellectual level for the time delay, but what is God's purpose in this? He now goes on to build on Habakkuk 2:3, a key verse for reflection on the problem in Judaism of the delay of the day of the Lord:

> For the revelation awaits an appointed time;
> it speaks of the end and will not prove false.
> Though it linger, wait for it;
> it will certainly come and will not delay.

Peter offers a theological understanding in terms that the Lord is in control and that the delay has a purpose: to delay the judgment in order to give an opportunity for repentance (v. 9). The scoffers were mistaken in characterizing the Lord as impotent and uncaring. Peter says quite the opposite – the Lord has delayed the judgment out of care for all.

On the basis of God's perspective and purpose, Peter now restates the reality of the second coming. Reflecting Jesus' parables (Matt. 24:43; Luke 12:39), he uses the image of the thief. The day will certainly come with a sense of unexpectedness and vulnerability (v. 10a). The Lord does not reveal everything to us about time and place and so to criticize him for not following our sense of time is foolish.

The second part of verse 10 has caused some difficulties of interpretation. The overall image is clear. Here we have an overwhelming act of God with a radical effect on the Universe.

First the heavens will disappear *with a roar*. This image of disappearing or 'passing away' is used in the Gospels (Matt. 5:18; 24:35; Mark 13:31; Luke 16:17; 21:33). *With a roar* is an onomatopoeic word communicating hissing, rushing, whizzing, cracking or roaring of flames. It could also refer to God's thunderous roar, which announces his coming, and if this were the case it would place more emphasis on judgment than on physical effects.

The *elements* as the NIV translates it may better be translated as 'heavenly bodies'. Although the word can be translated *elements* and reflects the belief that the Universe is made out of the four elements of water, air, fire and earth, 'heavenly bodies' referring to Sun, Moon and stars is a well-attested meaning in the second century AD. Some have argued that the 'heavenly bodies' are in fact angelic powers. This may be an additional meaning but does not detract from 'stars', as stars were believed to be controlled by spiritual beings.

Yet all of this uncertainty of meaning is overshadowed by the last part of the verse, *the earth and everything in it will be laid bare*. The basic meaning of the words in English is 'the earth and the works in it will be found', and the uncertainty of what this means has led to numerous varieties of translation and interpretation.

Some English translations use variant readings in alternative manuscripts to suggest 'will be burned up', 'will vanish' or 'will be found dissolved', but there is little evidence that these were original. The phrase 'will not be found' has two occurrences in ancient versions but not in the Greek manuscripts. This makes sense of the verse but it can only be a later emendation of text. Some argue that 'not' was missed out in an early version of the copying of the letter.

Other scholars argue for various emendations to give the meanings 'will be burned', 'will be consumed by conflagration', 'will flow together', 'will be singed', 'will be judged', 'will be healed', 'the earth and the works which are found in it', 'the earth and the works in it will be found useless', 'the earth and all that is in it will be found as chaos' or 'it shall be found to the earth according to the works in it'. Others question the reading, arguing that it is in fact a rhetorical question 'Will they be found?'

Such a variety of views caution against any hasty conclusions as to the meaning of the phrase. Yet the most attractive solution seems to be to take the words simply as 'the earth and everything in it will be found' in the sense of will be made manifest before God and his judgment. Thus the NIV is helpful in its translation of *will be laid bare*. Derek Tidball uses the illustration of a building damaged by fire where the roof and some of the walls have gone, showing whatever is inside. Nothing will be hidden from God's judgment.

It must be said that the Old Testament usage does not seem to support the absolute use of 'to find', meaning 'to subject to judgment'. However, as Bauckham suggests, general familiarity with that usage could have influenced the choice of words in 2 Peter 3:10. The verb 'to find' is used in the Old Testament in contexts concerned with moral or judicial scrutiny where sin or righteousness is found (e.g. 1 Sam. 25:28), someone is found righteous (e.g. Dan. 5:27) or where a criminal is detected or found (Exod. 22:8). This interpretation is supported by the suggestion that the passive form perhaps indicates a divine passive, that is, these things will be discovered or found out by God.

It is an interpretation with a long history. In the 1920s Wilson wrote that

with a fine sense of climax (the writer) makes the passing away of the heavens and the destruction of the intermediate spiritual beings, while terrible in themselves, even more terrible in that they lead up to the discovery, naked and unprotected on the earth, of men and all their works by God. The judgement is here represented not so much as a destructive act of God, as a revelation of him from whom none can escape.[229]

This interpretation further fits with the context, that is, of the parousia as a time of judgment. Bauckham rightly comments that 'the destruction of the universe is of interest to the author only as the means of judgment on men and women'.[230] In relating these biblical images to the future of the physical Universe we must always keep that as a primary concern.

Some commentators however argue that the physical Universe is the primary concern in these verses. They suggest that the *earth* must be the physical earth and *everything in it* must refer to the natural world rather than to the evil deeds of men and women. Of course *the earth* cannot mean human beings, but it can easily mean Earth as the scene of human history (cf. Matt. 5:13; 10:34; Luke 12:49, 51; 18:8; John 17:4; Rom. 9:29).

The phrase *the elements will melt in the heat* (v. 12) picks up verse 10 and derives from Isaiah 34:4:

> All the stars of the heavens will be dissolved
> and the sky rolled up like a scroll;
> all the starry host will fall
> like withered leaves from the vine,
> like shrivelled figs from the fig tree.

The verb 'to melt' is also used of the melting of the mountains at the eschatological coming of God (Is. 63:19 – 64:1). The promise of a new heaven and new earth also derives from Isaiah (Is. 65:17; 66:22). It is found throughout Jewish apocalyptic (e.g. 1 Enoch 45:4–5) and is taken up in other texts in early Christianity (e.g. Matt. 19:28; Rom. 8:21; Rev. 21:1).

What do we make of the cosmic dissolution described in verses 10–12? I have already pointed out the parallel to the flood used in verses 4–7. The writer sees such events as demonstrating a Creator God who is able to work in human history in a dramatic and physical way. Within the context of the apocalyptic images and the difficulty of recovering the original meaning, some intervention of God in the physical Universe accompanying a time of judgment is envisaged.

Destruction of the present creation cannot be justified by these verses. Bauckham concludes, 'Such passages emphasize the radical

---

[229] W. E. Wilson, in *Expository Times* 32 (1920–21), pp. 44–45.
[230] Bauckham, *Jude, 2 Peter*, p. 319.

discontinuity between the old and the new, but it is nevertheless clear that they intend to describe a renewal not an abolition of creation.'[231] Here is a Creator who can be trusted. Rather than breaking his promise (v. 4) he keeps his promises and brings about a new heaven and a new earth (v. 13). He is powerful and free to act in both spiritual and physical ways in his creation.

We need to be careful of the mistaken view today that the Lord will not return in judgment or indeed cannot work in the Universe. The dream of human progress can believe that the future is in the hands of science, education and technology with the Lord as simply an interested observer. As we have also seen, some theologians, in order to absolve God from guilt in the area of innocent suffering, suggest that he has limited his interaction with the world. In the extreme case God is relegated to a supreme being who sets off the world and then does no more than maintain its integrity. Such views may have a philosophical attraction in avoiding difficult questions about miracles and suffering.

Yet Peter would say that such views of God are mistaken. If he acts in the beginning of creation, then he should be able to act at other points in the Universe's history. Further, a God who creates a Universe with no purpose or point, and without any judgment of the moral evil in the world, in the words of Peter Baelz's criticism of deism, is to be more pitied than worshipped.[232]

## 3. Mistaken about discipleship

Verses 11–16 now turn to a description of the new heaven and earth and the type of people who are at home in such a world. The *day of God* (v. 12) is a reminder that the new heaven and earth is a direct work of God. It is important to note, as we have often done in this book, that the discussion of creation is not written for the purposes of theological speculation, but to give Christians hope and an ethical imperative to live lives consistent with the new creation in which righteousness is at home (v. 13).

Unfortunately a mistake has often been made in the link between eschatology and discipleship. Those who have interpreted the images here of this creation being destroyed and God starting again have thus seen no Christian responsibility toward issues of justice and the environment. After all, they say, if everything is going to be burned up, then there is no point in looking after the atmosphere or fossil fuels. Likewise, those who have stressed that Christians have

[231] Ibid., p. 326.
[232] P. Baelz, *Prayer and Providence* (SCM, 1968), p. 69.

already passed through judgment through Christ's death on the cross have sometimes lost the sense of preparing for the new home that awaits us.

Here in the approach of the scoffers, a world without judgment meant that there was no moral imperative at all. Evil desires could be followed without consequences. Peter asks the key question in the light of this, *what kind of people ought you to be?* (v. 11) The future thus controls the present. We live our lives now in the light of the future reality. The answer is thus clear: to be part of God's new creation we have to live *holy and godly lives* (v. 11).

What does it mean to speed the coming of the day of God (v. 12)? It could simply mean that as God delays for repentance, then from a human point of view repentance and holy living may hasten its coming. Does this not deny God's sovereignty? It is difficult in such a context to suggest that this is what Peter is saying. Is it more that God graciously takes human affairs into account? It is not easy to give simple answers to this.

Interestingly, the one feature about the new heaven and a new earth that Peter mentions is nothing to do the physical Universe, but has to do with morality, that is, in which righteousness is at home (v. 13). This reinforces the view that judgment is central to this passage.

If that is the nature of the new creation, Christians need to live righteously to be ready for it. There will be a judgment for Christians too, but not one leading to condemnation. The judgment will be one of transformation for those in Christ.

Thus a view of God's future has both negative and positive motives in terms of lifestyle and attitudes. It gives a negative warning but also a positive hope of the kinds of values that will one day triumph.

Far from gazing at the future of the Universe and seeing it as pointless, we look forward to God's future and live our lives in accordance with it (v. 14). This creation is not the end of the story. And those who put their trust in science or say the future does not matter should remember the coming of the Lord.

Peter's final comment in this passage is a reminder that far from the Lord's patience being a disappointment it in fact is an opportunity for salvation (v. 15). If this is the reality to come, then we need to reflect the Lord's patience and opportunity of salvation to others.

# 20. Revelation 21:1–8
# The Creator accepted

## 'Who knows what tomorrow brings, in a world few hearts survive'

*An Officer and a Gentleman* is a now dated movie that often makes an appearance on late-night television. Richard Gere stars as a young man going to military training, falling in love and getting past the stereotypical tough drill officer. Yet the movie has a little more depth to it. Alongside Gere's character is another young man for whom everything goes wrong. Unable to make it through training and rejected by the girl he thought loved him he commits suicide. For him there is no happy ending of carrying Debra Winger off into the sunset. The story is of course a modern parable of the uncertainty of the future. As Jennifer Warnes and Joe Cocker sang in the title song, 'Who knows what tomorrow brings, in a world few hearts survive.'

Who knows? The English philosopher and part-time footballer Paul 'Gazza' Gascoigne once said, 'I never make predictions – and I never will.' However, others have not been so reticent. There are those who are full of optimism. They believe the words of the theme song of Britain's New Labour election victory of 1997, 'Things can only get better'! If we have a problem, science and education will deliver us. In 1900 the philosopher Jeremy Bentham proclaimed that once we have universal education all our problems will be solved. Such optimism is still around today. Television programmes such as BBC's *Tomorrow's World* look forward to the inventions of science in the future and often paint a picture of a better world. On an individual level many of us hope for the better. The dream of winning the lottery is presented as life will be better for 'you'. Perhaps we shall meet that one special person and fall in love. Perhaps we shall get that new and apparently perfect job. Perhaps even we shall get a better pastor at our church!

In contrast, others are pessimistic about the future and interestingly enough enroll science on their side. Prince Charles paints a bleak picture of the havoc he believes will be caused by the genetic modification of crops. Movies such as *Gattaca* represent a world dominated by the new genetics as a place where true humanity is denied. Others fear the results of abuse of the environment or even of joining or not joining monetary union in the European community.

Scientists themselves can be quite pessimistic. Recently a newspaper reported that scientists had predicted the end of the world on Thursday 26 October 2028 at 6.30pm GMT owing to the impact of an asteroid on the surface of the world. In fact, looking behind the headlines, the scientists were a little less confident than the newspaper. The end of the world has been predicted a number of times. Michael Drosnin in his best-selling *The Bible Code* claimed the Bible itself contained a secret code that predicted the date of the Kennedy assassination and Armageddon in 2000 or 2006. This is nothing new. James Ussher (1581–1656), Archbishop of Armagh, calculated that the world was scheduled to end on 22 October 1996, and Paco Rabanne, the fashion designer, also predicted that Armageddon would begin in 1996. Yet the world goes on and clothes and perfumes still sell.

The recent arrival of the new millennium heightened people's fascination with the end. Publishers especially have pushed this theme. Since the historian Francis Fukuyama's *The End of History*, which speculated on the victory of capitalism, more than 140 books have been published on 'the End of...' We read of this theme from *Nature* to *Time*, from *Evolution* to *Education*, from *Comedy* to *Conversation*, from *Science* to *Economics* (twice), from the *House of Windsor* to *Medieval Monasticism in the East Riding of Yorkshire*!

If there are optimists and prophets of doom there are also those who view the future with indifference. The last words of Lord Palmerston were 'Die, my dear doctor? That's the last thing I shall do.' Perhaps the most complacent was the Union General in the American Civil War who pointed to some snipers far away and declared, 'They couldn't hit an elephant at this dist—.' It is easy to become complacent about the future. Time and human society rolls on. Wars come and go, and the poor are always there. A century of two world wars, the holocaust and the nuclear arms race can all be forgotten in a pizza and the week's latest video movie. As Scarlet O'Hara would say, 'Tomorrow is another day.'

For those, whether optimists or pessimists, who do think about the future, there is a common theme. That is, we want a better world. Very few people would want the world to go on exactly as it is. We thereby express our concern that something is not quite right about this world. We recognize that human beings can demonstrate depths of love, art and creativity. At the same time we recognize that human beings fall short of their potential, both as individuals and society. There is a dark side to our character that is shown in cowardice in the face of injustice, the taking of human life for our own greed, using others for our own sexual gratification and the worshipping of idols of money, sex, fame and power. Human existence is not dominated by joy and love all of the time, but affected by death, mourning, crying and pain. Will it ever get better?

The good news of the Bible addresses all of these positions. To the pessimists it says that there is a better world coming. To the optimists it says that we cannot bring about a better world by ourselves without God. And to the complacent it says, 'You'd better understand this, because the future affects the present.' We find this good news in Revelation 21:1–8:

> [1]*Then I saw a new heaven and a new earth, for the first heaven and the first earth had passed away, and there was no longer any sea.* [2]*I saw the Holy City, the new Jerusalem, coming down out of heaven from God, prepared as a bride beautifully dressed for her husband.* [3]*And I heard a loud voice from the throne saying, 'Now the dwelling of God is with human beings, and he will live with them. They will be his people, and God himself will be with them and be their God.* [4]*He will wipe every tear from their eyes. There will be no more death or mourning or crying or pain, for the old order of things has passed away.'*
>
> [5]*He who was seated on the throne said, 'I am making everything new!' Then he said, 'Write this down, for these words are trustworthy and true.'*
>
> [6]*He said to me: 'It is done. I am the Alpha and the Omega, the Beginning and the End. To him who is thirsty I will give to drink without cost from the spring of the water of life.* [7]*Those who overcome will inherit all this, and I will be their God and they will be my children.* [8]*But the cowardly, the unbelieving, the vile, the murderers, the sexually immoral, those who practise magic arts, the idolaters and all liars – their place will be in the fiery lake of burning sulphur. This is the second death.'*
>
> (Rev. 21:1–8)

This passage comes as part of a revelation given to John while in exile on the island of Patmos.[233] It uses language and images that can

---

[233] For a fuller discussion of the background of this passage and its context in Revelation see D. E. Aune, *Revelation 17–22*, Word Biblical Commentary (Word,

be quite strange to us, using apocalyptic images that often represent both future and present realities. This section describes the final defeat of the enemies of God, in particular the final defeat of Satan. It is framed by two parallel angelic revelations (Rev. 17:1 – 19:10; 21:9 – 22:9). Here in Revelation 19:11 – 21:8 we have described the final defeat of God's remaining foes. After the final defeat of Satan (Rev. 20:1–10) and a vision of the judgment of the dead (Rev. 20:11–15), John sees a transition to a new order of which two aspects are emphasized (Rev. 21:1–8).

## 1. The new creation will be different from the first

John sees a new creation in terms of a new heaven and a new earth (v. 1). The *then I saw* formula introduces a new section. Then possibly an angelic voice from the throne gives a commentary on the vision in reverse order (vv. 3–4) to emphasize its importance. Thus we have:

| Verses 1–2 | Verses 4–3 (reverse order) |
|---|---|
| first heaven and earth passed away | former things pass away |
| sea no longer exists | death and trouble no longer exist |
| holy city descends adorned as bride | God dwells with his people |

In addition, *new* (v. 1a), *first* (v. 1b), *passed away* (v. 1b) and 'no longer exists' (v. 1b) occur in reverse order in verses 4b and 5a. Verse 5 acts as a bridge into the next section identifying a voice from the throne as God himself. Some scholars argue that originally 21:3–4 and 22:3–5 were linked and that the section 21:5 – 22:2 was inserted later. Even if this was so the text as we have it links verses 1–4 and verses 5–8 quite skilfully.[234]

The phrase *a new heaven and a new earth* would encourage Jewish readers to think back to Isaiah 65:17–25 (see chapter 17). Here John introduces it boldly and without much elaboration. We therefore need to be cautious in overinterpretation. However, there seem to be a number of pointers in filling out its meaning.

Footnote 233 (*cont.*)
1998); M. R. Mullholland, *Revelation* (Eerdmans, 1990); G. K. Beale, *The Book of Revelation*, New International Greek Testament Commentary (Eerdmans, 1999); R. J. Bauckham, *The Theology of the Book of Revelation* (CUP, 1993); M. Wilcock, *The Message of Revelation*, The Bible Speaks Today (IVP, 1975); J. R. Michaels, *Revelation*, IVP New Testament Commentary Series (IVP, 1997).
[234] Aune, *Revelation 17–22*, p. 1116.

## a. New physical order

The *new heaven and a new earth* is contrasted to the *first heaven and the first earth* (v. 1). This means that God's purposes are beyond simply this present Universe. It is a caution against those who would see his purposes being wrapped up in this Universe. But what does it mean for the first heaven and earth to pass away? Is God going to destroy this Universe and make a new one? Is he going to start all over again? The problem with this is, what was the point of the first creation in the first place and will God really be defeated by sin to the extent that he has to scrap the lot and start again?

As in the interpretation of 2 Peter 3:3–13, most recent scholars see an image here of transformation rather than destruction.[235] This is emphasized in verse 5 in terms of *I am making everything new*. The word *kainos*, 'new', usually indicates newness in terms of quality rather than something new that has never been in existence. Here we have a qualitative contrast between the new and *first* creation. The college where I write this is situated in a number of historic buildings on the World Heritage Site of the Bailey of Durham Cathedral and Castle. The original houses have been transformed to make a new college that is home to hundreds of students. While the students would quickly point out that this is a long way from heaven (!), it is a new building. Not that the old buildings have been demolished but there has been a fundamental transformation maintaining the historic beauty while adapting it to college life.

The image indicates a radically changed cosmos but with continuity to the first cosmos. John does not give us the physics of the new creation. The only clue we get is the resurrection of Jesus, as the risen Jesus is the beginning of the new creation. The link between new creation following the pattern of the resurrection occurs in a number of passages.[236] Isaiah 65:16–17 is alluded to in 2 Corinthians 5:14–17 and Colossians 1:15–18. In Revelation itself Revelation 3:14 also alludes to Isaiah 65:17, seeing its prophecy beginning to be fulfilled in the physical resurrection of Christ: 'To the angel of the church in Laodicea write: These are the words of the Amen, the faithful and true witness, the ruler of God's creation.'

The word 'ruler' also means 'origin' or 'beginning'. This is a literary development of Christ's title in Revelation 1:5 which reads, 'and from Jesus Christ, who is the faithful witness, the firstborn from the dead, and the ruler of the kings of the earth.'

---

[235] G. B. Caird, *A Commentary on the Revelation of St John the Divine* (Harper & Row, 1966), pp. 260, 265–266; Mullholland, *Revelation*, p. 315; Bauckham, *Revelation*, pp. 49–50; Beale, *Revelation*, p. 1040.
[236] Aune, *Revelation 17–22*, p. 1116.

Now the second part of Revelation 3:14, that is, 'beginning/ruler of the creation of God', does not link Jesus to the original creation but, in the light of the reference to the resurrection in Revelation 1:5, his resurrection is viewed as the beginning of a new creation (see Col. 1:15–18).

If the resurrection of Jesus provides the pattern for new creation, then what do we see? First, there must be continuity between this creation and new creation, just as the continuity between the crucified Jesus and risen Jesus is emphasized by the Gospels:

- the risen Jesus is recognized by the disciples (John 20:19–20)
- he can be touched (Matt. 28:9; John 20:17; Luke 24:39)
- he eats fish (Luke 24:42–43)
- he shows his hands, feet and side (Luke 24:39; John 20:24–31)

However, at the same time there must be discontinuity. The Gospels portray the same Jesus but he seems to have different physical characteristics:

- he did not seem to be confined to space and time, as he appeared in rooms with locked doors (John 20:19–20)
- there is a sense of mystery to the resurrection appearances (Mark 16:1–8)
- the disciples have some trouble in recognizing Jesus, and indeed some continue to doubt (John 20:14; 21:4; 21:12; Matt. 28:17; Luke 24:37)

The transformation of the cosmos will have major differences. Once again we get tantalizing clues. One of these is that *there was no longer any sea* (v. 1). What does this mean? Does it mean that God is going to ban sailing, windsurfing and swimming for eternity! Once again we need to be careful to look behind the images, which would have had different meanings in John's time.

The understanding of sea in Jewish belief and within the book of Revelation is a little more complicated than some commentators state. It is often said that the Jews feared the sea because of the belief that the deep personified the power that fought against the deity at creation. Yet in Scripture the Lord is its Creator (Gen. 1:9–10), its controller (Ps. 104:7–9; Acts 4:24), compelling it to contribute to human good (Gen. 49:25; Deut. 33:13). Indeed, the sea utters God's praise (Ps. 148:7) and is completely under God's command (Is. 17:12; Jer. 6:23). At the same time, the sea is seen at times to be in conflict with God. God has to set a guard on the sea (Jer. 5:22; Job 7:12) and rebukes the waters (Is. 1:2; Nah. 1:4; Hab. 3:8; Pss. 18:6; 29:3).

In Revelation itself Beale suggests that the sea is identified in a number of ways:[237]

- the origin of cosmic evil (4:6; 12:18; 13:1; 15:2)
- the rebellious nations (12:18; 13:1)
- the place of the dead (20:13)
- the primary location of the world's idolatrous trade activity (18:10–19)
- a literal body of water sometimes used with 'earth' to represent totality of old creation (5:13; 7:1–3; 8:8–9; 10:2; 14:7)

It is probable that all meanings are reflected here. The new creation means no threat from Satan, other nations, death, no more idolatry, and no more conflict with God. Other commentators have also suggested that the sea represents separation between groups of people and nations and so such a separation will be no more, since all are in a new community with God and one another.[238] Others have suggested that the primary reference is to the heavenly sea, which served as a veil in the sky separating God's presence from earth, but will be eliminated from the new creation.[239] Richard Bauckham suggests yet another interpretation.[240] He sees in the reference to the sea an image of the removal of the threat of another flood. He notes that Revelation 11:18 alludes to Genesis 6:11–13, 17, making a parallel between the flood and eschatological judgment. The new creation is eternally secure, for the creation is beyond the threat of evil. Thus the emphasis is not on the passing away of the material elements of the old world but on the passing away of evil.

All these interpretations have some merit. At a basic level the parallels between verses 1–2 and verses 3–4 would identify the passing away of the sea with the passing away of the tribulations of human beings. One cannot help but wonder whether John, sitting in exile on an island cut off by sea from his loved ones and imprisoned by it, did not see a very strong image of hope in the sea passing away.

The new creation is therefore not a return to Eden. The new creation is better than Eden, in terms of its security against evil and its freedom from sin. It 'begins with the tale of a garden and ends with a city of gold' is not a bad summary of the Bible's view of creation and new creation.

[237] Beale, *Revelation*, p. 1040.

[238] M. E. Boring, *Revelation* (John Knox, 1989), p. 216; P. E. Hughes, *The Book of Revelation* (Eerdmans, 1990), p. 222.

[239] J. W. Mealy, *After the Thousand Years, Journal for the Study of the New Testament*, Supplement Series 70 (JSOT Press, 1992), pp. 192–212.

[240] Bauckham, *Revelation*, p. 53.

## b. New relationship

The second aspect of John's vision is the Holy City, the new Jerusalem (v. 2). This again takes us back to Isaiah 65:17–20. The new Jerusalem is prepared as a bride. The image of a bride is used of the church (see also Rev. 21:9 and 22:17) and in Isaiah is also used of returning captives (Is. 49:18; 61:10; 62:5). The adornment of the bride is in contrast to the adornment of the whore representing Babylon (Rev. 17:4). The image is a powerful way to represent the renewed relationship of God and his people. Some ten years ago I stood at the front of a church and waited for my bride. In the midst of her beauty, the dress and the congregation the most powerful thing was that she was doing this for me. She was prepared to be committed to me in a new form of relationship.

This depth of relationship likened to marriage is also about the presence of God. He will dwell with his people (v. 3), which resonates with God walking in the garden in Genesis and of the Word becoming flesh and dwelling with us (John 1:14). However, this relationship goes even further. He will live with his people and the covenant formula used in the Old Testament of 'I will be their God and they shall be my people' is heard again (Lev. 26:11–12; Zech. 2:10b–11; Ezek. 43:7; Exod. 29:45). Here is the fulfilment of God's promises and God's work in Christ establishing an intimacy and security for his people. As well as the image of marriage, of living in his presence and the obligations of covenant relationship, this intimacy is also picked up later in the image of *I will be their God and they will be my children* (v. 7b). This metaphor is based on ancient adoption law that becomes the basis of inheritance (v. 7a).

The Christian experience is not yet like this, although we experience parts of it. God's promises and the work of the cross make these things a spiritual reality in our lives. Yet at the same time, our earthly lives still have the experience of God being far away, of doubt, of fear and of sin. The work of sanctification in us is the work of transforming our human condition into the position we have in Christ. In the new creation that work will be completed and we shall experience joy, security and intimacy with God on a level that we have had just the smallest of insights into.

## c. New experience of life

This relationship with God in the new creation is something to look forward to. For God himself will take away the things that cause us tears. The image is once again of deep intimacy. Just as a parent wipes away a child's tears, so God will wipe away our tears. In this new creation there will be no more death, mourning, crying or pain. The *old order* has passed away. This surely refers to the order where sin dominated, but may also allude to the difference between this creation and God's new creation. In one sense this creation is always vulnerable to death and sin. But in new creation death will be no more.

Here is an experience of life that transcends our normal expectations of life. C. S. Lewis rightly objected to people talking about the shadowlands of the life to come as if our souls inhabited a grey world that was less than the full colour of our present existence. Lewis said that it is the other way round. This life is the shadowlands and the life to come will be in full colour. Those who thirst for healing, for complete reconciliation and fellowship, for righteousness and knowledge of God, will have their thirst quenched by the free offer of the spring of the water of life (v. 6).

### d. New community

Just as in our understanding of creation, we must not let our Western tradition of individualism cloud the corporate nature of new creation. In contrast to Revelation 1 – 3, which focus on the church's weaknesses, here the vision sees the church in its perfected eternal state. The vision focuses more on the glorified community of believers than on the physical universe. As we saw in chapter 2, God's plan is always about individuals in community, and so in John's vision we see a new community brought together by God's promises and work.

An old couplet goes, 'To live above with saints we love that will be our future glory. To live below with saints we know that's quite another story!' The reality of a fallen world is that sin divides us. Racism, sexism, ageism and denominationalism join with many other 'isms' to cause barriers, pain and hurt to the human community. Even in God's new community of the church these things exist. But in new creation these things will be wiped away. The church gives us a foretaste and should be a model to the world of what is to come. Indeed, our fellowship needs to reflect the future reality. A woman was asked why she worked so hard at getting to know other people in her church and at forgiving them quickly and readily. She replied, 'If I'm going to be with them in eternity, I'd better get to know them now.'

### e. Judgment

It is sometimes easy for Christians to paint a picture of heaven that is so sickly sweet that it bears more resemblance to never-never land than to the Bible. Revelation reflects the general biblical theme of a

265

coming judgment, although it may use different kinds of image to portray this. Verse 8a lists vices that have parallels with the Ten Commandments and indeed with other lists in the New Testament (1 Cor. 5:9–11); however, cowardice and unbelief occur only in Revelation. Cowardice was the designation in the Greek world for general moral degradation. That those who reject God's way will be punished is clear from the image. What is not clear is the nature of the punishment. Does the fiery lake of burning sulphur represent the annihilation of the person or eternal torment? This has become a big debate amongst evangelicals in recent years and lies beyond the remit of this present book. Yet we need to take the reality of judgment seriously, for whatever the punishment is, it is described in the most serious terms.

Here is a picture of the new creation as a renewed cosmos, an intimacy of relationship with God, life without pain and suffering, a new experience of community and a judgment of all that spoils the world. Does this picture excite you? It points us forward in hope. The philosopher Bertrand Russell's atheism led him to say, 'When I die I shall rot . . . There is darkness without, and when I die there will be darkness within. There is no splendour, no vastness, anywhere; only triviality for a moment, and then nothing.' Faced with such a bleak prospect some look to reincarnation, but that simply puts us back where we started. The Christian hope looks forward to a better time. The existentialist philosopher Jean-Paul Sartre commented, 'there is no purpose . . . no goal for mankind . . . the world seems ugly, bad and without hope. There, that's the cry of despair of an old man who will die in despair.' John's vision disagrees, and replaces despair with an exciting hope.

The biblical scholar Gordon Wenham tells of seeing an advert of the British Diabetic Association that read, 'No more blood tests, no more needles, no more watching food. Imagine the future. Imagine a cure.' Reflecting on the New Testament imagery, he suggests that the Bible promises, at the second coming of Jesus, a future of

No more crime, no more terrorism, no more wars, no more genocides.
No more heart disease, no more cancer, no more arthritis, no more suffering, no more death, no more sorrow.
No more anger, no more lust, no more bondage to unhealthy habits, no more sin.
No more injustice, no more exploitation, no more hatred.[241]

[241] G. Wenham, 'Decoding the Bible Code', *NB*, Supplement (April–May 1998).

I remember little of my grandmother, as she died early in my childhood. However, I have a clear memory of one thing. She had spent a great deal of her life in a wheelchair as she was unable to walk. I must have asked some question about this because before she died she said to me, 'When I go to be with Jesus I will be able to run!'

## 2. The new creation is a sovereign creation of God

Chris Rea in his song 'Tell me there's a heaven' sums up a fundamental human longing and wants it to be true. We want to believe in the eventual triumph of good over evil and the ending of death, mourning, crying and pain. Some may say this is a nice vision, but how do we know that it is true? Is it not just 'pie in the sky when you die'? How can we be sure that there is some purpose to all of this, and that there will be a new creation? In the words of one of the characters in the movie *Trainspotting*, surely our experience of life is that 'It is all a random lottery of meaningless tragedy and a series of narrow escapes.'

If the new creation were to be achieved by human beings, then this is a fair point. However, John's vision makes it clear that the new creation is all dependent on the work of God. The Christian hope is not dependent on the fickleness and sinfulness of human beings but on the character and revealed will of the God who brought this creation into being out of nothing.

Verses 5–8 summarize one of the central messages of Revelation; that is, just as this creation is the sovereign act of God, so the new creation will be a sovereign act of God. It is God who says, 'I am making everything new,' and this is done on his initiative and by his power (v. 5). This seems to be an allusion to Isaiah 43:19, 'See, I am doing a new thing!' Bauckham comments, 'The understanding of God as Creator was not only integral to Jewish and Christian monotheism; it was also essential to the development of Jewish and Christian eschatology. If God was the transcendent source of all things, he could also be the source of quite new possibilities for his creation in the future. Creation is not confined forever to its own immanent possibilities.'[242]

The hope for new creation is trustworthy and true because it comes from the God who can achieve it (v. 5b). John's vision sees a time when this new creation is accomplished – when God's work is done (v. 6). One cannot help but think back to John's Gospel when Jesus cries out that the work is accomplished (John 19:30). The defeat of sin and death on the cross is part of the process of God's new creation, while at the same time being a pointer to its reality. The cross

[242] Bauckham, *Revelation*, p. 48.

shows us that evil can never conquer the love of God, and that the domination of sin and death is not inevitable.

The title of *Alpha and the Omega, the Beginning and the End* (v. 6) was a widespread Hellenistic divine title emphasizing cosmic sovereignty and lordship. It is a phrase that is used in a cosmological sense. The Lord of creation was not thwarted in his work of creating the Universe and he will not be thwarted in his work of new creation.

God is the guarantor of new creation. What then does this mean for the Christian life now?

### a. Patience

First, it means patience in the midst of this creation. When my son was very young he and I watched England being eliminated from the Euro 2000 soccer tournament through a defeat to Romania. At the end of the match he was crying. Trying to comfort him I said, 'It's all right; there will be another chance in the next World Cup, which is only two years away.' He replied, 'I can't wait that long!' From the perspective of a six-year-old, another two years seemed to be an eternity away, whereas from an England fan of thirty-eight years of age and many disappointments, two years seemed to be just around the corner. From our human perspective, we often cry out for the pain and suffering of this world to be a thing of the past. We may pray, 'How long Lord?' and feel that we cannot wait for his coming again. Yet we must have a patient confidence that looks to the Lord. Confident hope of a new creation gives us patience.

### b. Action

Second, however, it leads to action rather than inactivity. We are not called to a kind of patience that simply sits back and does nothing. Unfortunately, Christians have often fallen into that trap. They have misused the hope of new creation to say that as everything will be perfect in heaven there is no urgency to change things in this creation, whether the conditions of the poor and the suffering, or abuse to the environment. Marx was right to see that often religion has been used as the opiate of the people. However, authentic Christianity is a stimulant, not a sleeping pill. Action is encouraged because we are confident of the end.

### c. Dream

Martin Luther King's fight against racism was because he had 'a dream'. The vision of the triumph of good over evil and of a new community gave confidence to those who suffered at the hands of an unjust system. The confidence and inspiration of the knowledge that the end was assured urged them into action. Lord Shaftesbury, the great campaigner for social reform, in particular of the exploitation of child labour, once said, 'I do not think that in the last forty years I have lived one conscious hour that was not influenced by the thought of the Lord's return.'[243] People need the dream. As Dave Andrews writes, 'A few people, with a big dream, can change the world . . . indeed it's the only thing which ever has.'[244] It is amazing how people flock to support a winning side. In this vision John shares with us that God will achieve the triumph of good. Confidence in him means that we reflect the concerns that will one day triumph, whether in caring for the environment or in working for justice in opposing racism, sexism, ageism and idolatry.

### d. Holiness

Finally, there is a challenge to holiness here. We are called to live a life now that fits with this eternal destiny. A mother knew her son was going to wed someone from another country. So the mother began to learn the language of that country because she knew that she would be welcoming a daughter-in-law into the family and wanted to prepare for that reality. We are called to overcome now those things within our own lives that do not reflect the beauty of our destiny as the bride of Christ. Whatever the final judgment for those who reject Christ, we who follow him now are called to put to death immorality and idolatry.

God is the one who knows what tomorrow will bring. For those who trust in him, it is not a matter simply of surviving but of over-coming (v. 7). That is what it means to be a child of God.

---

[243] Quoted in S. Travis, *The Jesus Hope* (Word UK, 1974), p. 49.
[244] D. Andrews, *Building a Better World* (Crossroad, 1998), p. 72.

269

# Appendix

## A 'brief history' of Genesis

Few passages in the Bible have raised such controversy as its opening chapters.[245] In terms of the large number of New Testament passages that allude to these chapters, it is clear that for Jesus and the early church they were as fully inspired by God as any other part of the Bible (e.g. Matt. 19:4–6; John 1:1; 1 Cor. 15:45, 47; 2 Cor. 4:6; Eph. 5:31; Jas. 3:9; 2 Pet. 3:5–6; Rev. 22:2).

All Christians would agree that Genesis 1 – 3 gives the basis that the Universe has God as its creator, and that everything owes its being, order and life to him. However, after that understandings differ. Does Genesis tell us how God created the Universe or is modern science to be believed? These are particularly difficult questions amongst those who want to assert the authority of the Bible strongly. In recent years a number of excellent books have appeared on these issues dealing with all the questions involved.[246] In the following sections I shall attempt only a summary of the different understandings with particular reference to the origin of the Universe. In all of this the main concern must be to let the text speak for itself.

## Seven-day creationism

This understanding is the most difficult to reconcile with modern science but is very attractive to those who want to assert the authority of the Bible. It sees Genesis 1 – 3 as literal history, that is, giving

---

[245] This section is adapted from D. Wilkinson, *God, Time and Stephen Hawking* (Monarch, 2001).

[246] See e.g. D. Burke (ed.), *Creation and Evolution* (IVP, 1985); M. W. Poole and G. J. Wenham, *Creation or Evolution – A False Antithesis?* (Latimer House, 1987); R. Forster and P. Marston, *Reason, Science and Faith* (Monarch, 1999); E. Lucas, *Can we Believe in Genesis Today?* (IVP, 2001).

a description of how the Universe was created, over a seven-day period a few thousand years ago (although strictly of course the actual period is six days).[247]

It is an approach that should not be underestimated either in its force or intellectual credibility. There is a tendency amongst scientists and theologians to ascribe it to a small group of fundamentalists who refuse to use their minds. This is not the case. The influential American Institute for Creation Research and the smaller but growing British Creation Resources Trust have a number of powerful scientists among their members.[248]

The approach denies that Genesis 1–3 contains figurative elements, but believes that it is quite simply history. The time of the creation can then be estimated by tracing back the genealogies in Genesis to Adam and Eve, and in this way an age of a few thousand years is derived. Part of its attraction is that identifying all the text as history means that little interpretation is needed as to what is history and what is not.

If the approach to the Bible is straightforward the approach to science is not. The generally accepted picture from science is that the Universe emerged from a rapid expansion of space-time some 12 billion years ago. The evidence for this is shown by the red shift of galaxies, the microwave background radiation and the observed helium abundance in the Universe.[249] The question is then how an age of about 10,000 years can be reconciled with the cosmological age of 12 billion years?

The answer takes two forms, which are not quite consistent with each other. One answer is to argue that the Earth only appears old. This was first argued by P. Gosse in 1857, suggesting that God created Adam with a navel. In modern astronomical terms it means that God created the Universe with light already in transit to the Earth from distant galaxies, making them only appear billions of light years away. Thus the findings of modern science are accurate, but they only tell us about appearances. The real age of the Universe is revealed only in the Bible. This position is logically consistent and science cannot argue against it. However, we shall come to theological difficulties in a moment.

The other answer (often put alongside the first, although they do say different things about science) is to argue that the majority of

---

[247] For a historical study see R. L. Numbers, *The Creationists: The Evolution of Scientific Creationism* (Knopf, 1992); *Darwinism Comes to America* (Harvard University Press, 1998).

[248] For those who would like more information and literature see the Creation Resources Trust website <www.c-r-t.co.uk>.

[249] See T. Ferris, *The Whole Shebang: A State of the Universe(s) Report* (Touchstone, 1998).

modern scientists have got it wrong and in fact science itself points to a Universe that is only thousands of years old.[250] Arguments used for such a young Universe include a decay in the speed of light, problems with ages derived from globular clusters and problems with the Big Bang. These are supplemented by evidence for a young Earth apparently shown by changes in the magnetic field strength, problems with radioactive dating, the explanation of the fossil record by means of the effects of a global flood and arguments against evolution. Some of these arguments do point to some inadequacies in current scientific theories, but have not convinced the vast majority of the scientific community that our picture of the origin of the Universe is mistaken. A further attack on the scientific models is to question their philosophical basis.[251]

This understanding of Genesis 1 – 3 however has four major problems. First, these chapters, which it takes to be literal scientific history, have within themselves indications that they should not be interpreted that way. That is, they contain clear figurative elements raising the question of whether they were written as scientific history. (See chapters 1–4 of this book.)

Second, as Lucas points out, the position assumes that God creates instantaneously rather than over an extended period of billions of years. However, the biblical literature does not require this. Even in Genesis God does not create instantaneously, but over six days, and Adam is created in two or three stages (Gen. 2:7). The same word 'create' is used also in contexts where a long period of time is assumed, such as in the creation of Israel (Is. 43:1, 15).

Third, if the argument is used that science only gives an 'apparent' age, then there is a theological problem. Is there any biblical warrant for believing that God has purposefully designed the nature of the Universe in order to deceive us? If the Universe was created a few thousand years ago, why does it appear to be expanding from a point of origin some 12 billion years ago? The growth of modern science stemmed from the Christian worldview that because the Universe was created by God, observations of that Universe could give us truth in some measure. If the Universe is designed deliberately to deceive us, then the whole philosophy of the empirical method

---

[250] H. M. Morris and G. E. Parker, *What Is Creation Science?* (Creation-Life, 1982); H. M. Morris, *Scientific Creationism* (Christian World, 1974); J. C. Whitcomb and H. M. Morris, *The Genesis Flood* (Baker, 1961); C. Mitchell, *The Case for Creationism* (Autumn House, 1995).

[251] This is usually done in the area of biology rather than cosmology, but the same approach is used in K. Ham, *The Lie Evolution* (Creation-Life, 1990); P. E. Johnson, *Darwin on Trial* (Monarch, 1994); P. E. Johnson, *Testing Darwinism* (IVP, 1997); C. G. Hunter, *Darwin's God: Evolution and the Problem of Evil* (Brazos, 2001).

(that science is about observation) and those biblical passages that speak of some limited revelation through nature are called into question (see Ps. 19:1 and Acts 17:22–31 in chapters 7 and 16 of this book; and also Rom. 1:19ff.; Acts 14:7). One may argue that it is our sin that deceives us rather than God's design and so leads us away from acknowledging his truth. This argument has some force, but in the end is very difficult to justify from Scripture. I have yet to see a biblical defence of this position.

Fourth, if the alternative argument is used that modern science has got it all wrong not in minor details but in the major concept, then this denies the work of the vast majority of research scientists, both Christian and non-Christian, whose results have been tried and tested by the scientific community. It is sometimes difficult to communicate the huge weight of evidence for a particular scientific theory. At the same time it is relatively easy to present holes in it, because every scientific theory has its strengths and weaknesses. There are unanswered questions in both the Big Bang and evolution and scientists should be honest about that. But there is also a great deal of evidence that is more powerful than the difficulties.[252] If one is to reject this balance of evidence, then one must be very sure that the text requires a literal understanding.

## The 'gap' theory

This attempt to reconcile the text of Genesis with the findings of science was introduced by the nineteenth-century Scottish preacher Thomas Chalmers. Its 'gap' is between verses 1 and 2 of Genesis 1. It argues that verse 1 refers to the original creation, which could be billions of years old. However, the fall of Satan is responsible for bringing ruin and destruction upon the creation and verse 2 is translated as 'The earth became formless and void'. The rest of chapter 1 is thus a six-day work not of creation but of reconstruction, which did happen thousands of years ago.

This has been attractive to many people although there are not many supporters of it today. Its problems are twofold. Most scholars do not think the translation of verse 2 as 'became' is allowable, and that is why most modern translations have 'The earth was form-

---

[252] E.g. in cosmology see Ferris, *Whole Shebang*; in geology D. A. Young, *Christianity and the Age of the Earth* (Zondervan, 1982); and in biology E. Mayr, *One Long Argument: Charles Darwin and the Genesis of Evolutionary Thought*; M. Ruse, *Darwinism Defended* (Addison-Wesley, 1982); S. Jones, *Almost Like a Whale: 'The Origin of Species' updated* (Doubleday, 1999); R. Dawkins, *Climbing Mount Improbable* (Penguin, 1997).

less and empty' (RSV). Second, there is little support elsewhere in the Bible that the fall of Satan had such a ruinous effect.

## Are the days really ages?

Another attempt at reconciliation, suggested in the nineteenth century by Hugh Miller, still attracts many supporters.[253] It sees the Hebrew word *yôm* (translated as 'day' in modern translations) in figurative terms of an unspecified period of time such as ages or the millions of years in the evolutionary process. It then argues for a general agreement between the order of the creative acts and the fossil evidence.

However, once again there are problems. Although *yôm* can be used as a period of time elsewhere in the Bible, it is highly unlikely that the writer of Genesis 1 was using it in that way. This is shown by the days being used as part of a week and with the emphasis of 'evening and morning' (e.g. Gen. 1:8). In addition, the agreement between the general order of creative acts and the fossil record is not exact. Trees appear before marine creatures (Gen. 1:11, 20) which is contrary to the fossil record, and evening and morning appear before the Sun and Moon (Gen. 1:5, 14).

## Days not of creation but of revelation?

This unusual understanding was put forward by a Jesuit priest Hummelauer, and in the middle of the last century by P. J. Wiseman.[254] It argues that the seven-day week of Genesis 1 is indeed a literal week, but that it is a week not of God creating but of God revealing to Adam how he created. Each day God reveals a new part of the story. This week of revelation would then be the thousands of years ago indicated by the Genesis genealogies, but the creation itself could be over an unspecified time before that. Wiseman points out that this explains some odd features of Genesis 1. Why for example did God rest on the seventh day when other parts of the Bible are clear that God never tires or grows weary (Is. 45:28)? Wiseman argues that the week is for Adam's benefit and God 'rests' in order for Adam to have time to contemplate what has been revealed.

Unfortunately, this understanding rests on Genesis 1:1 being translated as 'God made known the heavens and the earth' rather than

[253] H. Miller, *The Testimony of the Rocks* (St Matthews, 2001).
[254] P. J. Wiseman, *Clues to Creation in Genesis* (Marshall, Morgan & Scott, 1977).

'made the heavens and the earth'. The majority of scholars however do not accept this as a valid translation of the Hebrew sentence.

## The literary approach

This begins with the question as to what kind of literature Genesis 1 actually is? The Bible of course contains many types of literature such as poetry, prose, parables, allegory (e.g. Ezek. 16), fable (Judg. 9:8–15), history, correspondence, prayers, dreams and visions. It is important in understanding the Bible to be clear about what form of literature we are dealing with. For example some forms if taken literally are nonsense. The verse 'the eyes of the LORD range throughout the earth' (2 Chr. 16:9) does not mean that the Lord has optical nerves, but is a picture of God's knowledge and interest in the affairs of the world.

So if we address this question to Genesis 1 – 3, what kind of literature is it? As we see in chapter 1, there are indications that the meaning is essentially theological rather than scientific, as illustrated by the force of theological polemic in Genesis 1. Second, there are non-literal elements in Genesis 1 – 3. For example on the seventh day there is no mention of evening and morning, which some scholars suggest implies that the seventh day has not yet ended. Indeed, this assumption that we are still in the Sabbath of creation week is picked up by Jesus himself. When questioned about the Sabbath he replies, 'My Father is always at work to this very day' (John 5:17). Or when God creates man, does God literally 'breathe' (Gen. 2:7)? In addition, there are many wordplays: for example the word used for 'pain' is not the usual one for childbirth but is used because it sounds like 'tree' (Gen. 3:16). It is also interesting that the book of Revelation uses images of 'serpent' and 'tree of life' from Genesis, but uses them symbolically. Third, it is important to note that the structure of Genesis 1 makes excellent logical sense but not so good chronological sense. Fourth, there are also indications that Genesis 1 reflects a liturgical form; that is, it was used in worship. It is interesting that modern versions of the Bible like the NIV lay out the first chapter in the form of hymn or poetry rather than strict scientific history. It is a meditation on the work of creation so that we can understand that the creation is related to God.

Whether it is poetry, hymn or doctrine in narrative mode may never be settled. However, what we can say is that the chapter is a subtle interweaving of a whole number of literary genres. The indications above that Genesis 1 is not to be understood as literal scientific history do not mean that it contains nothing that is important

either to history or to science. Some scholars and popular commentators have gone to the position of saying that Genesis is nothing but
a story invented (or based on other ancient creation stories) in order
to give some comfort to an ancient people who lived in an unsure
world without the insights of modern science. However, this does
not have to follow from recognizing that the primary literary style
of Genesis is story or hymn. Real historical events can be described
in a symbolic way and Scripture itself has examples of this. Jesus
himself describes real events in a symbolic way, in the parable of the
wicked tenants (Matt. 21:33–41). Also this way of dealing with
events is not alien to our culture. In *King Lear* Shakespeare takes real
characters and events and presents them in story form in order to
convey a message. I am not of course suggesting that Genesis 1 can
be put alongside *King Lear*. Genesis 1 is from God, but the literary
medium through which he inspires the message to be written could
be closer to hymn or story than scientific history. This does not
negate the fact that there could indeed be historical and scientific
insights in it, but it does mean that we need to use care to identify
those insights.

In this literary approach, Genesis chapter 1 is viewed as truth. Its
truth is primarily theological rather than an account to be compared
directly with the scientific picture of contemporary cosmology. To
insist that it is simply scientific truth falls into the misleading view
that all truth is scientific truth. The writer of Genesis, inspired by the
Holy Spirit, is more concerned with who God is than how he made
the Universe.

## Genesis and science

Of all the understandings of Genesis outlined above, the latter one
seems to me to be the best understanding of the text itself. That is not
to say that the debate is closed, and Christians need to continue the
discussion. However, with an understanding of the literary form of
Genesis not as scientific history, then the Bible's view and science's
view can be easily held together in a complementary view of the
origin of the Universe.[255] Both are true but differ in the questions
that they answer and the form in which they give their answers. Such
a view can be seen in both Augustine and Galileo. Augustine saw
clearly that Genesis 1 had non-literal elements to it, and Galileo
famously said, 'The Bible does not tell us how the heavens go but

[255] H. Van Till, *The Fourth Day, What the Bible and the Heavens Are Telling us
about Creation* (Eerdmans, 1986).

how to go to heaven.' Building on this foundation, science and Christian faith are fruitful conversation partners in the contemporary setting.[256]

Some people say, 'But why did God not just write Genesis 1 as a textbook of modern cosmology?' 'Surely', they argue, 'this would remove the need for all this complicated talk of complementarity and the like.' The point is however that if Genesis 1 were to be written as a scientific textbook very few of us would understand it! Moreover, our scientific picture is continually being modified. Our scientific picture would be incomprehensible to a scientist of the sixteenth century. How then would God communicate to all peoples, regardless of whether or not they had a PhD in physics or the age in which they lived? The answer must surely be, in the form of a hymn or a story that could be understood and appreciated by all.

To others who will be reading this, this whole chapter will appear to be desperate biblical gymnastics – attempting to get the Bible and science to fit together whatever the contortion! I suggest that this may be a little unfair in that I have throughout attempted to be true both to the nature of science and the nature of the Bible. Science does not show us that the Bible is wrong. It however does help us to see when our *interpretation* of the Bible may be wrong. The different understandings of Genesis over the centuries are a record of Christians attempting to reach a better understanding of the Bible.

A robust doctrine of creation will mean that we shall not be afraid to bring God's two books, the book of his Word and the book of his works together. As Packer states:

> Our attitude must be determined by the principle that, since the same God is the Author both of nature and of Scripture, true science and right interpretation of Scripture cannot conflict . . . The truth is that the facts of nature yield positive help in many ways for interpreting Scripture statements correctly, and the discipline of wrestling with the problem of relating the two sets of facts, natural and biblical, leads to a greater understanding of both. Not only does the book of Scripture throw light on the meaning of the book of nature; the book of nature reflects some of that light back on to Scripture, so that we may read its message more clearly. It is through the ferment of thought created by such intervention

---

[256] For more information on this subject see the Christians in Science website <www.cis.org.uk> and the following books: A. McGrath, *Science and Religion: An Introduction* (Blackwell, 1999); R. T. Wright, *Biology Through the Eyes of Faith* (Harper & Row, 1989); M. A. Jeeves and R. J. Berry, *Science, Life and Christian Belief* (Apollos, 1998); R. J. Berry, *Real Science, Real Faith* (Monarch, 1991); D. Alexander, *Rebuilding the Matrix* (Lion, 2001).

that theological insight is deepened and the relevance of the gospel more fully grasped.[257]

We Christians can often differ in our interpretations of how to bring the two books together, but it is to be hoped that we would do so with grace. Most of all, we must not lose sight of the Creator.

---

[257] J. I. Packer, *Fundamentalism and the Word of God* (IVF, 1958), p. 135.

# Study guide

The aim of this study guide is to help you get to the heart of what the author has written and to challenge you to apply what you learn to your own life. The questions have been designed for use by individuals or by small groups of Christians meeting, perhaps for an hour or two each week, to study, discuss and pray together.

The guide provides material for each of the sections of the book. When used by a group with limited time, the leader should decide beforehand which questions are most appropriate for the group to discuss during the meeting, and which should perhaps be left for group members to work through by themselves or in smaller groups during the week.

In order to be able to contribute fully and learn from the group meetings, each member of the group needs to read through the section or sections under discussion, together with the Bible passages to which they refer.

It's important not to let these studies become merely academic exercises. Guard against this by making time to think through and discuss how what you discover *works out in practice* for you. Make sure you begin and end each study by focusing on God in praise and prayer. Ask the Holy Spirit to speak to you through your discussion together.

## The beginning of creation
## (pp. 15–77)

### 1. Genesis 1:1–25 The Creator of heaven and earth

1  Read, and study if you wish, the Appendix (pp. 271ff.), which gives various interpretations of the dating of the Universe and Genesis 1. Why does Wilkinson believe it isn't vital to the message of Genesis 1 whether the Universe was made in seven

days a few thousand years ago, or whether it was created over billions of years (p. 18)?

2   In what way is Genesis 1 a polemical text (p. 21)?

---

'God has set the revelation of the truth about himself into the thought forms and culture of the ancient Near East. Far from corrupting its purity, this gives the revelation even more power. God's revelation of himself is never in the abstract; it is in the reality of human history' (p. 22).

---

3   'Science may describe God's activity in creation and is to be valued for that. However, we must guard against language that suggests science is the creator' (p. 23). Give some examples of such language.

4   Describe how God creates with 'pattern and order' (p. 23).

5   What is the significance of the number seven throughout the Bible (p. 24)?

6   Explain how Christianity has contributed to the growth of what we now know as science (pp. 24–25).

7   Kepler is quoted on p. 26 as saying, 'Science is thinking God's thoughts after him.' Think about how you would defend sciences like engineering and technology as Christian ministries.

8   How does the Genesis account give a picture of God as the great artist (pp. 26–28)?

9   Give examples of the diversity of our 'extravagant universe' (p. 28).

10  'It is blasphemous to destroy the diversity of the world' (p. 29). How does this view contrast with your view of blasphemy?

## 2. Genesis 1:26 – 2:3 The Creator of human beings

1   In what terms does the Bible define human beings (p. 32)?

2   Wilkinson asserts that the work of creation involves all three persons of the Trinity (p. 34). How does he come to his conclusion?

3   Explain why early Christian commentators made a distinction between image and likeness (pp. 34–37). What is the biblical basis for such a distinction?

4   'The "image of God" means that we are sufficiently like God that we can have an intimate relationship with him' (p. 36). How is the truth of this statement shown in the relationship God has with Adam and Eve?

5   Jesus reveals what it is to be human in at least six ways (p. 37). List them.
6   Define how we are 'Human Becomings' (p. 38), rather than human beings.

---

*'Image is about both creation and redemption. Our capacity for relationship with God means that we reflect something of God in our human bodies, and to some extent we reflect his reason, the capacity for free action and moral sensitivity. Yet we need to see these things from the perspective of Jesus Christ' (p. 38).*

---

7   The book of Genesis records that the high point in God's creation was humanity. What is the real meaning, therefore, of the Universe (p. 39)?
8   It is a popular theory that God created the Universe because he was lonely. What is the fundamental problem with this idea (p. 39)?
9   Emil Brunner is quoted as saying that we 'are created for life in relationships that mirror or correspond to God's own life in relationship' (p. 40). Think about the implications of this statement for community living. How can we live more in line with God's will?
10  What does the current state of the environment say about our misunderstanding of our role in creation (pp. 41–43)? What should our motivation be in becoming more responsible?
11  'Written into God's creation is the necessity of rest' (p. 44). Give some examples of how our 24 hours a day, 7 days a week society makes us less human.

## 3. Genesis 2:4–25 The Creator provides

1   Contrast the distinguishing features in Genesis 1:1 – 2:3 and Genesis 2:4–25. What is the evidence for different sources for the two sections and why is it important to look at these details (pp. 46–47)?
2   In what way can Genesis 2:4–25 be described as a myth (p. 48)?
3   Another description of the style of Genesis 2:4–25 is 'proto-historical' (p. 48). Despite its helpfulness, how does this view cause problems?
4   Why is it so difficult to distinguish the different literary types in the Bible (p. 49)? Define how the written form of the Word of God can be taken more seriously.

5   Compare the similarities and differences between humans and animals (p. 50). What is the core difference?

> *'God is in the process of forming us from the dust. The image here is of a potter shaping clay. It is an image that communicates an artistic, inventive and intimate act, an act that requires skill and planning. God is not detached from the processes of the emergence of human beings. He is the choreographer of the DNA, the author of our genetic code, the sculptor of the human organs, the director of language, and the provider of life in all its fullness' (p. 53).*

6   Explain the importance of viewing life as a gift from God (pp. 53–54).
7   Look at the five possibilities given for what the *tree of the knowledge of good and evil* may mean (Gen. 2:17) (p. 55). Why do Wenham, Cassuto and Westermann, among others, take the last interpretation?
8   What are the consequences of living with or without God's wisdom (p. 55)?
9   Many people view work as a necessary evil. How would you argue otherwise?
10   Describe how Genesis 2:23 does *not* support the view that 'the man holds ultimate authority for decisions in marriage and the primacy of male leadership within the church' (p. 59).
11   Read the verse again. What hope does it give to the single person? How can the church and its leaders help the unmarried 'fulfil their humanity' (p. 60)?
12   Think about God's view of sex and Christians' view of sex (pp. 60–61). Why the disparity between the two?

## 4. Genesis 3:1–24 The Creator rejected

1   By what means does Genesis describe the origin of sin (p. 65)? How does the means of the description affect the way we view sin and its consequences?
2   'A great deal of Christian tradition has identified the serpent with the devil' (p. 66). Give the basis for this view.
3   Explain how you would communicate the concept of sin to someone with no understanding of it (pp. 67–68).

> *'The questioning of motivation can sour a good act or situation. The impression of a good sermon can be destroyed by*

*one sentence said in a conversation over coffee that ques-*
*tions the preacher's lifestyle or motivation. The truth that*
*God wants us to enjoy the goodness of creation, once separ-*
*ated from his concern for all human beings, can be a justifi-*
*cation for selfishness. We enjoy the goodness at the expense*
*of others, as many of our sisters and brothers in the devel-*
*oping world know too well. As C. S. Lewis pictured in* The
Screwtape Letters *the work of Satan is rarely outright*
*attack, but subtle luring and corrupting' (p. 69).*

4 List the ways in which seduction leads to action (p. 69).

5 Describe how Adam and Eve's hopes are unfulfilled after eating the fruit (p. 70). How does that event affect relationships between men and women today?

6 What are the consequences of sin for our relationship with God (pp. 70–71)?

7 Look at Genesis 3:11. How does God try to make Adam see that he is responsible for his sin (p. 71)?

8 John 16:8–9 teaches that 'part of the role of the Holy Spirit is to seek the lost and to make the connection between the consequences of sin and the reality of sin'. In what way can we 'differentiate between the convicting work of the Holy Spirit and other sources of guilt' (p. 72)?

9 Given that 'the consequences of sin are not confined to one generation' (p. 73), how will sin be defeated?

10 'Would Adam and Eve therefore have died if they had not sinned? If they had carried on walking with God in the garden, would they have been translated like Enoch without dying physically (Gen. 5:24)? Or is physical death without the negative effects of disrupted relationship with God simply part of being a creature on the Earth in this creation?' (p. 75). Discuss.

11 Reflect on the New Testament images of being clothed in the righteousness of Christ. Spend time with God in prayer or contemplation.

# The songs of creation (pp. 79–111)

### 5. Proverbs 8:22–36 The wisdom of God

1 Read Proverbs 8 – 9. Why is wisdom 'personified in the metaphor of Woman Wisdom' (p. 83)?

2   Describe how important wisdom is to God (pp. 84–85).
3   What is the argument used to show that wisdom is fundamental to the Universe (p. 85)?
4   How may humans share in the wisdom that is the source of joy (p. 86)?
5   Given that wisdom ultimately comes from God, how may we obtain it (p. 87)?

---

'The matrix of the patterns of the order of the world and human societies point us to a deeper reality. This reality is not a desert nor a nightmare, but is a world reflecting God's transcendence and immanence. Some people will see pointers to a deeper reality, but just as Neo has to take a step of faith in order to see reality as it is, we are encouraged to take a step of faith into a relationship of trust and obedience to God. In such a relationship we learn how to care for ourselves and the world rather than abuse it' (p. 87).

---

6   Consider renting The Matrix on video or DVD and discussing its themes in a small-group setting.

## 6. Psalm 8 The majesty of God

1   Think about pride. How does that lead us into getting things out of perspective (p. 88)?

---

'Within Western culture God is often relegated to the sidelines. He has become just a private belief on a par with the healing power of crystals or the "you will meet a handsome stranger" of the astrology pages in the newspaper' (p. 91).

---

2   Read Psalm 8. In what way does this piece of writing change our perspective (p. 92)?
3   When considering the vastness of the Universe it is easy to think of ourselves as insignificant. Describe how Psalm 8:5–6 shows us otherwise (pp. 93–94).
4   'My child you are more precious than silver . . . And nothing I desire compares with you' (p. 94). Reflect on the changed words of this worship song and thank God for his revelation in Jesus Christ.

## 7. Psalm 19 The glory of God

1  Explain Francis Bacon's concept of God's two books: the book of his works and the book of his Word (p. 96). Contrast the differing approaches of section one (Ps. 19:1–6) and section two (Ps. 19:7–14).

2  How is the glory of God revealed through section one (p. 98)?

3  Consider why some people only hear the voice of creation after they know Christ (p. 99).

4  What is the similarity between the role of the Sun (v. 6) and the divine law (v. 8)?

5  Look at the six aspects of God's Word (p. 101). 'Take one or two of these verses, be quiet in the presence of God and let your imagination engage. For example, what does it mean for the law of the Lord to be described as perfect?' (p. 102).

6  'The psalmist directs us to God's written Word' (p. 103). So what is the trap in following the 'letter of the law'?

---

*'We rightfully want to stand for orthodox doctrine. But we need to be careful that in desiring to be "sound" we in fact do not turn out to be "sound asleep" (p. 103).*

---

7  Define the key to hearing the voice of God clearly (p. 104).

## 8. Psalm 148 The universal praise of God

1  Read Psalm 148. Let it speak to you. Then look specifically at verses 1–6. In what way do these verses encourage praise (pp. 107–108)?

2  Compare the first section with verses 7–14. Note the similarities between them and Genesis 1. What is the theology here (p. 108)?

---

*'The worship of this insignificant people is seen as the centre of the praising Universe. God's people act as the worship leader commanding the choirs of the heavens and earth. The people who are close to his heart are the focus of the universal act of praise' (p. 109).*

---

3  Wilkinson gives six reasons for the relevance of praise in our local churches (pp. 109–111). Explain why praise is so important.

4  Imagine you are planning a no-holds-barred praise-and-worship service at your church. What does the service look

like in your mind's eye? How do you feel when you think about what it could be like?

# The Lord of creation
# (pp. 113–166)

## 9. Luke 8:22–25 The wind and waves obey him

1 Put yourself in the disciples' situation in the boat with Jesus (pp. 116–117). How do you think you would have reacted?
2 In terms of their vulnerability, what are the disciples being taught (pp. 117–118)?
3 What is the significance of this lesson being learnt in the midst of a storm (p. 118)?
4 'The world may be a fragile and evil reality, but Jesus is with us' (p. 119). Describe the second lesson the disciples learn in the boat.
5 Why does Jesus ask them where their faith is (p. 120)? Spend some time in prayerful reflection and ask yourself, 'Where is mine?'

---

*'Christians find it difficult to live through crises when our faith is put in other things apart from Jesus. We trust in our abilities, our church, money or even our own holiness. We therefore tell ourselves that we shall be fine in the storms of life. Yet none of these things has power over the wind and the waves' (p. 120).*

---

6 'In response to Jesus asking them about faith, the disciples respond with another question, *Who is this?*' (p. 122). How does their question show what is at the heart of faith and discipleship?
7 Think about how your church approaches evangelism. In what ways could a personal God be communicated more effectively (pp. 123–124)?

## 10. John 1:1–18 The Word became flesh

1 'A finite mind starting with a finite Universe can never get to an infinite God' (p. 126). What lead the British mathematician John Taylor to say this?
2 In what ways does John 1:1–18 speak to different audiences (p. 129)?

3  Why might some people have been shocked to hear that *The Word became flesh* (p. 129)?

4  Explain why the knowledge of the Word made flesh allows us to be more relaxed about the findings of scientists such as Charles Darwin or Stephen Hawking (p. 131).

5  Where was Jesus at creation and what role did he play (p. 74)?

6  John has used lots of different images to speak of Christ. Why did he use the term *Word* (p. 133)?

7  Read John 1:6–8 and 15. Define why history is important to God (pp. 134–135).

8  Reflect on the statement 'God pitches his tent with us' (p. 134). What does that say about God's attitude to the world?

9  If God came to us, how does that affect how we share our faith (pp. 136–137)?

---

'The Word becoming flesh is both an affirmation of this creation and a claim of lordship over it. That means that the whole of life must be brought under the lordship of Christ. Indeed, this is the heart of the biblical doctrine of holiness' (p. 136).

---

10  'We see in Jesus what creation is meant to be' (p. 138). Describe what it means to follow Christ in terms of our humanity.


## 11. Colossians 1:15–20 Supreme in all things

1  Identify the struggles the Colossian church was having (pp. 142–143). What is the common theme to them?

2  Outline the dangers this type of thinking poses to the church today (pp. 143–144).

3  Paul's argument against this thinking lies in the supremacy of Christ. Investigate his reasoning further (Col. 1:15–20) (p. 144).

4  Look at the parallels that emphasize the Son's role in creation and new creation (p. 145). What is the significant factor?

5  According to Paul, who is Jesus (pp. 146–147)?

---

'Paul's cosmic description of Jesus echoes the understanding of "wisdom" in some of the Old Testament. There God creates the world through wisdom. In 1925 C. F. Burney suggested that this hymn in Colossians applies to Jesus everything that could be said of the figure "Wisdom". Burney argued that Paul combines Genesis 1:1 with Proverbs 8:22 to suggest that the divine Wisdom has been

---

*fully embodied in human form. Here the creative work of
God is expressed not through a concept or personification of
a divine attribute or holy law but through a person. At the
heart of God's creative work is Jesus Christ' (p. 148).*

6 Read Colossians 1:16. How do the powers and rulers apply
   directly to the Colossian Christians (p. 148)?
7 In what way can we get a bigger picture of Jesus and his work
   (p. 150)?
8 Describe how God is supreme in (a) reconciliation, and (b) in
   all things (pp. 152–154).

## 12. Hebrews 1:1–14 Heir of all things

*'Western culture is cynical of finding reliable truth.
Postmodernism doubts whether there is one overarching
truth to be found, and our experience of a consumer- and
media-manipulated culture breeds in us doubt and questioning. In such a climate trust is not at a premium. The
peace process in Northern Ireland, or reconciliation in the
Middle East, has been a painfully slow process because of
mistrust on both sides' (p. 157).*

1 Why was the letter to the Hebrews written (p. 160)?
2 How does Hebrews 1:1–14 show that 'the revelation in Christ
   is consistent with the revelation of the Old Testament
   Scriptures' (p. 160)?
3 Describe how the diagram on p. 160 shows the nature of
   God.
4 'Jesus however is not just a spokesperson for God; he has the
   character of God' (p. 161). In what terms does the writer
   describe the Son?
5 Explain the importance for our salvation of Jesus being the
   great High Priest (p. 162).
6 Given that Jesus is superior to the whole created order, why is
   it relevant to know that Jesus is in particular superior to the
   angels (pp. 162–163)?
7 The writer of Hebrews highlights eight key problems of a
   Christian community in crisis. Compare them to the problems
   of the church today (p. 164).
8 In a confusing postmodern world, where all truth is relative,
   how can Christians make a stand (p. 164)?

# The lessons of creation
# (pp. 167–216)

## 13. Genesis 9:1–17 A new trust

1 To what extent does the Genesis account of the flood tie up with other flood stories (p. 170)?
2 Give the arguments for and against the flood being universal (pp. 170–171).
3 'If God does create the waters miraculously it heightens our final question, "Why did he do it?"' (p. 172).
4 How does God give hope in the midst of this disaster (p. 99)?
5 Contrast the flood story with Genesis 1. What are the similarities (p. 173)?

---

*'The world of broken relationships is very different from Eden, as the goodness of creation now exists side by side with suffering. The consequences of sin affect both the wicked and the righteous. Although Noah was saved, the flood had an impact on him. The investment in the building of an ark and the destruction of his home were not trivial matters, not to say anything of the smell of the animals in the ark!' (p. 175).*

---

6 'He gives the gift of responsibility again to men and women, whom he knows are sinful, have let him down and will let him down again' (p. 176). Reflect on this blessing and allow God to speak to you.
7 What is the main message of Genesis 9 (p. 176)?
8 Define God's covenant (Gen. 9:12–17) (p. 179). What is the sign of this covenant?
9 Why should we put our trust in God (pp. 179–180)?

## 14. Job 38:1 – 42:17 A new understanding

1 How is Job described as someone reflecting the wisdom tradition (p. 182)?
2 Describe the kinds of advice his friends give. Why are they misguided (p. 183)?
3 What do Job 38 and 40 say about the doctrine of creation (pp. 186–187)?
4 *Then the LORD answered Job out of the storm* (Job 38:1). Suggest what 'answer' may mean (pp. 185–186). What does that say about Job's relationship with God?

5  Job questions whether God is really in control (pp. 186–187). How does God answer him?
6  'A God who created the Universe is always bigger than our minds can comprehend' (p. 188). Outline the dangers of reducing God to our understanding.
7  Look at Job 39:7, 13, 18 and 22 (pp. 190–191). How does God use humour in his creation?

---

*'For those who want to find an easy answer to innocent suffering, the book of Job will be a major disappointment. In fact it warns us of the danger of the very attempt. Creation reminds us that we are creatures, not God. God is always beyond our human-centred expectations of him. We need to remember this in prayer and indeed in the way we think about the circumstances that affect us in life' (p. 192).*

---

8  If the purposes of suffering aren't clear, why does God allow it (p. 190)?

## 15. Isaiah 40:9–31 A new strength

1  Think about your relationship with God. To what extent do you trust him (pp. 195–196)?
2  How does the prophet answer the question of whether God can restore the nation (p. 196)?
3  Summarize the first two pictures God uses to reinforce his message through Isaiah (pp. 199–200).

---

*'Perhaps Israel herself had to learn that the pride, military power and success of the days of David and Solomon were not something to trust in or aspire to in the future as an imperialist dream. While the defence of a nation state and the health of its economy are important, they are not the things to trust in. Nationalism can be as much an idol as anything else that we worship or trust in. Ultimately, compared to the power, justice and love of God, they are nothing. Those who exercise power in our world need to remember that. Conversely, here is encouragement for those who are weak and oppressed in the world. The power of God is so much greater than human structures' (p. 200).*

---

4 Explain the danger of idolatry (pp. 200–201).
5 In what way are the people encouraged to see things from a different perspective (p. 201)?
6 Why does God share his power with us (p. 203)?
7 Read Isaiah 40:31. Define how we can obtain God's strength (pp. 203–204).
8 'Are we in a place and attitude in our own life where the power of the Spirit, the Lordship of Christ and the love of the Father are the motivating and empowering aspects?' (p. 204). Spend some time with God in prayer.

## 16. Acts 17:16–34 A new life

1 Why was Paul so angry when he saw the city full of idols (p. 208)?
2 Look at Acts 17:24–27, 30. How does Paul state the God he knows (pp. 208–209)?
3 Explain why Paul moved out from his comfort zone to preach in the market place (p. 210).
4 What was his motivation (pp. 210–211)?
5 'It has been easy for the church to build the barricades and retreat into a Christian subculture, afraid of those who sneer' (p. 211). Where is our Athens?
6 How does Paul witness to the meeting of the Areopagus (pp. 211–213)? From where has he adopted his message and what can we learn from his approach?
7 Describe what is at the heart of Paul's concern (p. 214).

---

*'If Paul was confident that Jesus could stand up in the Areopagus, he also believed strongly that this gospel claimed universal and public truth. This was not a privatized belief that had an intellectual attraction to it. It was more than just one of the latest ideas. When Paul makes his case that this gospel is for all and that the truth of this is written into the space-time history of the Universe in the resurrection of Jesus, he divides his audience (vv. 32–34)'* (p. 214).

---

8 'John Drane comments that two things characterized the early church. One was confidence in the power of the Spirit, and the other was vulnerability in the face of the world. What characterizes the church of today?' (p. 216).

# The fulfilment of creation (pp. 217–269)

## 17. Isaiah 65:17–25 The Creator of a new heaven and earth

1 Outline the problems for biblical theory caused by Isaac Newton's and Laplace's findings (p. 219).

*'We are at the mercy of the predictable world, yet our human spirit cries out for something more. We dream of a land "somewhere over the rainbow" where things are different, and a time when we wish upon a star and our "dreams come true". Such talk can be dismissed as childish fantasy, but the entertainment industry is full of escapism' (pp. 220–221).*

2 Describe how the Isaiah verses give a sense of hope despite the 'confines of Newton's mechanistic Universe' (p. 224). Where does this hope come from?

3 Explain how quantum theory and chaos theory have undermined Newton and supported the biblical view (p. 224). What does this mean on an individual level?

4 Contrast 'the former things' with 'the new creation' (p. 225). How can we interpret these pictures and what do they teach us?

5 Given that 'Christians believe that God always offers possibilities' (p. 227), how can we work with God for real change?

## 18. Romans 8:18–30 The Creator liberates

1 Richard Bauckham and Trevor Hart comment that 'the hope of bodily resurrection cannot stop at either the human individual, without human sociality, or at humans without the rest of God's creation' (p. 230). Why is the personal view of 'deliverance from this world to a new existence in heaven' (p. 230) unbiblical?

*'One of the important things about any narrative such as a detective story or a joke is that the beginning only makes sense from the perspective of the end, and indeed the end only makes sense from the perspective of the beginning. There is a tendency in Christian theology to separate the beginning of the story from the end ... Likewise we often talk about eschatology, that is, the end, without reference to the doctrine of creation' (p. 231).*

2 Read Colossians 1:15–17. In what way are 'creation and consummation' held together (pp. 231–232)?

3 In Romans 8:18–30 Paul sets out that we are 'heirs of God and co-heirs with Christ' (p. 234). How does that truth affect our view of suffering?

4 What is the relationship between 'creation' and 'new creation' (p. 237)?

5 Show why creation is waiting in 'eager expectation' (p. 238).

6 In what ways does creation groan (pp. 240–241)? In what way are the groanings birth pangs rather than death pangs?

7 Define what we can look forward to at the end of this age (pp. 242–243).

## 19. 2 Peter 3:3–16 The Creator transforms

1 To whom was the letter of 2 Peter written and why (pp. 245–246)?

2 Note the false teachings that were being taught at the time (p. 247).

3 In what way does Peter reassure his readers (pp. 247–248)?

---

*'We can have genuine sympathy with those who longed for the second coming, especially in situations of persecution and difficulty. Expectations of an imminent return would have an attraction, just as they had for many others over centuries of Christian history' (p. 248).*

---

4 How does he deal with the theological mistake about creation (pp. 248–249)?

5 Look at 2 Peter 3:7. What are the problems associated with understanding that the world will be consumed with fire (pp. 249–250)?

6 'There are many of us who would far rather take part in eschatological speculation than respond to the coming judgment of God on lifestyle and attitudes' (p. 250). How far would you agree with this statement?

7 Explain the error in thinking when understanding the delay in Jesus' return (p. 251).

8 Summarize Peter's defence to the accusation that the Lord had broken his promise by not coming back when he said he would (pp. 251–252).

9 Interpret the meaning of *the earth and everything in it will be laid bare* (2 Pet. 3:10) (pp. 252–253).

10   Given that 'the new heaven and earth is a direct work of God' (p. 255), why should we be good stewards of the planet?
11   What does it mean to 'speed the coming of the day of God' (2 Pet. 3:12) (p. 256)?

## 20. Revelation 21:1–8 The Creator accepted

---

*'Very few people would want the world to go on exactly as it is. We thereby express our concern that something is not quite right about this world. We recognize that human beings can demonstrate depths of love, art and creativity. At the same time we recognize that human beings fall short of their potential both as individuals and society . . . Human existence is not dominated by joy and love all of the time, but affected by death, mourning, crying and pain. Will it ever get better?' (pp. 258–259).*

---

1   Read Revelation 1:1–4. How will the new creation be different from the first (p. 260)?
2   'What does it mean for the first heaven and earth to pass away?' (p. 261).
3   Look at the picture of the crucified Jesus and the risen Jesus (p. 262). What evidence does this give for God transforming, rather than destroying?
4   Explain the significance of not having any sea in the transformed cosmos (pp. 262–263).
5   In what way is the new creation not a return to Eden (p. 263)?
6   Compare the depth of relationship in marriage to the relationship with God and his people in the Holy City (p. 264).
7   'This life is the shadowlands and the life to come will be in full colour' (p. 265). Reflect on this statement. What biblical understanding is behind the observation?
8   How should the church be a 'model to the world of what is to come' (p. 265)?
9   Describe what the Christian hope depends on (p. 267).
10   Wilkinson gives four pointers for what our Christian life should be now, given that God is the 'guarantor of new creation' (p. 268). Summarize and discuss.

# Study on the Appendix
# (pp. 271–279)

### Seven-day creationism

1 The seven-day creationist theory sees Genesis 1 – 3 as literal history. How then can an age of the Universe of about 10,000 years be reconciled with the cosmological age of 12 billion years?

2 What are the four main problems with the 'young Universe' theory?

### The 'gap' theory

3 Explain this theory and why it has little support.

### Are the days really ages?

4 Describe how the Hebrew word *yôm* is used to support this view.

5 Why is it unlikely that the writer of Genesis 1 was using it in that way?

### Days not of creation but of revelation?

6 On what translation of Genesis 1:1 does this understanding rest?

### The literary approach

7 What kinds of literature does Genesis 1 contain?
8 Why is symbolism important to understanding truth?
9 Define what the writer is most concerned about.

### Genesis and science

10 Galileo once famously said, 'The Bible does not tell us how the heavens go but how to go to heaven.' Why did God not just write Genesis 1 as a textbook of modern cosmology?